T0256045

The Internet City

CITIES SERIES

Series Editor: John Rennie Short, *Department of Public Policy, University of Maryland, Baltimore County, USA*

As we move into a more urban future, cities are the main setting for social change, economic transformations, political challenges and ecological concerns.

This series aims to capture some of the excitement and challenges of understanding cities. It provides a forum for interdisciplinary and transdisciplinary scholarship. International in scope, it will embrace empirical and theoretical studies, comparative and case study approaches. The series will provide a discussion site and theoretical platform for cutting edge research by publishing innovative and high quality authored, co-authored and edited works at the frontier of contemporary urban scholarship.

Titles in the series include:

The Internet City

People, Companies, Systems and Vehicles

Aharon Kellerman

University of Haifa, Israel

CITIES SERIES

Edward Elgar
PUBLISHING

Cheltenham, UK • Northampton, MA, USA

Published by
Edward Elgar Publishing Limited
The Lypiatts
15 Lansdown Road
Cheltenham
Glos GL50 2JA
UK

Edward Elgar Publishing, Inc.
William Pratt House
9 Dewey Court
Northampton
Massachusetts 01060
USA

A catalogue record for this book
is available from the British Library

Library of Congress Control Number: 2018960799

This book is available electronically in the **Elgar**online
Social and Political Science subject collection
DOI 10.4337/9781788973595

ISBN 978 1 78897 358 8 (cased)
ISBN 978 1 78897 359 5 (eBook)

Printed and bound in Great Britain by TJ International Ltd, Padstow, Cornwall

Contents

Figures

Tables

Preface

Cities have always served as foci for human connectivity and information transmission. Contemporarily, it has been for the Internet to become the ubiquitous urban communications and information technology, and at an unprecedented scale. The Internet connects people both locally and elsewhere. In addition, it connects people with all forms and types of information, as well as with their appliances. Soon the Internet will provide connectivity also for autonomous vehicles (AVs). The Internet connects companies with their customers, and it constitutes a major tool for local governmental actions. Furthermore, the Internet connects urban utilities and it connects devices with each other through the Internet of Things (IoT). As such, the Internet has become a leading element within growing local knowledge economies, specializing in the production and marketing of Internet-related products and services. Added together, then, all of these urban activities yield the Internet-based cities. Thus, the objectives of this book are to highlight and to interpret the Internet-based city, doing so by way of exposition of its numerous dimensions, side by side with attempted interpretations of the significances of this new phase of urban connectivity.

Generally, the Internet-based city consists of people, businesses, devices, systems, and governments, all connected and functioning through Internet communications and websites. In previous books, I have dealt separately with several of these numerous elements which jointly comprise the Internet-based city: the Internet (Kellerman 2002, 2016); people (Kellerman 2006, 2012, 2016); business (Wilson et al. 2013), and AVs (Kellerman 2018a). The leading motivation for the writing of this book is a strongly felt need to look at the role of the Internet from the rather unifying urban perspective, as compared to the more customary writings focused merely on specific Internet uses, such as individual uses or business use. The emerging extensive application of the Internet to all of the major dimensions of city life, invites its more comprehensive exposure, which is attempted by the following chapters of this book. Thus, this book will try to shed a fresh and updated light on connectivity and informational activities in cities, given that such activities are now broader than in pre-Internet times, including connected non-living entities, and that most of these activities are currently Internet-based.

To the best of my knowledge there does not yet exist any book that offers a comprehensive Internet framework for cities. Hence, this book may turn out to be helpful for both academics and practitioners in the fields of geography, urban studies, Internet studies, urban planning, and urban sociology. The book may be used for personal knowledge and future research, as well as for relevant courses. As such, the book may fit academic courses devoted to contemporary cities, and courses dealing specifically with the social and spatial dimensions of the Internet. I hope that academics who teach courses on a single urban dimension of the Internet will gain an opportunity, through this book, to examine any such specific dimension from wider urban and Internet perspectives. The book may further turn out useful for urban policy makers, since the planning of new urban projects, as well as the upgrading of existing urban systems, seem to require these days the incorporation of some form and level of Internet connectivity.

I would like to express my sincere gratitude to Prof. John R. Short, Editor for the *Cities Book Series* of Edward Elgar Publishing, as well as to Katy Crossan, Senior Commissioning Editor for the publisher, for their encouragement to pursue the writing and publication of this book.

I would like to thank the Research Authority of the University of Haifa for its assistance with the completion of the book through the funding of index preparation. I would like further to thank Noga Yoselevich, Department of Geography and Environmental Studies, University of Haifa, for the redrawing of all the figures.

I would like further to express my deep gratitude to my wife Michal, for her long-standing patience and understanding for her partner, an addicted researcher and writer. Her cooperation has been extended to my writing of this book, as well.

August 2018

Acknowledgments

I would like to acknowledge permissions granted for the following: Table 6.3 by Pon, B. (2015), 'Locating digital production: How platforms shape participation in the global app economy,' Paper presented at the AAG 2015 Workshop on Geographies of Production in Digital Economies of Low-Income Countries, accessed 5 June at http://cariboudigital.net/wp-content/uploads/2015/04/Pon -AAG-Platforms-and-app-economy.pdf. Table 6.4 by PPI, originally published in Mandel, M. and Long, E. (2017), *The App Economy in Europe: Leading Countries and Cities, 2017*, Washington DC: PPI (Progressive Policy Institute), accessed 5 June 2018 at http://www.progressivepolicy.org/ wpcontent/uploads/2017/10/PPI_EuropeAppEconomy_2017.pdf. Figure 9.3, Tables 7.3 and 8.1, Chapter 8 and parts of sections 9.3–9.5 by Edward Elgar Publishing, originally published in Kellerman, A. (2018), *Automated and Autonomous Spatial Mobilities*, Cheltenham UK and Northampton MA, USA: Edward Elgar Publishing. I would further like to acknowledge the free use of Figure 9.2, originally published in Alessandrini, A., Campagna, A., Delle Site, P. and Filippe, F. (2015), 'Automated vehicles and the rethinking of mobility and cities,' *Transportation Research Procedia*, 5, 145–160.

Abbreviations

ACT	automated container terminal
AEB	autonomous emergency braking
AGV	automated guided vehicles
ARPANET	Advanced Research Projects Agency Network
ARTS	automated road transport systems
ATM	automatic teller machine
AV	autonomous vehicles
B2B	business to business
B2C	business to customers
BITNET	But It's Time Network
CBD	central business district
CCTV	closed circuit television
CD	compact disc
DAB	digital audio broadcasting
DARPA	Defense Advanced Research Projects Agency
DOT	Department of Transportation
EFTS	electronic funds transfer systems
EPC	electronic product code
ERP	enterprise resource planning
ERS	electronic reservation system
ESC	electronic speed control
ESP	electronic stability program
FAA	Federal Aviation Administration
FCC	Federal Communications Commission
FCW	forward collision warning
Fin-Tech	finance technologies
FM	Frequency Modulation
GATS	General Agreement on Trade in Services

GPS	global positioning systems
GPT	general-purpose technology
G2B	government-to-business
G2C	government-to-citizens
G2G	government-to-government
HD	high definition
ICANN	Internet Corporation for Assigned Names and Numbers
ICT	information and communications technologies
IDDD	international direct distance dialing
IoE	Internet of Everything
IoT	Internet of Things
IP	Internet Protocol
ISP	Internet service provider
IT	information technology
I2V	infrastructure to vehicle
JANET	Joint Academic Network
KIBS	knowledge intensive business services
LAN	local area network
LBS	location-based services
LDC	less developed country
LKAS	lane keep assist system
M2M	machine-to-machine
MIT	Massachusetts Institute of Technology
MOO	MUD (multi-user dungeon/dimension/domain) object-oriented
MOOC	massive open online course
MP	Moving Picture
NSFNET	National Science Foundation Network
OPC	open platform communications
OTA	online travel agencies
PC	personal computer
PROMETHEUS	PROgraMme for a European Traffic of Highest Efficiency and Unprecedented Safety

R&D	research and development
RFID	radio frequency identification
SAR	Special Administrative Region
SHT	smart home technology
SME	small and medium-sized enterprise
SMS	short message service
TAM	technology acceptance model
TCP/IP	transmission control protocol/Internet protocol
3G	third generation
UA	United Architecture
UAS	unmanned/unstaffed aircraft systems
UAV	unmanned/unstaffed aerial vehicles
UHF	ultra-high frequency
UTAUT	unified theory of acceptance and use of technology
VoIP	Voice over Internet Protocol
V2I	vehicle to infrastructure
V2V	vehicle to vehicle
V2X	=V2I+V2V
WELL	Whole Earth 'Lectronic Link
Wi-Fi	wireless fidelity
WTP	willingness to pay
WWW	World Wide Web
YOFC	Yangtze Optical Fibre and Cable

PART I

Urban connectivity and informational activities

1. Introduction

This opening chapter for the book will begin with an exposition of the book objectives and structure. It will then move to brief discussions of the three primal notions, which constitute the basis for this book: information, virtual spatial mobility, and connectivity. The satiation of needs that emerge out of these notions comprise the essence for the double abilities of the Internet and its extensive implementation: a comprehensive and most powerful medium for the storing and transmission of all types of information, side by side with the provision of comprehensive connectivity among both people and things, notably within urban settings. In this book we are about to examine these two abilities of the Internet within urban contexts, bringing about the very basing of contemporary cities on Internet connectivity and information storing and transmission.

1.1   BOOK OBJECTIVES AND SCOPE

The objective of this book is to highlight and interpret the Internet-based city. The book will do so by way of exposition of the numerous dimensions of Internet-based cities. These expositions will be followed by discussions attempting at interpretations of the significances of this new phase of urban connectivity. The Internet-based city constitutes a wider concept than that of smart cities, a concept which we will highlight later, in Chapter 7. The Internet-based city assumes the application of a single technology, the Internet, for the operations of all the partners who share the urban scene, whereas smart cities assume the wider implementation of computing at large, and usually so for urban system operations only.

The book is divided into three parts. The first part deals with urban connectivity and information activities and it will provide three necessary backgrounds for the following two additional parts of the book. Thus, in this chapter we will focus on the basic notions required for understanding the Internet-based city. In the following chapter, we will review the traditional connectivity roles and operations of cities, whereas in the third chapter we will move to the exposure of the Internet and the Internet of Things (IoT), notably their development and structure. The second part of the book is devoted to urban Internet activities, presenting a series of expositions for the numerous urban uses of the Internet, as pursued by numerous partners of the urban scene.

First, by individuals in their consumption of urban services, highlighting their activities in this regard, as well as their functioning in dual (physical and virtual) or hybrid space. Second, by companies making use of the Internet, coupled with the Intranet and the hidden Internet, side by side with the emergence of local knowledge economies. Third, by local governments employing IoT for the operation and control of urban systems, and, fourth, by carmakers engaged in the development of the upcoming autonomous vehicles (AVs), which are about to be Internet-communicative. The third part of the book will focus on several interpretations for urban Internet activities from a rather general city perspective: first, some general features of the Internet-based city will be outlined, followed by speculations on possible changes in urban spatial organization. The book will conclude with interpretations of the Internet-based city from the perspective of the Internet as a general-purpose technology (GPT), followed by a proposed model for three phases for Internet applications yielding Internet implications.

The book chapters will be based on the existing literature in related fields, mainly within geography, mobility, urban studies, urban planning, urban sociology, and Internet studies. It will further be based on internationally comparative data, as recent as only available, side by side with original interpretations and analyses.

1.2   INFORMATION

'Information' is a term used somehow ambiguously, notably since the introduction of information technology (IT), which has permitted the storage, processing and transmission of enormous quantities of information in electronic formats (see Wilson et al. 2013). On the one hand, information constitutes a kind of an 'umbrella spectrum' containing within it a family of four communicative, mostly codified, classes of things: data, information, knowledge and innovations. On the other hand, however, the term information, in a rather restricted sense, constitutes a specific class of communicative material, which is included within the wider spectrum of information. The Internet stores and transmits all four classes of information. Sometimes, however, some specific attention may be given to specific information classes. For instance, when discussing knowledge economies (Chapter 6), innovation may be in the focus, whereas IoT transmits mainly data (Chapters 7–8).

As for information at large, Roszak (1991, 13) noted: 'in its new technical sense, *information* has come to denote whatever can be coded for transmission through a channel that connects a source with a receiver, regardless of semantic content'. Information at large is obviously something intangible, though its containers or media are tangible. Traditionally these have been paper-based products, such as books, magazines, letters, documents, lists and so on. The emergence of electronic transmission and storage media, mainly radio, TV, cassettes, numerous types of discs, coupled with computers and the Internet, have once again accentuated the intangible and abstract character of information.

The four classes of communicative materials, namely data, information, knowledge and innovation, have each received numerous independent definitions. Some basic definitions and observations for them are as follows:

1. *Data:* 'a series of observations, measurements, or facts in the form of numbers, words, sounds and/or images. Data have no meaning but provide the raw material from which information is produced' (Roberts 2001, 100).
2. *Information:* Information, as a sub-class of the more general wider spectrum of information, might be a statement or even just a word. It has received numerous definitions, estimated at over 100, proposed in about 40 disciplines (see e.g. Machlup 1983; Braman 1989). Information was further claimed to constitute several things, such as an activity, a life form and a relationship (Barlow 1994), as a resource, commodity, perception of pattern, and even as a constitutive force in society (Braman 1989).
3. *Knowledge:* Definitions of knowledge refer to its relation to information. Knowledge has, thus, been defined as 'the application and productive use of information. Knowledge is more than information … It involves an awareness or understanding gained through experience, familiarity or learning' (Roberts 2001, 100–101). For Roszak (1991, 105) '*ideas create information,* not the other way around. Every fact grows from an idea'. Other commentators, however, such as Boisot (1998, 12), argues that 'knowledge builds on information that is extracted from data'. In addition, a kind of two-way relationship between knowledge and information was illuminated by Postman (1999, 93), as follows:

> I define knowledge as organized information, information that has a purpose, that leads one to seek further information in order to understand something about the world. Without organized information, we may know something *of* the world, but very little *about* it. When one has knowledge, one knows how to make sense of information, knows how to relate information to one's life, and, especially knows when information is irrelevant.

Bell (1976, 175; see also Castells 2000, 17) added to the meaning of knowledge the communications element: 'knowledge is a set of organized statements of facts or ideas, presenting a reasoned judgement or an experimental result, which is transmitted to others through some communication medium in some systematic form'. On the other hand, knowledge may also be created without the involvement of information and communications: 'Information is acquired by being told, whereas knowledge can be acquired by thinking .... Thus, *new knowledge can be acquired without new information being received* (Machlup 1983, 644). Similarly also, 'information transfer is always necessary to knowledge exchange, the reverse is not always true' (Storper 2000, 56).

4. *Innovation*: Innovation may be defined as the creation of new knowledge, through an intrinsically uncertain problem solving process, based on existing knowledge and/or information. Innovative knowledge may lead to the introduction of innovative products or to the application of novel production processes, involving either radical breakthroughs or incremental improvements (Feldman 1994, 2; Feldman 2000, 373–375; Wilson et al. 2013, 13). Thus, knowledge may be viewed as an asset, serving as an input (competence), which may lead to the production of innovation as an output. Newly created innovations become new pieces of knowledge (OECD 2000, 13).

1.3   VIRTUAL SPATIAL MOBILITY

Spatial mobility in general has been outlined elsewhere (Kellerman 2018a), and our brief attention here will be given specifically to virtual spatial mobility. The recent telecommunications/information revolution has emphasized the virtual dimension of the term spatial mobility, referring to the human ability to move the rather abstract entity of information electronically over space, and thus carrying out virtual spatial mobility. Electronically transmitted information may constitute a virtual extension of the self, through a phone call or through an email. Alternatively, moved information may constitute public pieces of information, available through websites. Such website information is generally not being transmitted as one-to-one messages or as one-to-many messages, oriented from one user to some specifically denoted receivers. Rather, website information constitutes on-demand retrieved information.

Another type of virtually moved information is information sent to and from devices through IoT. Such information may move because of human actions ordering such movement. In other cases, a device may autonomously initiate such moving of information, as will be the case, for instance, with the future AVs.

The physical mobility of people has growingly involved, as of the 1970s, virtual transfers of their information, as well. For instance, information transmitted for travel booking and travel coordination, or for traffic control. Thus, communication has become a key for the management of people's physical mobility. From yet another angle of joint physical and virtual mobilities, it has become possible for individuals to move corporeally while simultaneously communicating virtually through smartphones. Moreover, even the mobilities of people and objects are interrelated: 'There are objects that enable people to travel across distance; there are objects that enable people to travel forming complex hybrids ... there are objects and people that move together' (Urry 2007, 50). The mass moving of objects has become increasingly organized and controllable through Internet-connected logistics as well as modal transportation. Individuals, on the other hand, tend, in many cases, to prefer individual mobility for their daily commuting, making use of personal mobility vehicles, that is, cars, cycles, and bicycles.

1.4   CONNECTIVITY

Connectivity may carry numerous geographical connotations, notably within biogeography (see Hodgetts 2018). Linguistically, connectivity was defined as 'the quality, state, or capability of being connective or connected' (Merriam-Webster 2018). Connectivity was originally attributed to humans and animals, implying both their physical and virtual mobilities. However, connectivity can currently be applied to non-living things, as well, since such things have become connective through IoT. For humans there are several ways and media for getting connected, and before moving to the highlighting of several specific communications technologies, in the following chapters, we will elaborate here on some of their comparative features, within an evolutionary framework, also in comparison to physical mobility via automobiles.

Wellman (2001) outlined several phases for the conduct of social relations, following the adoption of personal transportation and communications technologies, as compared to the mass media of radio and television, which offer one-to-many communications. Each of these phases was typified by some specific patterns of presence and co-presence. The first phase of social relations was defined as the traditional and non-technological *door-to-door* communications for people, for instance when walking out of home for visits with each other, visits which obviously involve face-to-face co-presence and direct connectivity. This type of communication required *synchronous presence* (or co-presence) of the communicating parties in a jointly attended location in physical space (Yu and Shaw 2008).

The automobile and the telephone have brought about the development of a second phase in social relations, namely *place-to-place* ones. These place-to-place social relations offered some flexibility in the location of people's social relations, so that they partially replaced the local door-to-door relations. Place-to-place communications and co-presence consist, therefore, of face-to-face ones in physical space using cars, side by side with virtual ones, over the telephone. These communications and co-presences were further termed as *synchronous telepresence* (or co-presence) (Yu and Shaw 2008).

The two media of automobiles and telephones have presented several features of contacting. The automobile has made it possible for people to reduce drastically the friction of distance for the meeting of fellow people located significantly far from their own locations, thus facilitating some additional face-to-face contacts. On the other hand, however, direct dialing through the fixed-line telephone fully nullified the friction of distance. In the past, long-distance calling involved high calling rates, thus permitting only a rather limited transmission of information routinely. In addition, past long-distance calling through fixed-line telephones required fixed locational co-presences of the interacting parties for the performance of audial and non-visual conversations (Kellerman 2006).

Later, but still within the second phase of place-to-place social relations, the introduction of the Internet has enhanced place-to-place relations and co-presences and has turned them more complex. Users of the Internet can engage in video calls, and they can further enjoy virtual face-to-face co-presences while being physically located in fixed physical locations, simultaneously with their locations in virtual spaces (see e.g. Kaufmann 2002, 28; Urry 2000, 71). This kind of face-to-face co-presence was referred to as simultaneous embodied and response presences (Knorr-Cetina and Bruegger 2002).

Internet communications presented a distinct mode of communications as compared to the telephone. On the one hand, Internet written communications, notably emailing, is both locationally and temporally flexible, since it does not require the synchronous attendance in time of the communicating parties at particular sites, next to their computers. Such Internet written offline communications constitute, therefore, *asynchronous telepresence* (Yu and Shaw 2008), and it does not imply co-presence by the communicating parties. On the other hand, however, Internet online written, as well as audial or audiovisual chats, constitute enhanced synchronous telepresence and co-presence, similar to those originally facilitated by the telephone.

The most significant contribution of the Internet to new patterns of co-presence has emerged through the introduction and wide adoption of portable communications devices, such as laptops, tablets, and above all smartphones, since these devices permit wireless, and thus placeless, communications. The use of portable communications devices implies the emergence of a third phase in social networking, namely that of *person-to-person* communications. Thus, in this type of synchronous telepresence or co-presence, both of the communicating parties can be fully detached from any fixed locations.

1.5 CONCLUSION

We noted in this chapter that information, in its wide spectrum, comprises the four elements of data, information in a stricter sense referring to statements, knowledge and innovation. People may communicate widely through virtual mobility media, currently led by the Internet. The levels and forms of human connectivity may differ by the chosen communications media. Devices can communicate contemporarily as well, through the IoT.

The three basic notions of information, spatial mobility and connectivity, which were briefly outlined in this chapter, present jointly the ability to move information to any connected others, whether they be humans or devices. This human ability and its pursuance have always constituted one of the essential elements of urban life. Human connectivity and informational activities have been upgraded, thus becoming most extensive as of the development of communications technologies and media, and peaking with the emergence of the Internet and smartphones. As we will note in the following chapters, these devices and media have facilitated full locational flexibility for human connectivity and informational activities. Furthermore, and as we will see in the following chapters, the Internet has further facilitated the instant transmission of all types of information to and from people, to and from wherever they are located or moving. Side by side with the expansion and upgrading of human connectivity, IoT has extended connectivity to non-living devices, as well.

2. Pre-Internet urban connectivity and informational activities

In this chapter, we will present the historical development and the contemporary patterns for cities as foci for connectivity. We will further outline the roles of cities in information production, transmission, gathering and retrieval, as pursued through pertinent media. The chapter will include several sections, highlighting informational and connectivity facilities and services in cities: face-to-face communications (in market places and cafés); informational institutions (libraries, universities, newspapers, and publishing houses); and electronic media invented prior to the Internet (telephone, radio and television). The common denominator for all of these facilities and media is that they serve people. Historical equivalents for IoT, as facilitators and media for communications between people and things, as well as among things themselves, probably have not existed prior to the introduction of the IoT.

It is of importance to look at the historical emergence of cities as foci for connectivity and informational activities, prior to the introduction of the Internet, which will constitute the focus of our discussions in the following chapters, for several grounds. From a historical perspective, cities in general have developed their functional activities in a cumulative manner, rather than deleting activities that were developed in previous periods, and this applies to connectivity and informational activities, as well. Thus, the introduction of the Internet has not nullified the previously developed connectivity and information media. From a technological perspective, the Internet is based on telephone, radio, and television technologies, side by side with its being based on newer computer technologies. Last, from a functional perspective, and as we will largely note in the following chapters, the Internet has become an alternative and/or a complementary arena for traditional urban connectivity and informational functions, such as books, newspapers, universities, market places, radio and television broadcasts and so on, side by side with their continued operations.

Since their early inception, cities have always served as foci for connectivity, a function that was accompanied by their operation as centers for information production, transmission, gathering and retrieval. In these activities, cities have served not just their own local residents, but additional populations, as well. Such additional populations could include people who live in a metropolitan area beyond city limits, some additional populations residing in the same region, and even people located in other regions and countries, all depending on city size and centrality.

These rather traditional urban features have become enormously amplified and sophisticated following the introduction and the massive adoption of the Internet, which has been universally applied for two categories. First, for human communications and informational activities in fixed locations as of 1995, as well as for people on the move, through mobile smartphones and additional mobile devices as of 1999. Second, for communications with and among appliances, vehicles, utilities, and other urban elements, through the IoT, as of 1999. Thus, cities in developed countries are engaged in a process of turning into Internet-based ones. This process is about to culminate with the possible upcoming wide adoption of the Internet-connected AVs, expected to be launched by 2022–2025, and probably reaching saturation in the car market as of the 2040s–2050s (Kellerman 2018a).

2.1   HISTORICAL URBAN CONNECTIVITY AND INFORMATIONAL ACTIVITY

It was already for Aristotle to declare, in the first century BCE, that 'Man is by nature a [political] social animal' (*Politics* 1.1253a), thus bringing about the emergence of human communities, urban and rural alike, celebrating togetherness. Towns and cities were further viewed as presenting a two-way relationship with connectivity, since they have constituted 'places and products of communications, and they provide spaces for interaction and/or observation' (Drucker 2005, 10). Towns and cities cannot be related to as merely big or giant villages, since their population size, and the urban, as compared to the rural, economic base of cities, have brought about the development of some specific formal and informal urban connectivity and informational activities (see e.g. Mumford 1961).

In the ancient Greek city, the *polis*, the theater served as the facility for the public transmission of artistic information, with the first one constructed in Athens in 530 BCE (Megan and Jessica 2012). Simultaneously, the agora served for the public distribution of governmental information, side by side with the informal connectivity facilitated by exchanges pursued through market activities, with the Athenian Agora originating in the early sixth century BCE (Roland 1951). The production of knowledge in the ancient Greek cities took place in scholarly sites, such as *Akademia* in Athens, established by Plato c. 387 BCE (Lindberg 2007).

As we will note in Chapter 4, these three basic functions of shopping, entertainment and high-education, typifying the early physical-space city, and continuing to develop there along history, are currently challenged by similar functions and activities available for performance in the virtual Internet. It has been since antiquity that cities have facilitated one-to-many communications, side by side with extensive one-to-one communications. These ancient and traditional modes of communication have been expanded contemporarily by many-to-many communications, made possible through social networking and email distribution lists (see Urry 2007, 158).

Most of the information production and transmission activities in the pre-printing eras were carried out orally, given that writing was expensive, and given that the majority of the population was illiterate. Thus, it was mainly for governmental, academic and religious authorities to make use of writing. In the medieval European city, churches functioned frequently as fora for the transmission of royal and other governmental announcements and information. In the late Middle Ages, a new facility for informal exchanges, the coffee shop, appeared, with the first one opening up in 1475, as the 'Kiva Han' coffee shop, in Constantinople (Istanbul) (Baskerville 2018). Coffee shops served as informal communications and information facilities, functioning side by side with information exchanges that took place in city streets, squares, and markets. Other urban places, which served also for informal communications, were personal care facilities, such as barbershops and public bathhouses (see e.g. de Vivo 2007; Buda et al. 2011).

The first production of paper in Europe occurred in the mid-twelfth century, and it was followed some 300 years later, by book printing, which was invented and introduced by Gutenberg in 1455, in Mainz (Germany) (American Printing History Association 2012). Interestingly enough, book printing was introduced just twenty years prior to the opening of the first coffee shop, thus implying an almost simultaneous enhancement of both oral and visual information transmissions in cities and by cities in Europe. Both inventions facilitated one-to-many information transmissions. Coffee shops did so orally for informal exchanges within a small and local crowd each time, whereas books did so more formally for wider, even national and international, markets of readers, notably so for religious and scholarly texts. Cities that specialized early in book printing gained a higher status in the production and transmission of knowledge. Among these cities were Mainz (Germany), Subiaco (within metropolitan Rome) and Venice (Italy), Bruges (Belgium), Oxford and Cambridge (UK), and Cambridge MA (US) (American Printing History Association 2012). Some of these cities, notably Oxford and Cambridge in the UK and Cambridge MA in the US, have preserved their leading status in the printing industry, notably for academic publishing.

More than a century after the first book printing, in 1605, the first newspaper was published in German Strasburg (American Printing History Association 2012), followed, half a century later, in 1650, by the first daily newspaper, also in German (Leipzig), and in 1702 by the first daily newspaper in English, the *Daily Courant* (London). The introduction of newspapers brought about the use of print for visual one-to-many daily information transmissions and communications, thus complementing and enhancing the oral informal transmissions of information, which was pursued already in city streets and cafés. Newspapers have assisted, in the longer run, the development of public awareness to national and international political and economic issues, as well as the emergence of public exposure to news in numerous other spheres of life, such as sports, foods and fashion (see e.g. Wilk 1999). Newspapers further have brought about the evolution of local identities, and the participation of citizens in public debates on local issues.

Another medieval urban institute for knowledge production and distribution, other than daily information, were the universities, which have also lasted until nowadays. The first university was the University of Bologna (Italy), established in 1088, followed by the University of Oxford (UK), established in 1167 (Rashdall 2010). Italy, the UK and Spain led, at the time, in the opening of medieval universities, whereas the first university in the US, Harvard University, was established much later, in 1636 (Harvard University 2018). A university located in town meant at the time an urban specialization in knowledge production and distribution, similar to urban specialization in printing. Again, for numerous cities, such as Bologna, Oxford, and Cambridge MA, this specialization in academic studies has continued until present times. Specialization of cities in knowledge production in universities was frequently coupled with their specialization in its distribution through book printers, as has been the case for Oxford and Cambridge in the UK, and Cambridge MA in the US.

2.2 MODERN URBAN CONNECTIVITY AND INFORMATIONAL ACTIVITY

From the perspective of urban communication and informational connectivity, the modern era in Western cities may be divided into three periods. The first one was the nineteenth century, typified by urban industrialization, with the appearance of electricity towards the end of the century, and the invention, but not the wide adoption, of cars and telephones, in its last quarter. This was the industrial period. The second period of the modern era in urban connectivity and informational activity was the twentieth century, typified by the adoption of telephones and cars, as well as by the introduction and adoption of the electronic public media of radio and television. Towards the end of the twentieth century, the Internet was introduced. Thus, this century was the media century. In the third period, as of the beginning of the twenty-first century, the Internet has become the dominant connectivity and information medium, as we will see in the following chapters. Hence, this century, so far, has constituted the Internet period.

All of the connectivity and informational institutions and facilities, which were established originally in the classical and medieval eras in Western cities, have been preserved and were moved into the cities of the modern era. These institutions and facilities include theaters, churches, market places, universities, book and newspaper printing, and coffee shops. Among these, the institutions that underwent some significant change, directly or indirectly, during the first period of the modern era, in the industrial nineteenth century, were the printing industry and universities.

The industrialization of printing implied the ability to print faster, cheaper, and, thus, more copies of both books and newspapers. This industrialization was enormously enhanced later, as of the second half of the twentieth century, when the industry became computerized, thus moving to virtual typesetting and automated text copying, which replaced the previous technology of material composition of printed texts, based on the use of metal letters.

The circulation of knowledge through books, as well as the distribution of information through newspapers, have become more extensive in the nineteenth century. This has meant for many people the ability to gain more knowledge from book reading, side by side with their ability to read more daily information concerning numerous spheres of life, through newspapers. The availability of books, side by side with increasing levels of literacy, as well as the need for high education for the changing urban economies, have brought about the growth of existing universities, side by side with the establishment of new ones. The libraries of universities expanded, and major libraries were established in the eighteenth century. However, fully open public libraries, offering subscription and circulating services, emerged widely only as of the second half of the nineteenth century (Stockwell 2001).

A century later, in the second half of the twentieth century, the printing industry was revolutionized, by turning the action of printing into a routine activity for the numerous computer users. The development of several technologies in the 1960s, such as laser printing, brought about desktop publishing in the 1980s (American Printing History Association 2012). Such printing amounted to the ability of end-users of personal computers (PCs) to print documents, making use of desktop printers, yielding print qualities preserved in the past for professional printers only.

We noted already that the ancient urban functions of shopping, entertainment and high-education, which we met first in the classical Greek cities, are currently challenged by the Internet. This applies even more so to the publication of books and newspapers. Books are published massively over the Internet, which is also the case for the availability over the Internet of printed newspapers, side by side with continuously updated news services offered through the Internet. We will discuss this virtual availability of urban services for individuals in Chapter 4.

Towards the end of the nineteenth century and continuing during the first half of the following one, three electronic media were invented and widely adopted: the telephone for connectivity, and radio and television for the broadcasting of public information. All of these three media are urban in nature, and in all of their dimensions. The production of these appliances takes place in plants located in cities, which is true also for information production, circulation and transmission facilities, almost all of which are located in cities. Needless to say, that the users of telephones, radio and television, have been mostly urbanites. We will look now separately at each of these three media.

2.3   FIXED-LINE TELEPHONE

The fixed-line telephone was the first personal one-to-one information technology, as compared to printing, which is a one-to-many technology. Further, as compared to printing, telephones have been operated routinely by nonprofessional individuals at their homes and in offices, in order for them to consume and produce information. Printing has been performed by professionals, who consequently serve as mediators between single information and knowledge producers, the book authors or newspaper writers, on the one hand, and readers who constitute end consumers, on the other. As we will note in the following chapter, the Internet has been based on and integrated into telephone technologies and systems, fixed and mobile alike, so that it has come to compete with fixed-line telephony. It is, thus, of importance to examine the emergence and social significance of fixed-line telephones, notably within urban contexts.

The fixed-line telephone was invented in 1876 in Boston US, and it has established itself as the most basic, as well as the oldest, appliance and medium for mechanized personal virtual mobility. The previously invented telegraph, first introduced in 1837, was not available to its users as a personal device, since this service was rather offered through post offices or by specialized companies (e.g. Western Union in the US). Furthermore, the telegraph proved itself as an expensive service, devoted solely to written messages, so that private people used it merely for urgent and essential communication. The tele-graph was followed in the mid-twentieth century by the telex system, which offered a telegram service for businesses, in which terminals were located. The telex declined, though, shortly after, following the introduction of desktop fax machines as of the 1980s (Kellerman 1993, 2006).

Fixed telephones were installed in the past in almost all households in developed countries, first in the US and later in Europe, side by side with their crucial service for the daily operations for business. However, the more recent wide adoption of mobile phones, notably smartphones, which we will discuss

Table 2.1   *Milestones in the development of fixed-line telephones*

Phase and year of innovation	Innovation	Country
Inventions		
1837	Commercial telegraph	US
1876	Fixed-line telephone	US
1924	Facsimile (fax) via telephone	US
I. Analog telephony		
1878	Commercial electromechanical telephone exchange	US
1900	Automatic telephone exchange for local calls	US
1950	Automatic direct distance dialing (DDD) service	US
II. Digital telephony		
1963	Commercial touch tone service	US
1965	Electronic telephone switching system	US
1970	International direct distance dialing (IDDD) service	US and UK

Source: Following Kellerman (2018a, Table 5.1).

in the following chapter, has brought about declining penetration rates for fixed telephones in both developed and developing countries. Thus, in 2017 the penetration rate for fixed-line telephones worldwide reached 13.0 percent, down from 19.1 percent in 2005, whereas the global penetration rate for mobile phones reached some 103.5 percent in 2017 (implying multiple phone subscriptions by individuals) (ITU 2018).

The history of the fixed-line telephone has been documented elsewhere (see e.g. Fischer 1992). It is important, though, to note here that the development of fixed-line telephone technology consists of two technological phases: analog and digital (Table 2.1). The very initiation of the telephone in 1876 was obviously intended for conversations between two users, directly connected by wire with each other. It took some additional two years before the first commercial telephone exchange was introduced in 1878, thus permitting the establishment of a commercial telephone service among multiple networked subscribers.

The original telephone service did not include any dialing by subscribers, and all connections had to be performed manually by operators hooking wires in the exchange system for any requested connection. Some 22 years following the introduction of the telephone, in 1900, the first automatic exchange for local calls was introduced, enabling subscribers to reach other local subscribers directly and instantly through their own dialing. Hence, as of the beginning of the twentieth century, urbanites gradually enjoyed direct electronic connectivity among telephone subscribers. Some additional fifty years were needed for the enhancement and upgrading of the electromechanical exchanges in order for them to provide automated direct distance dialing (DDD), allowing subscribers to reach fellow ones located elsewhere domestically (Hochheiser 2015). The last automated dialing phase, permitting worldwide direct, operator-less, dialing, namely international direct distance dialing (IDDD), was first introduced some twenty years later, in 1970. Before then, in 1965, computerized electronic switching systems were first introduced. These computerized switching systems were smaller and much more capable in their service provisions, as compared to the previous analog ones.

The development of the analog and digital telephone systems and their automation constituted American enterprises, assisted by the almost full ownership of the American telephone system by just one private company, the Bell system. In Europe, which initiated printing for both books and newspapers, as well as in other countries, the automation phases for fixed-line telephony began later and took longer, as compared to the US, with telephone services operated, at the time, directly by governments.

Under an operator-based telephone service, the subscriber could determine only the geographical destination of the call made to another fixed-line subscriber, whereas the transmission system and the operators, respectively, determined the routing and the timing of the call. Automation has meant that the exact timing of calls moved from its determination by operators to call timing by callers. Side by side, call routing, which has always been the responsibility of the telephone system, has become fully automatic, without transparency to regular callers. This latter nature of the telephone connectivity process was also typified later with Internet communications.

In the early twentieth century the facsimile (fax) machine, which permitted the transmission of still graphic documents via telephone lines, was introduced in the US, following the much earlier invention of fax machines for the telegraph in 1843. The first fax machines constituted the most cumbersome and space-consuming devices for textual and graphical transmissions over the telephone system. They served, therefore, at the time, mainly newspapers, meteorologists and security forces. Fax machines were digitized, automated, and miniaturized in Japan as of the 1970s, hence turning into desktop devices, installed widely in both offices and homes. The development of Internet technology has reduced the importance of fax transmissions, with the development of document scanning and the transmission of scanned documents through email.

Telephone connectivity in general and its automation process in particular, bear on a variety of social dimensions (see Kellerman 2006, 2012). It is of interest to note in this regard some of the major differences between the telephone and the private car, both constituting personal mobility media, mainly used for in-town virtual and physical movements, respectively. Whereas the initial mass-production of automobiles was geared to the household market, the early commercial introduction of the telephone was meant for businesses. Moreover, since the beginning of telephone penetration into households, in the US of the early twentieth century, telephone devices have always been small appliances, which normally have had to be attached to the user's body when used. Cars, on the other hand, have always been large-scale capsules enveloping the driver's body, and they were produced in numerous distinguished models differing from each other by their sizes and designs.

Telephone use implies speed, as it provides swift and instant two-way communications, features that were unattainable for communications through the previously available media of face-to-face meetings, or postal services and telegraph for remote communications, all requiring time and effort for their use. Following the full automation of calling procedures, which took, as we noted, several years, the telephone has become much speedier than the automobile, as it has not involved time and space frictions for call transmissions. Like automobiles, telephones provide plentiful opportunities for movements, once most households and businesses are connected to the telephone system.

Also like automobiles, telephones provide their subscribers with personal autonomy and individualism in their virtual mobility and social ties (see Fischer 1992), features which were at times of special significance for women and children, who were partially deprived of autonomy and individualism, prior to the wide household adoption of telephones. Telephones further involve the power of information sharing, as well as the pleasure associated with social contacts. Given the lack of time friction or traffic jams in their normal operation, once becoming fully automatic, the telephone assisted routine time organization and, therefore, it involved a reorganization of daily lives, notably once urban services could be reached over the telephone. As we will note in the following chapter, all of these features of the automated and universally available fixed-line telephone have been amplified later on with the wide adoption of mobile phones, followed by their provision of Internet communications.

The major differences between automobiles and telephones for their users are the lack of laws and regulations for the 'driving' of telephones or for 'passing through' communications lines, as compared to driving and road rules required for car driving. In addition, telephone use implies lower dependence on maintenance services, as well as on global supply industries, such as petroleum, as compared to cars. Furthermore, telephone use involves several features that are irrelevant for physical mobility such as co-presence, or the connected presence for calling parties (Tillema et al. 2010). It further amounts to 'disembodied sounds – of speech displaced in space and time from its origins' (Mitchell 1995, 36). The telephone is, thus, a time intruder, when somebody calls somebody else automatically, without a prior notification by an operator to the called party, as used to be the case in the early manual phase of telephone connectivity. All of these features of the telephone service, except for it being a time intruder, apply to email services, as well.

Early governmental initiatives, such as the 1934 American Telecommunications Act, attempted to assure universal availability of telephone services for all households, urban and rural alike, and assumed, therefore, that personal virtual mobility constitutes a basic right. In the American case, the telephone service was considered as a right, even though the service was not directly provided by government, but was rather channeled through private companies. Furthermore, the telephone service was considered as a right even at the early phases of telephone connectivity when it was not yet fully automatic.

Informal social relations, as expressed through telephone conversations, whether performed through fixed or mobile phones, may present some special nuances for audial social interactions, as compared to other modes of social interaction. Thus, some kind of 'telephone cultures' have evolved, for instance as to the way telephone conversations should begin, using words like 'hello' (English), 'hallo' (German), or 'pronto' (Italian), as well as for the ending and the structuring of telephone conversations, the preferred time of calling and so on. Such nuances and cultures might differ among countries, and callers are expected to abide by such domestic 'norms' and manners. Such norms have emerged, later on, also for written electronic messages, through emails or chats, but on a global rather than domestic basis, given the globality of reach of digital communications, without any procedural or cost differentiations among local, domestic or international destinations for messages.

Similar to the driving of private cars, telephone use for social contacts may facilitate increased contacts with other places, and such extensive contacts may bring about some decline in feelings of localism, possibly amounting to a degree of placelessness (see Relph 1976). However, despite its social importance, the wired telephone has not become a status symbol like automobiles, given it being a small appliance located inside homes, followed, recently, by its declining importance, at times of preferences for mobile smartphones.

From a spatial perspective, and contrary to automobiles, contemporary telephone infrastructures constitute a minor land-use, as most telephone cables are buried, and digital telephone exchanges have become much smaller. Until the introduction of digital telephone services in the 1960s, analog telephone exchanges required large buildings, so that telephone exchanges were present and visible in urban landscapes. Also contrary to automobiles, telephones have not been considered an environmental pollutant. Still, however, like automobiles, telephones have facilitated the suburbanization of population, services, and production (Kellerman 1984). As such, telephones do not necessarily contribute to social segregation, but they may facilitate some personal physical isolation of subscribers within their homes, while still permitting them to enjoy virtual communications through fixed-line, and even more so through mobile, telephones.

2.4　RADIO

The radio was the first electronic public medium, followed later by television and the Internet. Radio stations broadcast from one-to-many, with some possible immediate exchanges with their listeners, notably through talk shows. Audial radio broadcasting and listening are similar to the rather visual book and newspaper printing and reading, respectively, which we noticed before, in their constitution of one-to-many communications. Probably, radio has been even more accessible than books and newspapers, notably since its audial use does not require literacy, and listening to it can accompany other activities, performed simultaneously, such as driving. However, radio listening requires the purchasing and use of an electric appliance, similar to the current ebook readers, though the latter devices might be included in tablets, which can be used for other purposes as well. This, obviously, is not the case for printed books. One radio can be used for listening to numerous stations, whereas each book and newspaper contains only some specific contents. On the other hand, however, the durability of books for nonprofessionals can be much longer than some specific radio programs. Thus, there are normally no public radio libraries available to listeners.

The Italian Marconi invented the radio wireless transmission of sound some twenty years following the invention of the telephone, in 1896. The introduction of radio transmission was based on the prior practical identification of radio waves by the German Hertz, back in 1874. These two innovations were complemented by the invention of the diode valve by the British Fleming in 1904, thus facilitating the construction of radio appliances (Table 2.2). Some sixteen years later, in 1920, local broadcasting began in the UK and the US, followed by short-wave transatlantic broadcasting in 1925. These two basic phases of local and global broadcasting were followed in the 1930s with American efforts to expand radio reception through the introduction of the mobile auto radio in 1932, as well as by the introduction of higher quality broadcasting through FM (Frequency Modulation). Auto radios were later complemented by additional devices for recorded music, notably CD (compact

Table 2.2   Milestones in the development of radio

Phase and year of innovation	Innovation	Country
Inventions		
1874	Radio waves	Germany
1896	Radio	Italy
1904	Diode valve	UK
1947	Transistor	US
1995	Universal Internet	US
I. Spatial expansion of broadcasting		
1920	Local broadcasting	UK and US
1925	Long distance short wave broadcasting	US
1993	Internet webcasting	US
2001	Satellite radio	US
II. Spatial expansion of reception		
1932	Auto radio	US
1954	Transistor radio	US
1999	Smartphone	Japan
III. Broadcasting enhancements		
1939	FM (Frequency Modulation) broadcasting	US
1961	FM stereo	US
1995	Digital audio broadcasting (DAB)	EU

Sources: Coe (2006); Electronics Notes (2018); Greatest Achievements (2018).

disc) and MP3 (Moving Picture 3), thus bringing about an enhanced driving experience (Sheller 2007).

The introduction of computers in the 1940s has brought about gradual transitions in radio transmission and reception. Thus, the transistor, which was invented in 1947 for installation in early computers, permitted the replacement of the diode valves in radios, turning them into easily carried small appliances, as compared to the previous bulky home radios and the fixed ones for cars. Computer technology permitted further the introduction of FM stereo broadcasting, as of 1961.

The development of the Internet has implied major changes in the radio industry. The first Internet webcasting occurred in 1993, two years prior to the commercial and universal introduction of the Internet. Internet radio made possible the reception of any regular radio station worldwide being installed on the system, and in excellent quality. The Internet, thus, has permitted transmission beyond the terrestrial signaling of stations, which constituted a major restriction at the time. In addition to the provision of global range of listening for local radio stations, other radio stations could webcast as pure Internet radio stations, thus being unavailable for listening on regular radios. Several years later, the introduction of the smartphone in 1999 has led to mobile radio appliances being unnecessary, with radio reception pursued via smartphones, in addition to their provision for Internet radio reception. Side by side with the introduction of the commercial Internet in 1995, digital audio broadcasting (DAB) was adopted, thus solving the problem of wave availability for radio stations, notably in large metropolitan areas. This widening of the wave spectrum for radio stations was followed by the introduction of subscription services for station packages through satellite radio.

Radio technology was originally a European technology, developing, as we noted, in Germany, Italy, and the UK. The later emergence of computerization in the US, followed by the introduction of the Internet there, have implied also that most of the technological enhancement of radio broadcasting and reception, as of the second part of the twentieth century, have emerged in the US.

Radio has constituted an important element in the development of modern urban societies, and this was the case in several respects (see e.g. Coe 2006). Radio has provided wide and rather instant exposure to news, as compared to the delay in their availability through printed newspapers, which require time for printing and distribution, and charging their readers separately for each edition. In democratic regimes radio has assisted in the maintenance and prospering of democratic values, through the provision of free speech to broadcasters and listeners alike. Radio has further assisted citizens in their obtaining of civil and other rights. It has provided for popular general knowledge, and above all, it has been a routine daily source for music and entertainment. In the US, the flourishing of radio, or its 'golden age', were the three decades 1930s–1950s, which were later followed by the flourishing of television (Barnouw 1968).

Radio stations may constitute nonprofit national entities, run by governments or by public national authorities, or they may similarly constitute regional or local stations. They can further be commercial stations, frequently devoted to music broadcasting. An interesting type of radio station, notably as far as urban connectivity is concerned, are community stations, accentuating the cultures and interests of local communities, frequently of minorities, rather than being involved in the 'cultural homogenization', which may be promoted, implicitly or explicitly, by national stations (Keough 2010; Wilkinson 2015). Geographically expanded transmission through the Internet permits people with similar interests, but living or staying beyond the terrestrial signaling of a community station, to join the listening audience.

2.5   TELEVISION

Television followed radio as the second mass medium, broadcasting from one-to-many, and as being the first visual mass medium. Television is not merely an entertainment and news medium. More than other mass media, it brings the world into people's homes, whether in the form of live news broadcasts or in the way of viewers' exposure to other places and lifestyles through foreign cable-TV channels. Furthermore, it is even for domestic television channels to present films and programs, which focus on other countries. This global exposure of television broadcasting has become a catalyst for growing international tourism, thus decreasing the local-urban 'specialness of place and time' (Meyrowitz 1985, 125). As an entertainment medium, television provided for a virtual alternative to the theater and the concert hall prior the introduction of the Internet. As we will see below, television sets have contemporarily become integrated with the Internet.

Television was invented in 1925, close to thirty years after the invention of the radio (Table 2.3). Almost in parallel with the first TV station, which began to broadcast in 1928, the most important upgrade for television broadcasting was invented – color TV. However, it took some time until the first color TV station started broadcasting, back in 1940. Such lagging between invention and adoption has been the case for additional inventions, meant for the enhancement of TV reception. For instance, the transistor, which was invented in 1947, was installed in TV sets only as of 1954, and flat screens, which were originally introduced already in the 1960s, went into production only in 1997, while using another technology. The exception to this was the digital TV, introduced in 1998, just three years following the launching of the commercial Internet, at times of swift technological development of the digital realm at large.

From the customers' perspective, television has developed along the following sequence: b/w broadcasting (1928); cable TV (1948); color broadcasting (1951); flat screens (1997); and the TV/Internet merge (2005). However, this order constitutes mostly the American sequence, given that the initial adoption of TV has been foremost an American trend. In other countries, though, color TV might have been adopted before cable TV was introduced. The original development of TV technologies began in the UK, led later on by the US, with several inventions emerging in the UK and Japan.

As of 2005, a two-way relationship has emerged between television and the Internet, implying their merger. Television broadcasts can now be transmitted through the Internet and, they may, therefore, be viewed on computer screens and smartphones, serving as e-TV. Side by side with the emergence of e-TV, Internet websites and communications can now be viewed on smart TV screens, and such screens have recently become standard features for TV sets.

Table 2.3   Milestones in the development of television

Phase and year of innovation	Innovation	Country
Inventions		
1925	Television	UK
1928	Color television	UK
1940	HD (high definition) color	US
1947	Transistor	US
1954	Transistor TV	Japan
1962	Satellite transmission	US
1963	Home video recorder	UK
1995	Universal Internet	US
I. Watching enhancements		
1951	Color broadcasting	US
1989	HD (high definition) color	Japan
1997	Flat screen	US
II. Connectivity enhancements		
1928	First television station	US
1948	Cable television	US
1952	UHF (ultra-high frequency)	US
1998	Digital television	UK
2005–2006	Television on the Internet and the Internet on television (smart TV)	US

Sources: Polsson (2017); Jacobs (2018).

This two-way merger has expanded the availability of channels to viewers. Foreign channels can further be received through streaming technologies. This wide international availability of TV broadcasts makes it easier for migrants to live within other cultures (see e.g. Kosnick 2004). Such merger, or the two-way integration between television and the Internet, could not be the case for radio, given that both the Internet and TV are visual media, whereas the audial radio can only be available through the Internet, but not the other way around.

Urry (1999) termed the virtual information flows made possible through the Internet, as *weightless traveling*, whereas *imaginative traveling* referred to such flows through television. Though television broadcasts amount to one-way public transmission of predetermined information, they were compared to the rather personal physical mobility via automobiles by Bachmair (1991, 522), who claimed that 'television succeeded because it broadened and extended lifestyles associated with the motor-car; primarily those concerned with *mobility* as a shaping principle of communication'. Others termed mobility vis-à-vis television, as *transport of the mind*, in that 'television turns out to be related to the motor car and the aeroplane as a means of transport of the mind' (Arnheim, quoted by Morse 1998, 99).

2.6   CONCLUSION

Table 2.4 presents the leading urban facilities and services for informational activities and connectivity, which have developed in Western cities throughout history, and were highlighted in this chapter. These facilities and services have emerged cumulatively, rather than by the way of newer services and facilities replacing existing ones. Each of the informational and connectivity facilities and services has been shown to have its own functions, fulfilling needs for formal and informal informational activities.

Table 2.4   Leading urban facilities and media for informational activities and connectivity

Era and year of innovation	Facility or medium	Place and country of innovation
Classical era		
500–520 BCE	Agora	Athens, Greece
530 BCE	Theater	Athens, Greece
387 BCE	Academia	Athens, Greece
Middle Ages		
1088	University	Bologna, Italy
1455	Book printing	Mainz, Germany
1475	Coffee shop	Istanbul, Turkey
1605	Newspaper	Strasburg, Germany
Modern times		
1876	Telephone	Boston, US
1896	Radio	Bologna, Italy
1925	Television	London, UK
1969	Internet	Washington DC, US

One of these media and the newest among them all, the Internet, is of a special nature, in its comprehensive, multi-purpose and multi-media nature. We have noted the inclusion of radio and television webcasts within it. We will note in the following chapter the inclusion of telephone services within it, and we will further note in Chapter 4, the inclusion of all of the previously developed informational facilities and services within it, including markets, entertainment, books, newspapers, universities, and virtual meeting places. The Internet constitutes, therefore, an informational and connectivity hub, equivalent to this function pursued by physical cities. We will, thus, highlight in Chapter 9 the possible implications of the widening Internet uses on physical cities.

European countries and cities led the development of urban informational facilities and services until the introduction of telecommunications technologies, when the US emerged as a leader in both the innovation and the adoption of informational newness.

3. The Internet

This chapter presents the development, structure, and distribution of the Internet for people, as well as of the IoT for non-living entities. The chapter will highlight, first, the history of the Internet and its structure. In this discussion, special attention will be devoted to the comprehensive nature of the Internet, in its double role as a communications medium and an information service, as well as to its becoming mobile, as of the late 1990s. This exposition will be followed by a discussion of mobile phones, which developed into Internet-connected smartphones, thus turning the Internet fully mobile. We will then focus on digital gaps in the adoption of digital media, through the highlighting of geographical and social differential distributions of the Internet, smartphones and mobile broadband, within and among countries and cities. Finally, we will elaborate on the history and spread of the IoT, accentuating its role for connecting people with devices and services, as well as its role for the provision of connectivity among the devices and services themselves.

3.1   THE INTERNET

The Internet constitutes the first, and so far the only, comprehensive information and communications medium. Its comprehensiveness consists of the provision of storage and retrieval for all forms of information, whether textual, audial, graphic or streaming, through the Web, by users located in fixed locations, or while they are on the move. The Internet constitutes likewise, and simultaneously, a communications medium, facilitating textual, graphic, audio and audiovisual communications among its subscribers, again without regard of their fixed or mobile locations anywhere worldwide. Advances in Internet technology have also facilitated automated mailing, as well as automated sending of all forms of documentation.

As we will note later in this chapter, IoT, which has been advanced as of the late 1990s and early 2000s (Ashton 2009), has facilitated the remote operation and control of devices and services, as well as communications among things and services. This latter option will be of special significance for the upcoming AVs, as we will note later in Chapter 8.

The Internet, like other digital technologies, consists of computerized codes, which are transmitted through routers and servers to and from human, device, and system subscribers. These transmitted codes may contain specific user or device information, such as emails, as well as information transmitted to and from publicly available pieces of information, organized and located within websites. The Internet transmission system is based on routers, which offer wide spatial flexibilities in the choice of movement routes for the sending of informational codes, thus avoiding traffic jams during routine communication and transmission activities. This automated routing flexibility further provides for alternative movement channels during emergencies or disasters, such as 9/11 in New York in 2001. On the other hand, however, the public and rather open nature of the Internet infrastructure makes it vulnerable to a wide variety of criminal hacking activities (Warf 2013).

The Internet was originally developed in the US in 1969, within the project of ARPANET (Advanced Research Projects Agency Network), as an experimental alternative communications system for telephone services, developed for a potential replacement of the telephone system in case of nuclear disasters (Table 3.1). It was originally experimented through a network, which connected security headquarters with universities (Kellerman 2002). This early involvement of universities in the development of ARPANET led, as of the early 1980s, to the emergence of academic digital networks, mainly the international BITNET (But It's Time Network), the British JANET (Joint Academic Network), and the American NSFNET (National Science Foundation Network).

The Internet started its way as a restricted communications medium offering email exchanges (1972), followed by its experimental informational use, for the transmission of news and opinions, as public or semi-public textual information (1979). This transmission of information was followed by a third phase of Internet development, facilitating its users with the consulting of information resources, being permanently available through websites in which they were stored and accessible (1991). Still before its commercial introduction, the transmission of information and the options for communications among Internet subscribers were widened through the development of audial and visual information transmissions (1992).

It took some 26 years of incubation and development until the early security and academic electronic networks of communications and information eventually matured into a universally open and commercial entity, the Internet, as of 1995. During this interval, several technologies were developed for a variety of requirements: turning the network into a fully automated one; permitting its universal access for communications, facilitating its operations as an information library, and allowing the Internet to become a commercial service on a rather global basis.

The technological developments and tools, which accompanied the development of the Internet, have been analogous to urban construction of roads and buildings in physical space. Hence, first, in 1974 the TCP/IP (transmission

Table 3.1   *Milestones in the development of the Internet*

Year	Innovation	Country
1965	Two computers communicate with each other	US
1969	ARPANET (Advanced Research Projects Agency Network) initiated	US
1972	Networked email	US
1973	Internationalization of ARPANET, followed by the establishment of the NSFNET, BITNET and JANET academic networks	UK
1974	TCP/IP (transmission control protocol/Internet protocol)	US
1979	USENET for news and discussion groups	US
1981	Multiprotocol router	US
1985	Registered domains	US
1991	WWW (World Wide Web)	Switzerland
1992	First distribution of audio and video; Voice over Internet Protocol (VoIP)	Israel
1993	Mosaic, the first Web browser	US
1995	Commercialization and public availability of the Internet	US
1996	WebTV introduced	US
1997	Wi-Fi (wireless fidelity) connectivity certified	US
1998	Google search engine	US
1999	Smartphones	Japan
2001	3G (third generation) mobile broadband	Japan
2004	Facebook	US

Sources: Kellerman (2018a, Table 5.2); Zimmermann and Emspak (2017).

control protocol/Internet protocol) was released, permitting a standardization of signal transmissions by different networks, and thus enabling the creation of a unified one, the Internet. This protocol has, thus, been equivalent to the paving of a standard road system with standardized road signs for corporeal mobility, thus enabling universal automated 'driving' through it. The establishment of this virtual road system was followed in 1981 by the first release of multiprotocol routers. Routers can be viewed as virtual controllers, being equivalent to changing traffic lights in physical mobility, since they direct each message or information-browsing attempt to an available route. These two technologies for the moving of information and its control apply to the transmission of interpersonal messages, as well as to information retrieval.

Two additional major technologies have been applied mainly to the ability by users to store and retrieve information through the Internet. Thus, in 1991 the WWW (World Wide Web), or shortly the Web, was created, as the information storage system via websites, analogously to public and commercial buildings in cities. The establishment of the Web was followed two years later by the introduction of the first 'Internet information vehicle', the browser, which can be viewed as equivalent to cars in physical mobility, providing for the search and retrieval of information being stored in numerous websites on the Web.

The four major Internet technologies of the Internet protocol, the router, the Web and the browser, jointly led to the establishment of the Internet system, as a fully functioning automated information and communications virtual space entity, in 1995. The Internet has constituted a fully automated information and communications system from its outset, without intermediate phases in its development, which could have potentially lead to its commercial introduction in 1995. Such phases could have potentially involved mediators, for instance human operators or electronic ones, connecting between communicating subscribers, or between subscribers and their desired Web information. The current universal and wide-ranging availability of the Internet, as compared to its original restricted security and academic objectives and audiences, has been considered as the best example for the adoption of a technology for purposes completely different from those envisaged by its developers (Urry 2003, 63).

Following the commercial introduction of the Internet (1995), the transmission of information through it has become even more versatile with the development of WebTV (1996) and 3D (three-dimensional) transmissions. Side by side with these improvements of the Internet visuality, the search for information through the expanding Web became more efficient with the introduction of search engines (1998). Generally, the technological development of the Internet has taken place mainly in the US, both before and after its commercial introduction in 1995, though several of its innovative technologies were introduced in other countries, as well (UK, Switzerland, Japan, and Israel).

As compared to the diffusion of the telephone, the rapid adoption of the Internet, as well as that of mobile telephony, which we will outline in the following section, have had to do with the prior existence of fixed-line telephone infrastructures for their operations, so that new connections to the existing system could be conveniently established. Of no less importance, though, has been the emergence of the Internet, as well as that of mobile telephony, as leading applications of IT, which has brought about also the digitization of the previously existing telephone system, prior to the introduction of the Internet and smartphones. Furthermore, the Internet, the mobile telephone, and IT in general, have constituted technological components of the emerging information society, and vice versa: the information society has placed a special emphasis on the production, processing, transmission, and consumption of information, facilitated by IT (Kellerman 2000).

Another significant dimension facilitating easy adoption for the rather virtual Internet system by individual users was the adoption of an interface between the code language of the Internet system, on the one hand, and its users, on the other. This interface has been the metaphorical cyberspace. It was developed for human users of the Internet, and obviously not for connected devices, and it has consisted of a metaphorically spatial verbal language, using terms such as websites, surfing, homepage, and so on, side by side with a physical space like screen organization (Kellerman 2016).

As compared to the 26 years that were required for Internet development, it took for the Internet much less time, just six years following its universal introduction, to be adopted in 2001 already by one-half of Americans, either having access to it elsewhere, or being online at home. Globally, though, the Internet still presents a digital divide in its adoption patterns: some 48 percent of the global population made use of the Internet in 2017, albeit in less developed countries (LDCs) this percentage stood at 17.5 percent only, as compared to 81 percent in developed ones (ITU 2018). We will discuss these and some additional digital gaps, which have emerged in other geographical and social scales, in a later section in this chapter.

The Internet principle of free flow has been applied to the transmission of both communications and information, with seamless flows of messages and information, facilitated by the automation of both the transmissions and their control. This same principle of free flows has been applied also to Internet contents, which has been governed by an *open code*, considered by Lessig (2001, 246) as the 'heart of the Internet'. This open code nature of the Internet has become a major principle for the human use of the Internet. It has permitted autonomous access of subscribers to the Internet for the production of information, whether through the establishment of websites or through the writing of messages, unless such actions have been restricted by some governmental censorship (Warf 2013; Kellerman 2016). The open code principle typifying the Internet has further permitted an open access of Internet users to the consumption of Internet information, through the receipt of messages, as well as through their accessing of free of charge websites. In addition, the open code principle has facilitated the uncontrolled flows of information from any origins to any destinations, unless controlled by governmental censorship. At yet another end, the open code system has been crucial for innovative contents, as it has allowed innovations to be freely introduced, shared and adopted for both the production and the consumption of Internet information.

All of these activities for information production, consumption and innovation, have been unrestricted, neither by a minimal nor by a maximal age of users, so that the use of the Internet constitutes a completely informal activity, as compared to the requirement of age-restricted driving licensing for the operation of non-autonomous cars.

The open nature of the Internet, as a communications and information system, may be related to its origin and development in the US, a country that has been characterized by a social accent on the freedom of expression. The nature of the Internet as a mainly verbal-visual communications system, calls for literacy as a requirement for its use, as compared to car driving, which is based mainly on the recognition of road signs by drivers. As we noted in the previous chapter regarding the structuring and terms of conduct for telephone calls, there have emerged some informal codes for email correspondence, as well, using signs for smiles, agreement and so on, followed later by the practice of icon and emoji use, mainly for chat platforms.

Another informal requirement for Internet activity is a basic knowledge of computer operation for its efficient use. In addition, some knowledge of English is almost imperative, as illiteracy of the English language implies lack of access to information contained in over one-half of the website system (see Hargittai 1999; W³Techs 2017). Furthermore, the use of the Internet is not only facilitated by its accessibility, affordability, and the capabilities of its users, but also by the choices of preferred uses made by each of its subscribers (Kline 2013). Culture and religion are some additional informal dimensions that may influence, in some cases, the extent of use of the Internet, as well as its open code nature. This is the case notably when religious authorities attempt to restrict access to the system, or when they enforce some cultural censorships on its use, as well as on the contents of websites.

The flow experiences of individuals in their uses of the rather automated Internet, or their cyber-mobility experience, may resemble the use or the driving of traditional human-driven cars in cities. In driving, the specific structures of road systems, the driving alternatives that they may facilitate, and the eventual specific choices of roads made by each driver, as conditioned by levels of traffic congestion, may bring about varying experiences for the drivers, as far as trip lengths and driving conveniences are concerned. Similarly, flows in Internet transmissions, as experienced by individual users, may refer to the sequence of screens that follow each other in the use of some specific websites, notably in the use of those websites that provide a service. In such flow sessions, each screen may require some action by Internet users, for instance websites that require the engagement of their users in financial transactions, shopping, travel reservations and so on. Users may encounter friendly and logical flows of such activity processes/screens, or, in some other cases, rather cumbersome or complicated ones, making it difficult for them to follow through. Flows for individuals in cyberspatial contexts refer, therefore, to the flows of information, as well as to the interactions of users with websites (or with the servers behind them).

The Internet was considered to constitute 'a metaphor for the social life as fluid' (Urry 2000, 40), so that the notion of *Internetness* refers to values, practices, norms and patterns associated with the use of the Internet by individuals, involving the three social spheres of individuals, society and space (for a detailed discussion see Kellerman 2006). From a temporal perspective, the Internet cannot be considered a time-intruder for its users, unless it is used for incoming telephone calls through Voice over Internet Protocol (VoIP). In its other uses, the Internet facilitates its operation by users at any time of their individual choices, avoiding any intrusions or interventions of the Internet connectivity into their other activities.

From the perspective of individual users, the most dramatic trend in contemporary virtual mobility has been the turning of the Internet into a fully mobile and universal communications and information medium, thus enabling access to both email and the Web at any time and place. As we will note in the following section, these rather enhanced levels of automation and availability have been made possible mainly through smartphones equipped with the two leading technologies of Wi-Fi (wireless fidelity) and 3G (third generation) or 4G (fourth generation), of cellular broadband communications. These two technologies, coupled with the GPS (global positioning systems) technology, which has facilitated the determination of the location of mobile users through satellite communications, have become widely available as of the early 2000s. Thus, since then, people could get in touch with each other from anywhere to anywhere. Furthermore, these technologies have made it gradually possible for Internet users to connect with their homes and their devices via IoT, which has been the case for inter-device communications, as well. As far as people are concerned, the simultaneous introduction of social interaction platforms (Web 2.0) as of the early 2000s (e.g. Facebook, Twitter, WhatsApp and Viber), has brought about the emergence of a rather continuous use of smartphones for both interpersonal communications and information gathering and transmissions.

The Wi-Fi and 3G connectivity technologies have widened the geographical extent of access to the Internet, as well as its quality. The ITU (2018) reported for 2017, that some 56.4 percent of the world population and some 97.1 percent of the population in developed countries possessed active mobile broadband subscriptions, mainly for their mobile phones. The critical importance of broadband for the growing use of the Internet and the widening applications of Internet communications cannot be scaled down. Thus, it was for Mossberger et al. (2013, 3) to declare that 'broadband has become the standard for Internet use'. Furthermore, Castells (2009, 65) stated that mobile broadband is for the Internet what the electric grid has been for the provision of electric power, that is, it permits universal distribution of Internet connectivity, though electricity use does not involve human capabilities, such as literacy. The two technologies of Wi-Fi and 3G have integrated the two virtual mobility media of the Internet, as a communications and information system, on the one hand, and mobile phones and as communications and information devices, on the other. Such an integration is true also for the fixed PCs.

As Mossberger et al. (2013) have strongly argued, the use of mobile broadband cannot function as a full substitute for fixed broadband. It is for mobile broadband, notably when installed in smartphones and tablets, to be used mainly for routine communications, as well as for some basic information retrieval. However, it is rather for fixed broadband when being connected to desktop PCs, or to big-screen laptops, to permit and to facilitate much wider uses of the Internet, notably for production processes, as well as for innovation purposes and opportunities. Both the fixed and the mobile uses of the Internet involve two new conditions for the behavior and action of their users: simultaneous co-presence in physical and virtual spaces, as a new mode of behavior, and the online experience of action in virtual space, as a new mode of action. We will briefly outline these two conditions in the following two chapters.

3.2   THE SMARTPHONE

Smartphones constitute upgraded mobile phones, facilitating connectivity to the Internet and GPS, side by side with their provision of audial and textual mobile telephony. Hence, we will look first at the emergence and adoption of mobile telephones, followed by their upgrading into smartphones.

Mobile telephone technology was originally invented back in 1906 in the US by Lee de Forest who claimed already by then that 'it will be possible for businessmen, even while automobiling, to be kept in constant touch' (Agar 2003, 167). However, the first limited mobile phone service was introduced in the UK much later, in 1940, followed by a similarly limited service in the US in 1947 (Table 3.2). The universal availability and wide adoption of mobile telephony began much later, in the late 1970s, awaiting two developments: the release of proper wavelengths for the system by governmental authorities, and the emergence of IT, which has brought about the miniaturization of the telephone devices and the automation of their calling and operational systems.

The release of proper wavelengths by the FCC (Federal Communications Commission) in the US was slow and rather late, so that the inauguration of mobile telephone service, as well as further technological development of mobile telephony, were shared by the UK, Japan and the Scandinavian countries. The leadership of the Scandinavian countries in the adoption of telecommunications services began already with the veteran fixed-line telephones, whereas Japan, jointly with South Korea, led the development and adoption of Internet uses through smartphones (Kellerman 2002, 2014). Thus, universal commercial availability of mobile telephone services began only in 1979, in Japan and Scandinavia, and its automation came right after, in 1981 in Scandinavia. This two-year interval between the beginning of mobile tele-

Table 3.2   *Milestones in the development of smartphones*

Phase and year of innovation	Innovation	Country
Inventions		
1906	Cellular telephone	US
1973	Handheld cell phone	US
I. Mobile telephony		
1940	First commercial mobile call	UK
1979	First cellular phone service	Japan and Scandinavia
1981	First automated cellular phone service	Scandinavia
1993	SMS introduced	Finland
II. Smartphones		
1990	GPS for car navigation	Japan
1997	Wi-Fi (wireless fidelity) connectivity certified	US
1999	Smartphone introduced	Japan
2001	3G (third generation) mobile broadband established	Japan

Source: Following Kellerman (2018a, Table 5.1).

phone services and their automation was much shorter than the 22 years that passed between the inauguration of fixed-line telephone service and its initial local automation, and the 92 years which passed until full dialing automation was reached (see Table 2.1). This fast pace of automation for mobile telephony emerged given that mobile telephony began its initial universally commercial operations in the digital era.

Two additional features of mobile phones have contributed to its enormous success. The first feature was their ability to transmit written text transmission through SMS (short message service), which was originally introduced in 1993 in Finland, and which became widely adopted as of 2000. SMS was originally invented for text messaging, and it was extended later on for video messages transmitted through mobile phones. Text messaging has turned mobile phones from an audial medium only, thus being similar to fixed-line telephones, into an audiovisual one, requiring literacy for its textual operation. The second feature of mobile phones, leading to their success, was their turning into smartphones, connected to the Internet and GPS, innovated in 1999 in Japan. The condition of literacy requirement has become even more striking when mobile phones turned into Internet-connected smartphones.

Mobile broadband connectivity, required for turning mobile phones into smartphones, has been based on two technologies, which we mentioned already: Wi-Fi, certified in 1997 in the US, and 3G broadband transmission, established in 2001 in Japan. In addition to Internet and GPS connectivities, smartphones included some other features, in the form of early applications, notably calculators and calendars.

Though originally introduced in the early 1990s, Wi-Fi was widely adopted only as of the second half of the 1990s. Its adoption required, first, the development of tiny communications components installed within smartphones, side by side with the need to install all over towns numerous fixed Wi-Fi antennas, each covering a limited spatial range of reception. The second mobile transmission system, 3G, permitting broadband transmission through mobile phone networks, has made it possible to use the Internet extensively through mobile phone service subscriptions without a need for Wi-Fi coverage, but for charges made by mobile phone companies.

The availability of Wi-Fi and 3G communications technologies for mobile Internet transmission, as of the early 2000s, turned smartphones into hand-held computers, facilitating full Internet use and traffic. From that point on, mobile telephony and the Internet have developed hand-in-hand, with much of the use of the Internet by individuals pursued through smartphones on a continuous location-free basis, rather than through location-fixed PCs.

The fully automated smartphone, provided with multiple connectivity, including phone calling, Internet communications and information, and GPS navigation, implied an autonomy of the mobile devices for the determination of call routing, as well as for the determination of the destinations of calls and messages, in case calls are placed to other mobile phones, rather than to fixed-line telephones. The flexible routing of mobile phone calls, using wireless routes, has permitted wider routing possibilities, as compared to the cable dependency of fixed-line telephones, thus turning mobile phones into highly autonomous devices in their operations. However, it continues to remain for mobile phone subscribers to decide on the specific personal destinations of their calls, as compared to the determination of the locational destinations of the called party, as is the case for fixed-line telephone calls. Coupled with the determination of the exact timing of calling, mobile phone users enjoy their own autonomous power to reach calling parties wherever they are located, and whenever they wish to reach them.

Mobile phones have been rapidly adopted as of the 1990s, coupled with a reduction of both the size of the devices and the subscription rates for their use (Lacohée et al. 2003; Rogers 1995, 244–246). Recently, the mobile phone has turned into the globally most widely diffused communications device, with a global penetration rate of 103.5 percent in 2017, attesting to multiple subscriptions by individuals. This high penetration rate for mobile phones was coupled with some 95 percent of the populated areas worldwide covered by a mobile phone signal already as of 2009. The penetration rate of mobile phone subscription in LDC reached some 70.4 percent in 2017 (ITU 2018), and this high penetration rate represents an even wider availability of mobile phones in LDCs, given that in some developing countries people may rent out their mobile phones to others for single calls or SMSs as a commercial service.

Already as of 2002, the percentage population worldwide owning a mobile phone line has been higher than that having a fixed line (ITU 2018). Numerous factors contributed to differences in the growing adoption rates, such as country, gender, and age (Castells et al. 2007; Kellerman 2014). Digital international gaps still pertain, however, as far as access to mobile broadband is concerned. Thus, and as we noted already, in 2017 some 56.4 percent of the world population enjoyed access to mobile broadband, but this was divided between 97.1 percent in developed countries, as compared to merely 22.3 percent in LDCs (ITU 2018).

The constant carrying of mobile phones by their users and the automated constant connectivity that they provide have affected the public urban sphere. The use of mobile phones has blurred the common distinction between the private and the public, as well as that between indoors and outdoors (Kopomaa 2000), into what Sheller (2004) termed 'mobile publics'. Such mobile publics have become the standard urban human landscape, with numerous people making use of their telephones in public, either for audial calls or for visual Internet activities. Whereas telephones and computers have been traditionally considered devices to be used indoors, and involving some privacy of communications by their users, the newly emerging wirelessness as of the 1990s, has implied less privacy and a change of social boundaries, due to the emerging norm of acceptance of audial communications activity in the public sphere (see Kellerman 2006).

3.3   DIGITAL DIVIDES

The adoption processes of the digital media, which we have discussed so far, have involved divides or gaps, some of which, as we will see, still persist. Digital divides or digital gaps were defined as 'differences in people's access to information and communications technologies (ICT)' (Atkinson et al. 2008, 479; see also Van Dijk and Hacker 2003). Such differences relate to the availability and utilization of a variety of ICTs, notably the Internet, the mobile phone and mobile broadband. Of these ICTs, special attention has been devoted to the Internet, which still presents wide gaps in its adoption levels at the global scale. This digital gap may reflect the Internet implying the availability of a wide spectrum of information and communications activities, all of which require literacy.

Digital divides may be identified both geographically and socially. Geographically, divides may emerge at several scales: globally among conti-

Table 3.3   *Global adoption percentages of selected communications media 2017*

Communications medium	World	Developed countries	Less developed countries
Internet	48	81	17.5
Mobile phone	103.5	127.3	70.4
Mobile broadband	56.4	97.1	22.3

Source: ITU (2018).

nents or between developed countries and LDCs; internationally, among countries; domestically among regions and locally within cities. Digital divides may further reflect sectoral differences along gender, age, income, as well as level of education. As we noted already, digital gaps are still there between the developed and the developing world, coupled with differences among nations. Thus, the emergence of Internet-based cities is currently more typical of cities in the developed world, characterized by high penetration rates of the Internet among the populations of those cities.

From a global perspective, Table 3.3 presents divides among two blocks of countries, developed and LDCs for 2017, most of which we noted already in previous sections. Interestingly enough, this summary table shows that the ranking of media by their adoption rates is similar in both country blocks, the developed ones and LDCs. Thus, mobile phones lead, followed by mobile broadband and the Internet, in this order. In LDCs, this ranking may reflect lower levels of literacy, thus restricting the utilization of the Internet. However, in developed countries, this difference may reflect a preference for enhanced spatial mobility made possible through the adoption of mobile phones. The role of literacy, side by side with that of the cost of Internet services, find their expression also in the rather extremely high gaps between the low adoption rate of the Internet, as compared to those of mobile phones and mobile broadband in LDCs, whereas in developed countries these differences are rather small.

At the international level, the presentation of gaps in Internet access and use by country has been presented elsewhere (e.g. Wilson et al. 2013; Warf 2013; Kellerman 2014). An in-depth statistical analysis for international digital divides was performed by Pick and Nishida (2015), who studied differences in the availability and utilization for all the three ICT media for 110 countries, making use of 2007–2009 data, and employing independent variables representing a variety of economic, social and governmental forces. They were able to show that globally 'the most important correlates are tertiary education, capacity for innovation, and judicial independence. Of lesser importance are freedom of press, foreign direct investment and females in the labor force'

(Pick and Nishida 2015, 6), with some variation among the studied media. For the developing continents of Africa and South America, they found that 'the correlates of Internet use are tertiary education, freedom of press, and foreign direct investment' (Pick and Nishida 2015, 12). These latter findings accentuate the roles of knowledge, openness and economic development in levels of Internet use.

A specific investigation of gender differences in the use of the Internet at the international level revealed that there were numerous Latin American and Caribbean countries in which women led in the rate of use of the Internet (Kellerman 2016). This tendency regarding females' use of the Internet in Latin America constitutes just one aspect of a more general trend for these countries. Thus, it was reported by the World Economic Forum that 'Latin America and the Caribbean is the region that has made the most progress at closing the gender gap over the last ten years' (Ugarte 2015, compare with Warf 2009).

Divides in the adoption of digital media used to be substantial in the past also within countries in the developed world, whether among regions or among population sectors, whether along gender or by socioeconomic sectors, and these gaps were studied extensively (see e.g. Castells et al. 2007; Graham and Marvin 1996; Malecki and Moriset 2008; Gilbert and Masucci 2011). Some of these gaps were attributed, at the time, to the reflection that 'the Internet is a social product that is interwoven with relations of class, race, and gender and increasingly subject to the uses of power' (Warf 2006, xxvii). However, with the contemporarily achieved high adoption rates of the Internet, as well as of those for mobile phones and mobile broadband in developed countries, the gaps among regions, as well as within cities, seem to be of declining significance. Thus, in the US in 2018, some 90 percent of the population utilized the Internet, and this rate was equally divided between women and men (Pew Research Center 2018).

In less developed peripheries within countries, digital gaps continue to persist. A study in the Russian periphery suggested that the use of the Internet has been more restricted there, since Internet information has been considered by residents there as unreliable (Dovbysh 2013). The digital divide between urban and rural areas has drawn the attention of numerous governments worldwide, leading them to activate development plans for its reduction. This has been the case, for example, for India (James 2003); Mongolia (Ariunaa 2006); Hungary (Pósfai and Féjer 2008); and Chile (Kline 2013).

At the intra-city level, Crang et al. (2006) noted, at the time, the differences in speed of action and everyday practices within neighborhoods, depending on levels of Internet and other ICT connectivities, thus producing multispeed urban landscapes, consisting of slow and fast paced neighborhoods. Studying two neighborhoods within the city of Newcastle upon Tyne (UK), they were able to point to differences in media adoption, with the fixed-line telephone considered essential by all residents. Similarly, studying the town of Albury (Australia), Atkinson et al. (2008) were able to show that age, education, and level of income determined the level of people's access to the Internet, at the time.

3.4 THE INTERNET OF THINGS (IoT)

The emergence of IoT technology and its adoption for communications of human beings with devices and services, as well as for communications among devices and services themselves, occurred only after the Internet was already pretty widely adopted by both individual and company users, with the term IoT coined back in 1999 (Ashton 2009) (Table 3.4).

Table 3.4   Milestones in the development of the Internet of Things (IoT)

Phase and year of innovation	Innovation	Country
Inventions		
1945	RFID (radio frequency identification)	Soviet Union
1995	Internet	US
1999	Smartphone	Japan
Development		
1999	The term Internet of Things (IoT) coined	US
2002	Web of Things	US
2003	EPCglobal (electronic product code)	US
2006	OPC (Open Platform Communications) UA (Unified Architecture) protocol	US
2008/9	More devices than people connected	N/A
2022–2025	Autonomous vehicles (AVs) introduced	?

Sources: Postscapes (2018); Desjardins (2018); Atzori et al. (2017).

However, the vision for IoT, as well as the development of several pertinent technologies, which permit machine-to-machine (M2M) communications, date much earlier (Atzori et al. 2017). Basic among these technologies were, at the time, RFID (radio frequency identification) technologies, originally invented in the Soviet Union in 1945. These technologies facilitate radio signal transmissions from objects. RFID has become widely applied as of the early 2000s, following the introduction of miniaturized and rather cheap tags attached to communicating devices. RFID tags of newer generations being attached to objects, have become interconnected via the Internet through the

EPCglobal (electronic product code) network as of 2003, using Web technologies and resources through the Web of Things.

As we noted earlier in this chapter, interactions among both individuals and devices have been massively widened and upgraded through the introduction of the wireless and fast transmission technologies of Wi-Fi (as of 1997) and mobile broadband (as of 2001). These technologies have facilitated the turning of mobile phones into Internet-based smartphones. Furthermore, these technologies have provided also for inter-object communications to become Internet-based. Using Wi-Fi and mobile broadband technologies for IoT applications has thus widened the scale of IoT applications.

However, the most important boost for the wide diffusion of IoT was brought about by the release in 2006 of the OPC (Open Platform Communications) UA (United Architecture) protocol, which provided for secure communications among devices. In addition, numerous other relevant procedures, standards and protocols, have been developed since then, with current efforts centered on the 'cloud of things' technologies, which attempt to automatically and autonomously interconnect people, objects and services within the so-called 'future Internet' (Atzori et al. 2017).

Thus, side by side with the increase in human Internet activities and human Internet users, there has developed a fast quantitative growth in the extent of IoT implementation as well. Thus, as of 2008/9, more devices were connected to the Internet than humans were, and this latter trend may possibly peak even further, once the Internet-communicated autonomous vehicles (AVs) are introduced, probably by 2022–2025 (Kellerman 2018a). Still, however, IoT applications need to be trusted by human users in order for them to be applied for sensitive uses (Atzori et al. 2017).

As we will note in Chapter 7, IoT has turned into an essential technology for the very operations of smart cities, notably as far as the addition of connectivity to the operations of urban systems is concerned, so that utilities have become remotely operated, as well as interconnections established among urban systems. The adoption of IoT for smart city development involves the deployment of numerous wired and wireless sensors throughout cities, installed in smart homes, in traffic lights, in utility central facilities, as well as in environmental monitoring stations and so on. These sensors are connected to control centers through Wi-Fi, Bluetooth and mobile transmission networks of various generations (Rathore et al. 2016; Talari et al. 2017; Mehmood et al. 2017).

The development of the basic technologies for IoT has been shared, at the time, by the Soviet Union, the US and Japan. However, most of the following protocol developments have taken place in the US, similarly, and side by side with, the development of Internet protocols and software.

In her pioneering study, Xu (2017) attempted to portray some basic notions for geographical interpretations of IoT. Thus, IoT may be involved, as humans are, in the production and use of tacit knowledge, though IoT does so obviously through technology-leaned means. Also in similarity to the Internet, IoT functions simultaneously within two contextualities, from the local to the global, as well as from the physical to the digital. These contextualities involve a rather diversified production of services through IoT, for the benefit and convenience of individuals and households, for increased productivity of organizations and industries, as well as for societal sustainability and service provision through cities, regions and nations.

Adoptions of IoT along these socio-spatial size scales may involve also some risks, such as a potential hurting of privacy for individuals, data security for companies, and regulatory risks for governmental applications. However, IoT may be used in numerous cases for rather innocent new or upgraded applications, sometimes through combinations between the Internet and IoT. For instance, the control panels within elevator cabins may be turned into Internet-connected touch screens, thus permitting a choice of language by users, as well as the presentation of time, external temperature and changing announcements. These new functions may serve as additions to the control of floor access by users and their floor selections, as well as the collection and analysis of information on the patterns of use by elevator riders.

3.5   CONCLUSION

We focused in this chapter on the emergence of the Internet in the wider sense of the application of this technology, including smartphones and the IoT. As far as the Internet per se is concerned, we noted its comprehensive nature in its constitution of both a communications and information system, facilitating the transmission, storage and retrieval of all forms and formats of information. Mobile phones turning into smartphones connected to mobile broadband and GPS constitute the leading medium for the use of the Internet in a rather location-free and mobile manner. Digital gaps in the adoption of the Internet still prevail at the global and international levels, whereas mobile phones have become widely adopted even at the global level. IoT development and use have flourished as of the late 1990s, so that IoT has been applied at an enormously wide scale, and it will probably peak even further with the upcoming introduction of AVs.

The Internet has enabled the construction of a metaphorical space including sites, addresses, vehicles (search engines and browsers), and transmission systems (mobile broadband). Smartphones permit their users to reach this metaphorical space for a wide variety of uses from anywhere and at any time. The wide availability of this virtual city-like Internet system calls for a more detailed examination of the activities performed by urbanites within it, as well as the experience of Internet users being simultaneously present in both the material and virtual cities. These dimensions will constitute the foci for the following two chapters, respectively.

The three technologies which were described in this chapter, the Internet, the smartphone and IoT, have reached an integration among them from their users' perspective, in the sense that smartphones serve as always-there mobile terminals for connectivity to the Internet, as well as to those IoT applications, which are designed for human communications with devices and services (see Chapter 7). Communications among non-human devices are channeled through servers, which provide for connectivity between the Internet and the IoT, as well.

The growing communicational complexities presented by the Internet in its wider sense, bear also on the nature and measuring of digital divides. These divides should not be measured anymore merely along the traditional parameters of Internet and smartphone adoption levels, since these latter measures do not expose the possible emergence of complex smart systems in some cities or countries, as compared to others. Such smart systems include mainly smart homes, smart cities, and smart cars, all of which will be discussed in Chapters 7 and 8, respectively. The emergence of such smart complexities imply the availability and use of sophisticated operational and control systems. Thus, wide adoption rates of mobile phones and the Internet by individuals do not imply by themselves the emergence of Internet-based cities, since the latter require the implementation of complex control systems and technologies for the communications of urban systems, as well.

PART II

Urban Internet applications

4. The Internet for individual users

The first part of the book was devoted to urban connectivity as well as to urban informational activities, and the Internet was introduced within this framework. We will move now to the second part of the book, which will focus on the rather wide variety of urban Internet activities, as pursued by individuals (Chapters 4–5); companies and organizations (Chapter 6); urban systems (Chapter 7); and, finally, by the upcoming AVs (Chapter 8).

This chapter will elaborate on the uses of the Internet by urbanites for their obtaining of urban services, which were previously pursued solely in physical space (see also Kellerman 2014). In the following section, we will discuss the advantages in the obtaining of urban services via the Internet, followed by elaborations of specific urban services currently consumed, at least partially, also through the Internet. These elaborations will be complemented in the following chapter, by an exposition of the dual-space city, experienced by Internet users, and consisting of both physical and Internet spaces.

The urban 'e-' (electronic) services and actions, which are currently available through the Internet, include mainly, but not exclusively, social interaction, shopping, banking, travel reservations, learning, health, and governmental services. However, as we will see, the use of the Internet for full-time telework is less popular, since most employees do not prefer to work permanently from their homes only. In later sections of this chapter, we will expose the nature of these Internet services, and we will further examine some comparative data on their consumption by Internet users in various countries. For the EU countries, we will use mainly the official EU data for 2017, as released by Eurostat (2018). However, for countries in other parts of the world, updated country-by-country data have not been available. Thus, we will make use of OECD (2018) data for an e-government parameter for numerous countries, as well as some country-specific data for other e-services, gathered from numerous sources.

There are additional individual routine activities, of a more cultural nature, which may be viewed as urban services, and for which the Internet does not constitute the sole digital alternative to physical attendance. Virtual alternatives to the theater and the concert hall have emerged already before the introduction of the Internet, through television and audio home systems, as well as through the more contemporary mobile MP3 devices. However, it seems that people still mostly prefer to use these latter digital options rather than the

Internet for such activities (for some European data see Eurostat 2018). At yet another arena, that of religious services, the Internet may offer an alternative to churches and temples, thus bringing about even the development of online religious communities (see e.g. Kong 2001).

4.1 ADVANTAGES OF INTERNET URBAN SERVICES

We may identify several advantages, from the perspective of Internet-using urbanites, for their growing tendency to consume urban services via the Internet. These advantages include the freedom of choice for arenas that facilitate service consumption; changes in the service industries; the availability to individuals of numerous types of devices for Internet communications; and, finally, the ease of use of the Internet for service consumption. We will shortly outline below each of these advantages.

First, the availability of Internet services, side by side with their availability in urban physical space, provides for freedom of choice, as far as the time and location for the obtaining of services are concerned, thus implying enhanced locational opportunities for service consumption for individuals, or their self-extension, through the distanciation of their availability into virtual space (Giddens 1990). Thus, Internet subscribers are able to consume services, and to explore opportunities for their consumption wherever they are located (Kellerman and Paradiso 2007; Kwan 2001).

Second, the possible splitting of service consumption between physical and virtual spaces may, potentially at least, bring about some complementarity, rather than substitution, between the services offered by the two spaces, so that the performance of some specific service activity may be split between the Internet. For example, price comparison for some commodities may be pursued over the Web, whereas the eventual shopping of these commodities takes place in physical space. However, repeated uses of Internet services may, potentially at least, change the balance between services offered through facilities located in physical space and within easy bodily reach of potential customers, on the one hand, and similar services provided through the Internet, on the other. Such possible change of balance between the two spaces would obviously be in favor of the virtual and at the expense of the physical, as current trends show (see Chapter 9). Alternatively, the competition with services available over the Internet may potentially bring about some structural changes in service facilities located in physical space, making them more attractive for potential customers.

Third, the contemporary scene of the information age presents to individuals a wide choice among media that permit a variety of performances over the Internet, including mainly PCs, laptops, tablets and smartphones, as well as combinations among these appliances. It has become possible, therefore, for a person being on the road, to communicate with websites, while the location of the hosting servers for these websites may simultaneously change (e.g. through peering). In other words, new sophisticated virtual mobilities permit individuals to act virtually without any regard to the location of the cities or countries from which they communicate, nor with regard to the internal spatial structures of the cities from which they communicate (Kellerman 2014, 100).

Fourth, the operation of contemporary personal communications media by their users, notably PCs and smartphones, is assumed to be rather convenient and user-friendly, and thus barrier-free for virtual service consumption. Once communication between a user and a chosen website is initiated, the speed of reach of the website is normally instant. Moreover, users of communications media expect constant enhancements in communication speed through IT innovations, as well as through upgraded Internet and mobile infrastructures. Thus, the global traffic of mobile data has grown by some 50 percent in one year (2016–2017), and is expected to grow by this annual pace at least until 2021 (Statista 2018a). This traffic of mobile data is led by video transmission for entertainment, as well as by e-commerce as a service activity.

4.2   HOME-BASED WORK

Home-based work, or as it has variously been termed telework, telecommuting, or tele homework, assumes that people's work can be fully and continuously performed by many workers from their homes. Home-based work requires appliances and communications infrastructures that are available already within households in developed countries: PCs or laptops equipped with cameras; multipurpose printers (facilitating printing, scanning copying and faxing); fixed-line telephones; and broadband Internet.

Home-based work has probably been the first, as well as the continuously discussed virtual activity, bringing about potential locational opportunities for individuals (see Kellerman 1984). For Halford (2005), work at home implies the spatial relocation of work from offices to homes, coupled with its dislocation from physical space into cyberspace. Work at home, fully or partially, became potentially possible as far back as the 1970s, following the introduction and diffusion of the Telnet technology, which facilitated remote access to mainframe computers through computer terminals and later on through PCs. The introduction of the Internet some twenty years later, in the mid-1990s, could have potentially turned the option of working from home into a standard mode of work. The Internet has offered extremely wide options for instant information transmission, and it has been widely adopted by households in developed countries. Furthermore, the Internet was introduced following the previously accumulated twenty years of experience in computerized remote work from home via Telnet.

However, as things have turned out, work from home, as an exclusive location for workers, has not matured into a favorite option, neither for employers, nor for employees, or for the self-employed. Employers have preferred to maintain their on-site supervision of workers, as well as the holding of face-to-face staff meetings on a regular basis, and employees, on their part, preferred to meet face-to-face with their colleagues, on a daily or almost daily basis, and be bodily present in their offices. Women in particular have tended to prefer a locational separation between home and work duties (for reviews of these preferences see Halford 2005; Hislop and Axtell 2007; Felstead et al. 2005; and Loo 2012). Still, though, partial work from home, notably after work hours, has become routine for many workers, who were viewed, at the time, as 'nomads' (see e.g. Castells 2000). Thus, Finnish findings have shown that telework is more common among knowledge-intensive workers (Merisalo et al. 2013). Work at home does not normally imply a higher quality of life for workers, though productivity was reported to be higher among workers from home (Halford 2005).

Home-based workers may be classified into three groups: partial or hybrid (working both from their offices and at home); full-time; and 'mobile workers', with the latter ones being those workers who work at dispersed locations, such as at clients' facilities (see Malecki and Moriset 2008). Of these three groups, people who work online fully from home are of special interest, since their daily professional action space has become completely virtualized. Among these teleworkers, even more interesting are those self-employed workers who work fully from home, so that they serve their clients through the Internet, and perform their work through the Internet as well, for instance text editors and translators or consultants.

Data on home-based work by country are frequently too general, without distinctions among types of teleworkers. In the US in 2017, some 2.9 percent of the total workforce worked from home at least half of the time. Though this share of the workforce is small, it represents a 117 percent growth from the 1.8 percent reported for 2005 (Flexjobs 2017). In the UK, by 2014, some 5 percent of those at work did so within their homes or its grounds, with some additional 8.9 percent of those at work using their homes as their bases, but still working in different places. These rates were the highest since records on telework were collected first in 1998 (Office for National Statistics 2014). In China too, the percentage of home-based workers was low, standing at 3 percent only in 2012 (Luo 2015).

4.3   ONLINE SHOPPING

Online shopping has further been termed B2C (business-to-customers) e-commerce, as compared to B2B (business-to-business) e-commerce (see e.g. Loo 2012). Online shopping systems permit potential customers to perform virtually all the phases of shopping processes, and in similar ways as compared to their performances in physical space stores, with the exception of touching and trying. These phases include search for products; search for vendors; viewing of products and reading information on them; price comparisons; and eventually the very act of purchasing. The reach of product information, as well as extensive and instant price comparisons, available through the Web, are unparalleled in physical space stores. Furthermore, virtual shopping constitutes the silent, but also the much less experiential, option for shopping, as compared to the noisy and rather lively experience offered by physical shopping malls and urban streets alike.

Shopping has become extended into a potential global 'opportunity', when shopping through global stores and virtual shopping malls can be accessed via the Internet on a 24/7 basis (Loo 2012), so that online shopping frees customers from spatial barriers, as well as from temporal frictions and restrictions. Frequently, customers prefer to split a specific shopping activity between physical and virtual vendors, notably when it comes to the purchase of major appliances and other highly priced commodities, so that touching and trying are made in a physical store, whereas the very purchase is possibly pursued in a virtual one. Such fragmentations of action, as a common characteristic of shopping activities by individuals, implies that at least some shopping in physical stores is continued, side by side with people's shopping in virtual ones (Couclelis 2004; see also Schwanen et al. 2008). The relationships between online and in-store shopping may turn out as complex from behavioral perspectives, as well. Thus, for example, it was found for China that online shoppers prefer to shop online during weekdays, whereas their in-store shopping is the preferred mode during weekends (Ding and Lu 2017).

The beginnings of online shopping, in the early 2000s, were typified by a focus on information products, 'soft' ones such as reports, music and books, side by side with 'hard' ones, such as computers of all types. Several years later, online shopping has widened its scope and, as of the 2010s its offerings include mainly clothing and other consumer products.

The emergence of online shopping in North America, Europe and Asia in the 2000s and up to 2012 has been outlined elsewhere (Kellerman 2014). During this period, the US led in the percentage of the population shopping online with some 71 percent of the population doing so in 2011, followed by China with some 55 percent of its population shopping online in 2012 (Table 4.1).

Table 4.1   *Percentage of Internet users shopping online in leading countries 2010–2017*

Country	2010–2012	2017
China	55 (2012)	83
South Korea	37 (2012)	83
UK	53 (2010)	82
Germany	47 (2010)	81*
Indonesia	26 (2012)	79
India	26 (2012)	77
US	71 (2011)	77
Taiwan	N/A	76
Poland	35 (2010)	75
Thailand	23 (2012)	74

Note: * Eurostat (2018) has reported for Germany 75 percent (Table 4.2).
Sources: 2010–2012: Kellerman (2014, Tables 7.1–7.2); 2017: Statista (2018b).

Other countries presented, by then, rather modest shares of their populations shopping online, with the differences among them, notably in Europe, related to country size, coupled with people's preferences for shopping in physical stores. Shoppers' habits, lower trust in online vendors, and uncertainties about online financial transactions were suggested, at the time, as the main obstacles on the road of expanding online shopping (see Kellerman 2014).

Just 5–7 years later, in 2017, the percentages of the population going online for shopping has grown widely in most countries in the developed world, and the global leadership and the geographical patterns for online shopping have changed as well. The US percentage of population shopping online grew from 2011 to 2017 by a mere 6 percent to 77 percent, bringing about its losing of the global leadership in shopping online to China and South Korea, each of which has some 83 percent of their populations shopping online, thus presenting a remarkable growth. The leadership of these two countries, as well as the high adoption rates of online shopping for Indonesia, India, Taiwan and Thailand, have to do with the remarkable penetration of smartphones in Asian countries, and their use for m-shopping (mobile shopping). As we noted already in the previous chapter, smartphones and mobile broadband were introduced first in Asia, in Japan.

In Europe, numerous countries presented for 2017 online shopping rates of 80 percent and even slightly over (UK, Germany, Denmark, Luxembourg, and Sweden) (Table 4.2). Thus, the European leadership in online shopping was shared by then by both small and big countries, located in both West and North Europe. This mixed pattern of leadership attests to a growing maturity

The Internet city

Table 4.2   *Percentage of Internet users pursuing selected online services in the EU and other countries 2017*

Country	Shopping	Govt. (2016)	Banking	Travel	Learning	Health	Networking
Austria	62	33	57	43	5	54	51
Belgium	60	35	67	45	8	52	72
Bulgaria	18	N/A	5	11	2	34	50
China	83	21	49	40	20	N/A	77
Croatia	29	N/A	33	17	2	53	47
Cyprus	32		28	40	4	58	63
Czech Republic	56	12	57	48	3	51	48
Denmark	80	71	90	58	9	64	75
Estonia	58		79	39	11	59	60
EU (current)	**57**	**35.6**	**51**	**42**	**7**	**51**	**54**
Finland	71	60	87	61	16	69	66
France	67	49	62	43	6	44	43
Germany	75	17	56	58	6	63	51
Greece	32	26	32	28	5	47	50
Hungary	39	24	38	23	4	58	65
Iceland	76	N/A	93	57	20	56	89
Ireland	53	48	58	42	4	37	59
Italy	32	12	31	27	5	33	43
Latvia	46	31	61	18	4	43	60
Lithuania	38	N/A	56	18	7	55	54
Luxembourg	80	35	76	71	9	65	68
Malta	52	N/A	49	40	6	59	70
Netherlands	79	55	89	56	10	71	67
Norway	77	62	92	57	14	63	83
Poland	45	19	40	23	4	45	48
Portugal	34	29	31	24	5	51	56
Romania	16	N/A	7	12	3	33	52
Serbia	31	N/A	N/A	24	5	52	48
Slovakia	59	15	51	35	4	50	59
Slovenia	46	17	39	39	5	54	45
Spain	50	32	46	46	12	57	57
Sweden	81	48	86	57	18	64	71
Switzerland	77	N/A	66	N/A	N/A	N/A	53

Country	Shopping	Govt. (2016)	Banking	Travel	Learning	Health	Networking
UK	82	34	68	56	13	57	71
US	77	N/A	69	46	N/A	64	81

Sources: EU, except for government, Eurostat (2018); government OECD (2018), for China, Warf (2017, 41); shopping for US and China, Statista (2018b); banking for US, Statista (2018f), for China, China Internet Watch (2018); travel for US, Credit Suisse (2018), for China, Wang (2018); education for China, Statista (2018g); networking for the US, Statista (2018h), for China, Statista (2018i).

of online shopping within Western Europe. We will meet more homogenous leadership patterns in the following sections, relating to some additional online activities, which are less mature in their adoption patterns by European Internet users. Romania and Bulgaria presented the lowest rates for online shopping in Europe, with 16 and 18 percent respectively. The lagging of the transitional economies of East Europe will repeat itself for the adoption rates of other online services, reflecting lower economic development and related lower penetration rates of Internet services. Shoppers still preferred to carry out big purchases through PCs rather than via mobile devices (Statista 2018c). Generally for retail trade, the total share of sales through online shopping out of the total value of retail trade in 2017 reached some 17.8 percent in the UK (Statista 2018d), and just 9.1 percent in the US (Statista 2018e). However, this share has been growing in recent years simultaneously with the growing population percentages tending to shop online. We will discuss the outcomes of these growth rates of online shopping for the number of physical stores in cities in Chapter 9.

4.4   E-GOVERNMENT

E-government, or digital government, was defined as 'attempts of governments to automate and facilitate the use of e-technologies in governmental processes, whereby individuals and organizations interact directly with governments for various reasons' (Loo 2012, 37; see also Yildiz 2007). E-government can be classified along several service categories, in similarity to those that we noted for e-commerce: government-to-business (G2B); government-to-government (G2G); and government-to-citizens (G2C) (Warf 2013). Given our focus on urban services available over the Internet for individuals, our discussion will mostly deal with G2C. From a governmental managerial perspective, or the supply side of e-government services for citizens, the development of e-government for citizens involves efforts pursued by governments for the modernization, higher efficiency, and enhanced quality of the routine day-to-day services offered by them to their citizens-clientele, such as licensing and tax paying.

Governments may opt to provide additional online services, other than 'managerial' ones, to their citizenries, notably voting services ('consultative'), and public opinion channels ('participatory') (Chadwick and May 2003; Warf 2013). The development of managerial e-government services presents a bottom-to-top evolution, starting with mere one-way presentations of services by governments online, and culminating with full two-way interactions with citizens, including payments by citizens and transmissions of documentation by governments. This latter maturity of e-government may emerge following computerized integrations of inputs by numerous levels of governmental administrative departments (Layne and Lee 2001). Typical obstacles in the process leading to the offering of full e-government services include the authentication of citizens, mobilizing the bureaucracy for change in service structure and means, and computer capabilities of the citizenry (Loo 2012).

G2C online services differ from other 'e-' activities, such as shopping, learning, banking and travel arrangements, in that government services in general constitute compulsory and uncompetitive ones. Thus, one may choose which products to buy online and where to buy them, which is true also for the obtaining of other commercial services, such as banking and travel. However, people are forced to consume governmental services from single governments only, including the payment of taxes and fees, submissions of applications for permits, and the receipt of documentation. This compelled system of services applies to all governmental levels: local, regional and national. Thus, one cannot choose, neither among governments, nor among suppliers of governmental services and their virtual offerings. If citizens wish to change their suppliers of e-government services, they have to move to a new residential location, but still, even in their new location they will find again a similar uncompetitive and compulsory governmental service system.

The other side of this coin of compulsory and uncompetitive service is that the option for interaction with governments electronically, mainly via the Internet, presents a major advantage for citizens, since digital interactions with governments imply major timesaving, as compared to the attainment of traditional face-to-face governmental services. Furthermore, automatic service systems may turn out, in some cases, as being friendlier to their clientele, as compared to face-to-face ones. The use of managerial e-governmental services by citizens might be either 'passive' in the sense that citizens may merely access information presented on governmental websites, or it might be 'active', involving transactional e-government services, so that citizens interact with their governments by sending information and/or payments to governments.

The geographical patterns of availability for G2C e-government services present digital gaps, so that they are rapidly emerging in developed countries while being frequently still in their infancy in developing countries, with some exceptions among developed countries, notably the low adoption rates in Japan (Loo 2012; Warf 2013). The digital gap between developed and developing countries in this regard reflects the need for literacy in order for citizens to make use of e-government services. The international gaps in the provision of e-government services is further coupled with intra-national ones, with lower potential uses among the poor and the elderly.

Countries differ widely in their adoption rates of e-government, such as among Asian countries (Warf 2017). Thus, for 2016 the OECD reported an average rate of 35.6 percent of individuals in OECD countries using the Internet for sending filled forms via public authorities (OECD 2018) (Table 4.2). With the majority of OECD member countries reporting on this issue, it was for Denmark to lead by then (71 percent), followed by Estonia (68 percent), Norway (62 percent), and Finland (60 percent) (Table 4.2). Thus, the long-standing leadership of Nordic countries in the adoption of telecommunications services has been well kept (Kellerman 1999; 2014). Generally, it seems that transactional e-government services are still within the process of becoming widely adopted. 'Passive' uses of e-government services are more widely adopted (Kellerman 2014). Citizens may prefer to avoid using transactional governmental services if the operational procedures for these services seem for them to be cumbersome, and/or distrustful.

4.5   ONLINE BANKING

Like other Internet services, online banking, or digital banking, offers its customers swift, continuous and universal banking services. For banks, money constitutes a product, to be bought and sold, exchanged and deposited. As such, money has been the only material product so far that has been turned into information, as part of the computer-based information age, thus bringing about a new condition in which 'nowadays money is essentially information' (Thrift 1995, 27). This transition emerged already before the introduction of individual online banking through the Internet. Hence, we may recognize four phases in the development of online banking.

The first steps in the emergence of digital transmission of funds applied, as of the 1970s, to bank offices and employees only, facilitating electronic transfers of funds among banks, maintained through electronic funds transfer systems (EFTS) (see Malecki and Moriset 2008; Warf 2013). The second phase in the development of electronic transmission of funds emerged in the 1990s, focusing on cash money, and this time for transmissions carried out by individual bank customers, carried out through Automatic Teller Machines (ATMs).

The introduction of the Internet in the mid-1990s brought about a third phase in automated banking, in which it became possible for banks to establish online banking services, operating through websites which have imitated physical bank branches. As such, bank websites have facilitated the execution of bank operations, such as fund transfers, stock exchange activities, depositing and withdrawal from saving accounts and so on. This latter phase had to await at the time the solution of security issues, side by side with proper domestic legislations and licensing.

In the final and fourth phase, banks have developed special versions of their websites as applications for smartphones, so that the services of banks became available to their customers continuously and universally. The introduction, though, of purely virtual, branch-less banks failed several times, mainly because some specialized services, such as credit management, securities trading, life insurance and tax consulting, still required face-to-face meetings in physical branches, even for highly capable customers, as far as their ability to operate online banking (Malecki and Moriset 2008). More recently, however, fully online banks have been successfully opened up in North America, Europe, Asia and Australia.

For the banking industry, the adoption of online banking has permitted more efficient and less costly transactions, coupled with the possible provision of better services to the clientele and meeting its demand, and yielding in the overall a saving of some 40 percent in the operational costs of banks (Takieddine and Sun 2015). On the demand side, the percentage of Internet users adopting online banking for selected countries, mainly in Europe, by 2017, is presented in Table 4.2. The variation in the adoption rates of Internet banking is extremely wide, ranging from 5 percent in Bulgaria to 93 percent in Iceland. Thus, within Europe only, there are countries, again the Nordic ones, which have actually reached full maturity in the operation of banking online services, as far as the mass adoption of online banking is concerned, side by side with other countries, mainly East European and Mediterranean ones, which are still in the early stages of adoption of online banking. The factors for the differing levels in the adoption of online banking were examined for the 33 EU member countries for 2013, and were found to reflect cultural differences, as well as varying national economic indicators, as well as differing levels of Internet access, speed and security (Takieddine and Sun 2015).

Surprisingly, the percentage of Americans who use online banking has been relatively modest, standing at 69 in 2017. It seems that the use of the Internet for banking involves not only a reasonable capability by customers to make use of banking websites and to understand well the basics for financial activities, but it implies also customers' trust, mainly in the security measures provided by the banks for their Internet services. Thus, online banking in the US is, probably, more popular among younger, educated and affluent customers.

4.6 TRAVEL ONLINE

'With the exception of finance, no economic sector more clearly demonstrates the path breaking power of Internet-based electronic platforms than the travel industry' (Malecki and Moriset 2008, 110). However, travel online, or digital travel, differs from the online activities that we have addressed so far. Online travel does not constitute an end by itself, like online work, shopping and banking, since it rather constitutes preparatory activities for yet another activity that takes place later in physical space, namely the very travel away from home, whether for business or pleasure. Browsing through websites, which provide information for destination cities or sites, hotels, and attractions, has become a routine step taken prior to out-of-town travel, whether domestic or international. From the perspective of cities, the Web has turned into a major medium for the promotion of touristic visits, side by side with the ability of tourists to use tools offered through the Web, in order for them to plan and execute their touristic visits (see e.g. Paradiso 2012).

Furthermore, and even more important, individuals are able to reserve flights, hotels and car rentals online, similar to such reservations being posted by professional travel agents. Individuals might do so directly with airlines, hotels and car rental companies, or through online travel agencies (OTAs). Still, however, even those who prefer to reserve their travel fully online may need to consult a travel agent or an airline agent over the phone or face-to-face, in cases of complex travel itineraries. Online preparations for travel are pursued at times and spaces other than the flight itself, at one's home or office, and at any time of the day or the week. Such actions constitute indispensable components of the flight itself, since normally flights require reservations and tickets. Hence, the preparatory phases for travel and the travel activity itself jointly present a kind of disembedded hybridity between aerial action spaces, on the one hand, and virtual activities, on the other.

Similar to the development of automated bank services, airline reservations have been digitized first for the supply side of the system, namely for and within the airline industry, as well as for travel agents, through the development of electronic reservation systems (ERSs), before the introduction of the Internet. Only later on, following the introduction of the Internet, have such systems become accessible to potential passengers as well, leading browsing Internet users directly to specific airline websites, or to websites of online travel services, which present routes and prices to potential passengers (see Malecki and Moriset 2008).

Online reservations systems have been developed also for railway and other terrestrial and maritime transportation systems, side by side with equivalent reservation systems for lodging and car rental services. The growing availability of online reservation systems for potential passengers has brought about mergers of travel agencies, located in cities, as well as the closing down of others, so that less such retail offices are visible in urban landscapes, as we will note again in Chapter 9.

The use of the Internet for online travel seems, so far, to be much less popular in Europe, the US and China, as compared to the adoption of online banking. Thus, the highest adoption rate for travel online for 2017, was presented by Luxembourg (71 percent), and was followed again by Nordic countries (Table 4.2). The EU average adoption rate for travel online stood at 42 percent, as compared to 51 percent for banking. Low percentages were again presented by the Eastern European transitional economies, though not as low as the rates for online banking. It seems that the counselling and professional knowledge of human travel agents are still appreciated by travelers, but the currently growing popularity of low-cost airlines may bring about growing uses of travel online services.

The Nordic leadership in the adoption and use of telecommunications services was noted already before. For Luxembourg, the higher popularity of travel online might reflect frequent travels from this small but most connected country. East European countries seem to lag behind in the adoption of travel online, as part of a more general slowness in the adoption of Internet services, which we noted already, given lower levels of economic development and related lower adoption rates for Internet income-related services.

4.7   E-LEARNING

E-learning, also variously called distance learning and online learning (or education), offers academic (and other) studies through the Internet, in domestic institutes of higher education, as well as through cross-border global education platforms. Such studies amount to the attainment of codified knowledge online. The Internet further permits students who are engaged in traditional frontal studies to gain wide tacit knowledge. Such tacit knowledge may be acquired by the students through their consulting of websites, which are relevant to their studies, or through virtual consultations with remotely located colleagues, possibly enriching students' traditional frontal study. Codified knowledge, on the other hand, may be gained online either through study in single formal courses or through full academic degree studies. The acquisition of tacit knowledge is informal, by its very nature, it may range in its intensity of seeking from time to time, and it is similar to other forms of informal personal communications and networking among individuals. Formal degree studies, or purchases of codified knowledge, might be viewed as being similar, somehow, to e-commerce, in that a product, knowledge, can be bought online. There are, however, some differences between the sale of products and services (such as airline tickets) over the Internet, on the one hand, and the provision of formal codified knowledge through the Web, on the other, and some of these differences are highlighted in the following paragraphs (see also Kellerman 2014, 117–118).

From the supply side, language is a much more crucial element in e-learning than it is for e-commerce, by the very nature of the learning process. Standards of quality for formal study are another dimension that differentiate e-learning from standards of quality for products and services. Some internationally recognized quality standards for products and services (e.g. ISO9000) have been widely adopted worldwide, but domestic, as well as cross-border academic degrees have to be recognized by national or regional higher education councils in the country of residence of the studying student, as well as by potential domestic employers of the graduating student. Efforts have been made in recent years at the international level of high-education for the establishment of some international standardization of academic study, in response to the circumstances of an opening and globalizing world of higher education. Such efforts are, for instance, the EU Bologna agreements, as well as global GATS (General Agreements on Trade in Services) agreements (Knight 2006). In other cases, the prestige of globally leading universities offering online courses may bring about domestic recognition, though some professions, such as law and medicine, may require, in any case, some domestic adjustments for their practice.

From the demand side of potential students, the purchase of full online degree programs implies a prolonged purchase process spanning several years, as compared to the few minutes required for the online purchasing of other products and services. E-learning further implies a much more extensive investment by its customers, including the financial costs of tuition, extensive time allocation, and intellectual efforts, notably when studying within virtual and rather individual contexts, rather than within a group composing a frontal course. The intellectual efforts, which are required for academic study, may make online studies look inferior to the richer experiences offered by face-to-face ones, from the perspectives of students and universities alike. From yet another perspective, the product durability of an academic degree is lifelong, as compared to the disposability or limited lifespan of commercial products and services.

The very option of online formal academic education has been a widely debated issue, with supporters noting the widening of accessibility for higher education facilitated through e-learning, and with opponents arguing for the crucial importance of face-to-face teaching and class discussions (for debates see e.g. Breton and Lambert 2003, and for a review see Huh 2006). The need to overcome traditions, habits and conventions by potential students, as well as the hesitation of many universities and colleges to fully teach over the Internet, have brought e-learning into fast growth only in recent years (see Kellerman 2014).

There are universities, such as MIT (Massachusetts Institute of Technology), which have posted on the Internet the video filmed lectures of their entire faculty, for the purpose of self-non-degree study, side by side with numerous additional universities, which offer full or partial formal e-learning services. However, the adoption of this option by students has been partial, even in the United States, which pioneered at the time in distance learning. In the 2010s, a new trend has emerged in distance learning, namely the offering of Massive Open Online Courses (MOOCs), or the offering of stand-alone full online interactive courses that can be studied freely or for tuition, on a course-by-course basis, rather than as partial or full-degree programs.

Thus, in 2011, two academic entrepreneurs, Daphne Koller and Andrew Ng, established Coursera as a global academic online study service (Coursera 2018). It began by offering courses by leading American universities on a full online basis, including interactions among the students themselves, as well as by the offering of paid-for credit for these courses. In 2018, Coursera included some 2,800 single courses, offered by 164 universities located in 28 countries, as well as a small number of fully online degree programs. The teaching language in the internationally offered courses is mainly English. Another leading global online course system, jointly developed by the American Harvard University and MIT, is Open edX (Open edX 2018). This system offers development services to interested faculty, as well as maintenance services for existing courses. In 2018, the system included c. 2,000 courses offered by about 130 universities.

The partial use of online teaching within traditional frontal courses, sometimes called hybrid e-learning, or h-learning, has become another option for university instructors (see e.g. Selim and Chiravuri 2015). In addition, full online courses may be integrated within degree programs consisting mainly of frontal courses. This way e-learning in frontal higher education has gradually become a routine option for students, so that by 2016 some 28 percent of American students were enrolled in at least one online course (OLC 2016).

From the perspective of Internet users at large, the percentage of Internet users taking online courses is obviously much lower, as compared to other daily uses, such as shopping and banking (Table 4.2). China presented a high percentage of 20 percent for online learners in 2017, possibly given the wide geographical spread of its population. The EU statistics present data for a wider online study, measuring the percentage of Internet users taking any course online, including non-academic ones. These data show a European average of

7 percent of e-learners for 2017, led again by Nordic countries, with Iceland at the top with a rate of 20 percent. E-learning may be of special importance in Nordic countries with scattered populations and winter conditions which may restrict traveling. Bulgaria, Croatia and Turkey presented the lowest rate of 2 percent for e-learning, as part of the general trend of lagging adoption rates of the Internet and its online services.

4.8   E-HEALTH

The use of the Internet by individuals for health-related matters has received numerous names, both general and specific. Telemedicine is the oldest term, dating back to pre-Internet times, when telegraphy and telephony were the major available telecommunications media. Thus, telemedicine was defined as 'the use of telecommunication technology for transfer of medical data from one site to another' (Pal et al. 2002). Obviously, it was mostly for medical practitioners to transmit medical information at the pre-Internet times. Currently, telemedicine has turned into a more specific term referring to distance medical treatments (Smith 2004), and thus, defined as 'the use of advanced communication technologies, within the context of clinical health, that deliver care across considerable physical distance' (Breen and Matusitz 2010). The term e-health was considered, at times, as related to the provision of health information mostly as a commercial service (Pal et al. 2002), and later on more generally as the supply and availability of medical information online, including information on diseases, medications and so on (Breen and Matusitz 2010). The term telehealth was suggested as an even broader one, including, for instance, distance learning for health professionals (Smith 2004). Others, referring mainly to the online search for medical information by individuals, suggested the term health online (PewInternet 2013).

We will refer in our discussion here to the term e-health, as a wide spectrum of health-related online services, which includes the use of the Internet by individuals for three main health-related activities: management, consulting and treatment. First, the management of one's health includes activities such as appointment fixing with doctors, viewing the findings of laboratory and other medical tests, and ordering and receiving medical prescriptions. Second, medical consulting, or health online, which involves, above all, people's search for Web information on health issues, such as diseases, medications and so on. Third, medical treatment, or telemedicine, performed at a distance, through the Internet, such as teleradiology. The first two e-health options have received wider uses through the adoption of smartphone applications, bringing about the so-called m-health (mobile health).

As compared to other virtual services, such as e-banking, travel online and e-government, e-health is not fully automatic. For many of its functions, notably for telemedicine, it involves people, such as expert physicians or other medical workers, performing treatments or sending prescriptions, online with patients, or offline. However, health management and consulting activities are similar in most of their functions to other e-activities. On the other hand, telemedicine, which involves remote medical treatments, differs from online shopping, government and travel services, in that it requires the development of specialized equipment, software, and specialists for its operation. E-health has its own nature, from yet another perspective, as compared to other online activities. Shopping online, as well as other online services, such as banking and travel, involve some activity performed by Internet users, whereas e-health may sometimes involve information search and gathering only. Online social networks, which we will discuss in the following section, may include network discussions over health issues, either within dedicated medical networks or through general ones, thus complementing or replacing people's searches for health information on the Web (Griffiths et al. 2012).

Several negative implications for the use of telemedicine, and of e-health in general, were outlined by Breen and Matusitz (2010, 67):

> (1) lack of real-time interaction between the patient and provider, (2) the possible lack of reliability or accuracy of information provided by e-health resources, (3) the public health concern over consumer use of the Internet to self-diagnose conditions that may be life-threatening, (4) the inaccessibility to e-health by a certain number of disadvantaged and isolated groups, and (5) the deep intercultural differences among the patient and the healthcare provider that e-health services have not improved.

There are several additional problems involved in the operation of telemedicine. First, the need to insure the practitioners acting at a distance from the patients. Second, the partial recognition of health problems discovered at distance for payment or reimbursement by health insurance providers. Third, the frequent lack of expertise in the operation of technology and equipment in remote areas (Breen and Matusitz 2010). Fourth, the assuring of confidentiality of medical information transmitted over the Internet, and, finally, the need for cross-border licensing of medical practitioners (Pal et al. 2002).

It was estimated for the US that some 64 percent of the patients there used a digital device for their health management in 2017 (McCarthy 2017). However, the percentage of Internet users in the US that sought for information or diagnosis for diseases stood at about 33 percent only, and reflected digital gaps along demographic and socioeconomic parameters (Jacobs et al. 2017). In Europe, the EU average for the seeking of health information stood at 51 percent by 2017, with a peaking at 71 percent in the Netherlands, followed by Luxembourg and the Nordic countries (Table 4.2).

4.9 SOCIAL NETWORKING

'Man is by nature a social animal' (Aristotle's *Politics*, originally written in 350 BC). This basic and ancient statement has been true not only for human social contacts in physical space, some of which we discussed in Chapter 2, but for the use of the Internet in this regard, as well. Social contacts over the Internet apply mainly to interactions through social networks that have emerged as of the early 2000s, using the so-called Web 2.0 system for their Internet platform. However, it applies also to video calls as well as to chats for social, personal and intimate purposes, pursued through PCs or mobile phones (see Kellerman 2014).

Rainie and Wellman (2012, 21) portrayed the contemporary online social networking from a societal perspective, claiming that:

> [S]ociety is not the sum of individuals or of two-person ties. Rather, everyone is embedded in structures of relationships that provide opportunities, constraints, coalitions, and work-arounds. Nor is society built out of solidary, tightly bounded groups – like stacked series of building blocks. Rather, it is made out of a tangle of networked individuals who operate in specialized, fragmented, sparsely interconnected, and permeable networks.

Online networks, like those in physical space, are supposed, therefore, to offer numerous qualities for their participants, and they may facilitate the emergence of a social space for varied activities, similar to those offered by cafés, parks and other physical meeting places, which have traditionally been facilitated by cities.

Online social networking possesses yet another special feature, namely its very use of information technology. Thus, websites for social networking were defined by boyd and Ellison (2007; see also Davis 2010), as 'Web-based services that allow individuals to 1) construct a public or semi-public profile within a bounded system, 2) articulate a list of other users with whom they share connection, and 3) view and traverse their list of connections and those made by others within the system.' Thus, the Internet permits individuals to maintain an extended geographical spread for their social contacts, and it further facilitates the management of wide social contacts, as well as the management of the contents shared among them. These traits of online social networks stem from the very constitution of the Internet as an informational system, so that, normally, such traits cannot be used for people's traditional face-to-face social networks, based in physical space.

At the heart of Internet social networking stand the networked individuals, namely people who are 'networked as individuals, rather than embedded in groups' of whichever type, such as families, work units, neighborhoods, or social groups (Rainie and Wellman 2012, 6). Furthermore, these networked individuals present a new sense of personal, albeit connected, autonomy, expressed also through increased personal mobilities (Rainie and Wellman 2012; Kellerman 2012). Networked individuals may interact with several people at a time, while simultaneously being also engaged in some other activities. However, online social networking is demanding, so that 'networked individualism is both socially liberating and socially taxing' (Rainie and Wellman 2012, 9). Online social networking is liberating in the sense of the immense widening of social ties which it permits, but it is also taxing by the time and effort it requires for its use, and potentially, at least, also by the weakening of ties in physical space which it may possibly bring about.

The very nature of the social relations, which are developed online through social networks, as well as their potential impact on social relations in physical space, has been widely debated in recent years. This debate has taken place in parallel with the massive adoption of social networking by Internet users globally, so that societies worldwide are still in search of balances between physical and virtual social spaces, notably regarding the social relations, which take place in them. Furthermore, since Web 2.0 and the major network platforms based in it are relatively new, it might be still too early to firmly and decisively describe and assess the new world of social relations being activated and existing simultaneously in physical and virtual spaces (Kellerman 2014).

Castells (2000) identified and developed, at the time, the notion of 'network society', based mainly on the 'space of flows', and consisting of business ties among cities globally. However, in parallel to this network society of business, which may include elite segments of society, there has gradually emerged the more popular network society, which opened its gates, mainly through Web 2.0 applications, to all interested individuals who have been permitted to do so by their governments and by their cultural values. This latter widely spread process of social networking among people who belong to all societal strata, has brought about the emergence of the 'networked information economy' (Benkler 2006).

Virtual written social networking nested within the mainly academic email and Gopher systems, which operated before the inception of the Internet and its declaration as a wide and open access system in the mid-1990s. Thus, some global networks developed initially around a physical location, for example, the San Francisco-based WELL (Whole Earth 'Lectronic' Link) network (see Rheingold 1993), whereas others, such as MOOs (MUD [Multi-User dungeon/dimension/domain] Object-Oriented), were organized around metaphorical cities, thus directing exchanges by topic, time of the day into specific 'rooms', 'buildings', or 'neighborhoods' (see Schrag 1994).

A second generation of social networking, becoming popular as of the mid-1990s, consisted of online exchanges, via systems such as ICQ (I Seek

You) and MSN (Microsoft Network), and these were followed by blogs that were instituted as of 2002 (Herring et al. 2005), but were basically initiated in different forms much earlier (Gopal 2007). Blogs constituted, at the time, part of the first generation of globally wide and free self-publications of personal materials of all types by individuals over the Internet, spreading widely through blog interlinking, within what was termed, at the time, as the 'blogosphere' (see Bruns 2008; Jones et al. 2010; Warf 2013; Kellerman 2014).

The social networking dimension of the Internet has become extremely popular in the third phase of social networking, commencing with the emergence of Web 2.0, the Internet framework that has flourished as of the early 2000s, with a focus on social networking. Web 2.0 has hosted since then several swiftly adopted networks, or platforms, for online social networking, led mainly by Facebook, Twitter, Myspace, LinkedIn, and Second Life. The last one, Second Life, differs from the other online networking platforms in that users deliberately create avatars that communicate with each other, whereas in the other networks this is only an option. The very use of social networking over the Internet does not automatically imply globally stretched networks created and attended by all of their subscribers. Facebook has become, for example, a framework for virtual interaction among school kids whose location may not stretch beyond a single neighborhood (see Rainie and Wellman 2012, 130–131).

The barrier-free, constraint-free (in most countries) and cost-free virtual social networking has exhibited a tremendously fast adoption rate, with some 71 percent of Internet users worldwide attending at least one social networking system (Statista 2018h). The comparative dataset in Table 4.2 presents the rates for Internet users involved in social networking online in at least one networking system, for European countries, the US and China. Leading among these countries in 2017 was Iceland with 89 percent of adoption, in an island country with extreme winter weather conditions. Compared to the adoption rates of Internet services, which we reviewed in previous sections of this chapter, it was not for East European countries this time to present the lowest adoption rates for social networking, but these lowest rates were rather presented by France and Italy, with 43 percent in each. Thus, the levels of adoption of social networking are not related to levels of economic development, as we will note specifically for Facebook in the following paragraph. The US presented a high, but not leading, adoption rate of 81 percent, whereas in China some 77 percent of the Internet users subscribed to domestic networking systems.

Facebook has become the most popular global system for social networking. It was established back in 2004, and it offers subscribers several services, including, first, the presentation of personal profiles, side by side with the presentation of commercial pages and websites. Facebook further offers the online publication of personal materials, distributed to specifically identified friends, who are subscribed to the Facebook system, side by side with the publication of reactions written by these friends.

There are several striking elements in the global distribution of penetration rates of social networking, as demonstrated by the percentages for Facebook adoption in 2017 (Internet World Stats 2018). First, some countries present very high levels of Facebook use percentages, notably in Latin America, sometimes reaching 100 percent of the total population. Second are the leading countries in Facebook usage, which are neither the US nor Scandinavian countries, but countries such as Brazil, Colombia and Honduras. Third are the identities of the 'lagging' countries, namely those with extremely low rates of Facebook subscription, notably China with some 0.2 percent in 2017. We will attempt to explain these tendencies in the following paragraphs.

The extremely high values for Facebook adoption seemingly imply multiple Facebook subscriptions maintained by numerous subscribers. This tendency has probably to do with domestic cultures, which tolerate fake identities over online social networks, or because domestic cultures do not permit open and free networking among people, notably from the opposite gender, as was noted for instance for Morocco (Hassa 2012) as well as Thailand (Hongladarom 2011).

The popularity of online social networking in industrializing or developing countries, accentuates the difference between online networking, on the one hand, and other online services, on the other. Online social networking does not require any financial costs for network subscription and its maintenance, nor does it involve the purchase of any products and services. The only cost pertaining to online social networking is the pay for the very use of the Internet. For many users in developing countries who cannot afford the purchase and maintenance of Internet hardware and subscription, the access to the system may be achieved through low-cost access offered by Internet cafés, or by Wi-Fi communications via cheaply priced smartphones.

Therefore, the use of online social networking is almost completely separated from the levels of national and personal economic development, whereas the use of other online services, such as shopping, banking, government and so on depends on personal incomes of the users, as well as on Web infrastructures developed by the relevant businesses. The only requirements for the use of online social networking are literacy and the little money which might possibly be needed for the use of publicly available Internet access. Furthermore, and from a social perspective, online social networking permits users to bypass social, cultural, religious, and political taboos on social relations that may prevail in physical social space.

The extremely low rate for Facebook subscription displayed by China does not imply lack of interest in online social networking, but it rather presents the banning of Facebook by the Chinese government for political reasons, so that domestic alternative online networking platforms are available to Chinese Internet users. Similarly, in previous Soviet Union countries, Internet networking services are offered by the popular *VKontakte* system, and domestic systems are also widely used in Japan, by *Mixi*, as well as in Korea, through *Cyworld*.

4.10   CONCLUSION

We have examined in the previous sections some eight major services that can be obtained over the Internet: work; shopping; banking; government; travel; learning; health and networking. We will examine them now comparatively, first by their varying nature and by their diversified significances in people's lives, and then by their differing global adoption rates. As a final note for this chapter, we will briefly comment on the need for new balances for urbanites as service consumers in physical and virtual spaces, a topic that we will address in the following chapter, as well as for their cities as service suppliers, a topic which we will discuss in Chapter 9.

Work extends for most adults over at least one-third of each weekday, and it is by far a leading human activity with major implications for people's present and future lives. This crucial significance and role for work in the lives of individuals may have led to a continued global hesitation by workers to divert their physical locations while at work, fully or partially, from their offices to their homes. This preference has prevailed despite the growing performance of work activities by many workers through computers, whether located at work or at home.

The purchase of an online degree program is somehow similar to work in its being a rather prolonged purchase process, spanning along several years, as compared to a few minutes required for the purchase of other products and services online. Online study further requires a much more extensive investment by the customer-student, in terms of its financial costs, the extensive investment of time involved in its pursuance, and the required intellectual efforts, notably when studying virtually and thus individually, as compared to being part of a physically present group assembled together in a real classroom. This latter intellectual effort involved in online study may make it be considered as inferior to face-to-face ones, from the perspectives of both students and universities and colleges. Another difference between learning and the purchase of goods and services is their durability, which for an academic degree is lifelong, as compared to the disposability, expiring or limited lifespan of commercial products and services.

Shopping online is a more widely adopted service activity as compared to learning online and full-time telework. The adoption of online shopping is usually partial for each customer, because a preference for shopping in physical space still prevails for certain products, and shopping online may be split between browsing and shopping, with possibly just one of these two phases taking place online. As compared to shopping online and the wide choice of merchants and merchandise which it offers, e-government is a rather compulsory and uncompetitive service, forcing citizens to consume governmental services, such as tax and fee payments, submission and receipt of documents, from the governments of their local, regional and national locations.

Travel online differs from other 'e-' activities in that it does not constitute an end by itself, like telework, online shopping and online banking, but it rather constitutes a preparatory phase towards business or pleasure travel. E-health is not a fully automatic service, such as online banking, travel online and e-government, other than for health management and information seeking. For many health functions, e-health involves people, such as expert physicians or other medical workers, as well as specialized equipment for telemedicine. Furthermore, in most cases telemedicine may involve treatment at the patient's end performed by nurses or technicians.

The Internet facilitates the management of wide social contacts, as well as the sharing of contents with them. These traits of online social networks stem from the very constitution of the Internet as an informational system. The barrier-free, constraint-free (in most countries) and cost-free virtual social networking has exhibited a tremendously fast adoption pace. However, the very use of social networking over the Internet does not automatically imply globally stretched networks attended by large numbers of subscribers. In developed countries, online social networking is as popular as other services obtained online, notably shopping, whereas among Internet users in developing countries, social networking is more popular than in developed ones, whereas other online services are more weakly adopted, given the lower incomes there.

The worldwide adoption of available online services is complex and is still in the making, some 22 years following the commercial and universal introduction of the Internet, back in 1995. Thus, if we take the EU 2017 averages for the adoption of virtual services, taking into account the varied levels of economic development and Internet penetration levels pertaining to its member countries, the chance is that only every second European consumed shopping, banking, travel, health, and social networking over the Internet by then (Table 4.2). In addition, only one out of three residents in OECD countries consumed e-government services. However, the variations between the highest country-levels of adoption and the lowest ones are wide in some cases. Banking constitutes the most striking case with a level of adoption of merely 5 percent in Bulgaria, as compared to 93 percent in Iceland, attesting to differences in economic development, geographical location, and traditions of adoption of telecommunications means and services. Interestingly enough, the highest levels of adoptions for several services stood equally at 71 percent, but these were split among several countries: government (Denmark), travel (Luxembourg), and health (the Netherlands).

The US presents higher levels of adoption for Internet services, as compared to the EU average, and these adoption rates are, in some way, similar to those of large European countries (UK, Germany and France) (Table 4.2). As for China, representing the rising Asian countries (see Table 4.1 for shopping), the adoption levels are more varied, ranging between high levels for shopping (83) and learning (20), and low ones for government services (21).

It seems that worldwide two services have reached wide levels of adoption: shopping and social networking. However, whereas shopping online has become most popular in developed economies, social networking peaks in developing ones, thus presenting different adoptions of Internet services for people living under varying economic conditions.

The global leadership in the adoption of Internet services was shared until a few years ago by the US and Scandinavian countries (Kellerman 2014). The US led given its being the major inventing and introducing country for most new information technologies, and a country that enjoys a tradition of adoption of newness. This leadership has been lost in recent years, attesting to the slow but progressing maturing of the global Internet economy. The Nordic countries have shared with the US the leadership in the adoption of Internet services, and they still lead in the adoption levels of numerous services, side by side with other small European countries (the Netherlands and Luxembourg). The Nordic countries have developed a history of fast adoption of telecommunication newness, coupled with their location implying extreme winter conditions, thus inviting wide adoption rates for Internet services (Kellerman 1999). It seems that in the upcoming years, leading Asian countries, notably South Korea and China, will take the lead in the adoption levels of Internet services, beginning with shopping. The extremely fast and wide adoption of smartphones by the population in these two countries, side by side with their current leadership in smartphone production and enhancement, contribute to this direction.

In a comparative study of 45 countries using data for the late 1990s, Park (2001) claimed that the adoption of the Internet and its use have been heavily influenced by cultural aspects. Generally, he claimed, the level of penetration of the Internet has depended on the social distance of countries from the US, the country that has been most reflected in the Internet. Thus, it was difficult at the time for the Japanese to adopt email services, which permit rather 'horizontal', and open interactions by their users, without regard to hierarchical 'vertical' social structuring and status, contrary to the societal patterns prevailing in Japan. Hence, Shiu and Dawson (2004) stated that the level of adoption of emailing may differ from the adoption of online shopping, which on its part might be attractive when the time budget of individuals becomes restrained, thus making technology overcome cultural-national values. These two internationally comparative studies further claimed that a dominance of feminist and individualist values in countries may assist the adoption of the Internet, as compared to countries with prevailing collectivist and uncertainty avoidance values, since emailing permits free networking, a routine which may be preferred by women.

The recently emerging use of the Internet for the obtaining of urban services, side by side with their traditional obtaining in physical cities, may involve a need for two balances: for the individual Internet users, or the demand side for service consumption, and for their cities, or the supply side for service provision. Users of Internet services within virtual image environments of computer and smartphone screens, which attempt to imitate the traditional physical ones, require some balancing between their very physical presences, side by side with their virtual one. We will address this dual-space condition in the following chapter. Cities, which traditionally have offered a wide variety of services and service suppliers, have to cope now with a new reality, in which the Internet offers a similarly rich variety of services and suppliers. A possibly newly emerging balance between the physical-urban and the virtual-urban suppliers of services will be discussed in Chapter 9.

A special case for the need for new balances are social relations, which can take place physically and virtually through numerous platforms and in plenty of places, and which do not involve any financial transactions. The very nature of social relations, which are developed online through social networks, as well as their potential impact on social relations in physical space, has been widely debated in recent years. This debate has taken place in parallel with the massive adoption of social networking by Internet users globally, so that societies worldwide are still in search of balances between real and virtual social spaces, as far as social relations are concerned.

5. The dual-space society

In the previous chapter, we outlined numerous services that urbanites have traditionally obtained in urban physical space, and which they now growingly pursue through the Internet. Individuals, who use their Internet connectivity, whether fixed and/or mobile, for the performance of service activities, find themselves simultaneously present in physical space bodily and within Internet space virtually. Hence, this chapter is devoted to an exposure and interpretation of the emerging hybrid dual-space society, consisting of the double presences of individuals in urban physical and Internet virtual spaces. The chapter will focus on the very conception of hybrid dual-space and its emergence, followed by an exposure of the ways in which urbanites experience it, as well as function within it.

The chapter will explore, first, three phases of interpretation for the spatial status and the human meaning and experiencing of the Internet, thus laying the ground for a continued relevance for the hybrid dual-space approach, tying together the physical and Internet spaces. The chapter will then focus on the numerous conditions, which are required for the emergence of dual-space. First among them, and in order for Internet space to function dually with physical space, the Internet has to function under three conditions: available accessibility of users to the Internet; universal reach of websites by users; and instant information transmissions by the Internet connections available to users. Second are four conditions required by Internet users, in order for them to function within dual-space: presence in both spaces; personal identification; personal autonomy; and, finally, experiencing the use of dual-space. If all the Internet and user pre-conditions for the emergence of hybrid dual-space are met, then users may engage in three types of service activities within dual-space: interpersonal interaction; social networking and service action, and these three activities will be briefly outlined. Finally in this chapter, we will discuss the numerous and interrelated spatialities involved in the performance of service activities online.

5.1 PHASES IN THE SPATIAL INTERPRETATIONS OF THE INTERNET

It was shortly after the introduction of the commercial Internet, back in 1995, that geographers began to speculate on the status and meaning of virtual space, as compared to the well-known physical space (see Adams and Warf 1997). Over the years since then, it has turned out that the spatial meanings and identities of relevant dimensions and applications of the digital realm constitute a complex issue. This complexity has grown even further, as new technologies (e.g. GPS), appliances (e.g. the smartphone), and applications (e.g. online shopping) have emerged and become widely adopted (see Kinsley 2014; Ash et al. 2018; Kellerman 2014).

The digital realm in its basic and most general instance constitutes merely computer codes, hosted by servers as well as by user end-stations (see Kitchin and Dodge 2011), and these codes have received several spatial connotations over the years.

At the first phase of attribution of spatial meanings to computer codes, starting already before the introduction of the Internet, the visual interfaces between computer codes and their human users have employed spatial metaphors (de Souza e Silva 2006; Kellerman 2016), and spatial concepts have served as organizational principles for online content (Leszczynski 2015). At a second phase, physical and digital spaces were assumed to jointly constitute hybrid space (Kluitenberg 2006), and at a third phase, the locational connectivity of selected digital systems, and/or the spatial contents of such systems, were viewed as loading them with relevant spatial dimensions and meanings (Leszczynski 2015). Thus, the three phases of spatial interpretations, which were attributed to relevant digital systems are cyberspace; hybrid space; and spatial media. We will review these three approaches, notably from the perspective of the Internet, the spatial meanings and practicalities will be in our focus later in this chapter.

The viewing of selected digital systems as cyberspace, focused, first, on relevant classes of image space, followed later by some specific attention devoted to the Internet, as a sub-class of cyberspace (Ettlinger 2008; Kellerman 2016). The three relevant classes of image space are, first, the widest one of virtual space, which includes within it the digital media, art and photography. Within this wide class of image space nested cyberspace, consisting of the digital media, and within the latter one emerged the Internet, as a rather specific digital medium. All of these three classes of image spaces were interpreted initially as spatial entities, being separate from physical space. Thus, cyberspace 'has been considered a "parallel" universe to our own' (Grosz 2001, 76), and 'the Internet can be thought of as a space attached to the earth' (Wang et al. 2003, 383).

Cyberspace was argued to have its own geography and to be symbol-sustained (Benedikt 1991, 123, 191; Batty 1997), and it was further suggested that digital space might possess its own materiality (Kinsley 2014). From yet another perspective, Bolter and Grusin (1999, 179) interpreted cyberspace as a virtual mode of Augé's (2000) non-places, originally proposed for physical unpopulated spaces, such as airports. For Graham (2003, 179), though, cyberspace carries a double spatial connotation. It 'is conceived of as both an ethereal alternate dimension which is simultaneously infinite and everywhere (because everyone with an Internet connection can enter), and as fixed in a distinct location, albeit a non-physical one (because despite being infinitely accessible all willing participants are thought to arrive into the same marketplace, civic forum, and social space)'.

The conception of cyberspace was coupled with a wide metaphorical application of geographical terminology for Internet use, such as surfing, home page, and website. This use of spatial metaphors amounted to a process of spatialization (Kellerman 2007), employing orientational metaphors (Lakoff and Johnson 1980, 14). The rationale, at the time, for the application of spatial metaphors for Internet use, was that spatial experience has accompanied humans since 'early in life and is essential for survival' (Tversky 2000, 76; see also Couclelis 1998). The use of spatial metaphors for Internet operations was further interpreted by Couclelis (1998, 214–215), as involving 'the mapping of one domain of experience into another, more coherent, powerful, or familiar one ... the metaphor performs a cognitive fusion between the two, so that the things in the source domain are viewed as if they really belonged in the target domain'.

Side by side with viewing the Internet as a separate space, it was also assessed as being embedded within physical space, from the perspective of its hardware infrastructure, including servers, cables, and antennas, all of which being rooted within physical space (Cai et al. 1999; Li et al. 2001, 701).

The second phase of thought opposed the separation between physical space and cyberspace. Already back in 1998, Internet space was viewed as interacting with physical space, in that the two spaces 'stand in a state of *recursive interaction,* shaping *each other* in complex ways' (Graham 1998a, 174). This view matured into the idea of hybrid space, as connecting physical and digital spaces. It emerged, at the time, in light of the development of the Internet into a most versatile, comprehensive and powerful information system, enhanced even further through its integration with new technologies, notably GPS as of the early 2000s. GPS technologies have imported physical space images and locations into Internet space, through applications such as Google Maps and Google Earth for satellite images, and Google Street for physical space pictures (Zook and Graham 2007a, 2007b, 2007c; Crutcher and Zook 2009).

The idea of convergence between physical and Internet spaces has further developed in lieu of the introduction and wide adoption of smartphones (as of 1993), broadband (as of the late 1990s), mobile broadband connectivity (as of 2001), and Wi-Fi (as of 1997). These technologies have facilitated a wider range of uses for the Internet, coupled with users' permanent and mobile access to it. Thus, a convergence between physical and Internet spaces for the performance of several routine activities has emerged, such as for shopping and social networking, activities in which, as we noted in the previous chapter, physical and Internet spaces may complement each other, even simultaneously (Kellerman 2014).

Kluitenberg (2006) was probably the first one to suggest the convergence and interfolding of physical and virtual spaces, notably within mobile contexts, into a joint 'hybrid space', and this notion was further developed by de Souza e Silva (2006). The term hybrid space, and the duality which it involves, have received numerous nuances, such as 'doubling-of-space' (Moores 2012), and 'more-than-real' (McLean 2016; McLean et al. 2016), side by side with additional phrases relating to relations between the spatial and the digital in general (see Ash et al. 2018; Kinsley 2014).

The notion of hybrid space and its derivatives has been largely developed through feminist interpretations of the digital, which criticized, for example, the 'sweeping erosion of locational privacy involved in the mediation of everyday life by digital media' (Leszczynski and Elwood 2015, 22). Thus, the idea of hybrid space refers to 'a world where the digital and the material are not separate but entangled elements of the same processes, activities and intentionalities' (Pink et al. 2016, 1; see also Wilson 2014).

The notion of hybrid space does not fully oppose the viewing of Internet platforms as metaphorical cyberspace, since the digital/virtual space within hybrid space is still merely metaphorical, even when hybridized with physical space. Spatial hybridity implies an 'always-on' connection, while our very moving 'transforms our experience of space by enfolding remote contexts inside the present context' (de Souza e Silva 2006, 262). The locations of hybridization, notably within cities, constitute 'net localities' (de Souza e Silva and Frith 2012; see also Farman 2012). Hybrid space constitutes further a networked space, so that the connection between the far and the contiguous is carried out in a rather borderless way, without the feeling of 'entering' the Internet, and so that a 'hybrid reality' is experienced, in which social practices occur simultaneously in physical and digital spaces within a mobile context. Moreover, 'flows through and beyond online spaces produces reality' (McLean 2016, 509), which involves 'materialities in which potential becomes actualized and through which digital mediation is afforded' (Kinsley 2014, 365).

Based on Crampton (2009, 2014), it was for Leszczynski (2015; see also Timeto 2015) to go one-step further in the search for spatial identities for digital systems, when she focused on the notion of 'spatial media', as the third phase of spatial interpretations for digital systems. Spatial media 'refers to both new technological objects (hardware, software, programming techniques, etc.) with a spatial orientation, as well as to nascent geographic information content forms produced via attendant practices with, through, and around these technologies' (Leszczynski 2015, 729). Thus, the spatial identity of digital systems, notably the Internet, has moved from spatial metaphors attached to them, and, subsequently, their hybridity with physical space, to their own possible possession of spatial orientation and/or spatial content. This interpretation of the spatial in the digital applies not just to the Internet, but also to much wider digital systems. Furthermore, through the use of spatial media we may view contemporary human life as a product of mediations among technology, space and society, and our spatial experiences in physical space as supplemented by spatial information.

The notion of spatial media/tion offered by Leszczynski (2015) for digital systems makes it possible to identify some 'true' spatial elements within digital systems, such as their orientation and content. However, the nexus technology–space–society, which stands at the basis of the spatial media/tion thesis, remains theoretical or conceptual, focusing on the very nature of digital systems, without reference to human agency, or the everyday uses of digital systems, notably the Internet, by individuals. For Internet users, the Internet has come to constitute an action space or arena, even if only metaphorical in nature, in which users can perform activities that they traditionally used to carry out in physical space (Kellerman 2014).

In essence, one may conceptually refer to Internet space in a variety of ways: as a metaphorical entity of cyberspace, as a spatial medium, or alternatively, just as a digital system. We believe that, from the perspective of its users, the Internet has turned into a space-like entity that permits its users to perform physical-space-like human actions within and through it. Thus, when interpreting human action vis-à-vis the Internet per se, rather than theorizing the spatial meanings of the digital realm in general, the use of the term 'Internet space' is called for. The dual-space society, introduced in the following section, focuses on Internet users who function within a mix of separate physical and Internet spaces, side by side with their operation within a hybridized space that mediates between physical space and digital media, with the latter being metaphorically space-like.

5.2   THE DUAL-SPACE SOCIETY

Following our discussion of the three spatial interpretations proposed for digital systems, we will move now to the exposition of the dual-space society, based on the notion of hybrid space. Dual-space is based on the three elements of physical space, Internet space and individuals, with the latter acting within both spaces. Each of these three elements is based on some basic features or conditions. The most basic spatial features of physical space consist of its provision of terrestrial locations for humans and their facilities, side by side with the rather costly and time-consuming friction of distance involved in moving about it (Figure 5.1). The basic spatial conditions for humans include their

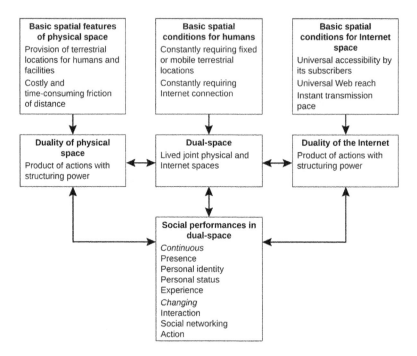

Figure 5.1   *Spatial conditions, dualities, and social performances in*
                dual-space

constant requirement for fixed or mobile terrestrial locations within physical space, side by side with their contemporary need for continuous Internet use, whether being located in fixed or mobile locations.

The Internet system must meet three spatial conditions, in order for it to provide for an effective action space. First, the system has to be universally accessible by its users, so that subscribers may use their appliances, notably smartphones, worldwide. This requirement for users' universal accessibility to the system is equivalent to the required constant terrestrial fixed or mobile location for all humans. The second spatial requirement from the Internet system at any location is its provision of universal reach for its users to all websites worldwide, and third, is its facilitation of an instant pace of transmission for information/data. The universal reach of all publicly available Internet addresses and the instant pace of information transmissions are required for the Internet in order for it to offer advantages in its use over physical space and the friction of distance implied in movements about it. Internet users may experience restrictions for all of these three basic conditions, because of low-level infrastructures at some locations, thus limiting system access and pace, notably in developing countries, as well as censorship restrictions on website reach in a variety of countries (Kellerman 2016).

The very simultaneous existence of both physical and Internet spaces, side by side with the operation of individuals within them, bring about the dual-space society. In this dual-space society, individuals can be continuously and jointly located within physical space and the Internet. They may experience things, communicate with people, attend events or places, make use of information, or pursue activities. They may do so at any time, and through any of the two spaces, which are always at their choice and disposal. Furthermore, they may act separately in each of the two spaces, or they may prefer to act simultaneously within both of them as hybrid space. Thus, dual-space is not a synonym for double-space, since the latter term implies the existence of two spaces, being separated and situated next to each other, whereas dual-space implies a permanent and continuous duality of the two spaces from the perspective of their users.

The continuous dual-space location of individuals, and the permanent choice of action channeling available to them, either for action within any of the two spaces (physical and Internet) separately, or simultaneously within the two of them, has become an integral element of routine daily lives for smartphone and PC/tablet users, notably in developed countries. Thus, for example, individuals may be located within a store in physical space, standing next to a desired item displayed there for sale, and noting its price. They may simultaneously communicate via their smartphones with a virtual store noting the price of the desired item there, and then finally make a decision, whether to buy the product through the physical store or whether to purchase it through the virtual one, while being still located within the store in physical space. In another case, people may have a choice, at a specific moment, to perform a video call with a friend over the Internet, or rather go across the street for a face-to-face meeting with her/him.

The new spatial conditions and options offered to citizens of the dual-space society for their very existence, experiencing and action, require the extension of several notions, which were originally developed for physical space within social space theory. It was for Lefebvre (1991), at the time, to propose a classification of social space, focusing on its human experiencing, into three classes: material spatial practices, the representations of space, and the spaces of representations. These classes jointly constitute human social space/spatiality. Harvey (1989, 220–221) interpreted these three classes as relating to human (direct) spatial experiences, to individual perception, and to the imagination of space, respectively. For Soja (1996: 6, 66) these three classes rather constituted a trialectic of human perception, conception and living of space, respectively. Material spatial practices, or *Firstspace*, for Soja (1996), include people's flows, transfers and interactions, or their mobilities, in physical space. Soja

(1996) further coined the representation of space as *Secondspace*, relating, for instance, to the work of urban planners, whereas *Thirdspace* referred to the spaces of representation, or lived space, as interpreted by writers, artists and philosophers.

These classifications were extended and applied for Internet social space, as well, so that spatial practices over the Internet, or its firstspace, include flows, transfers and interactions, as pursued by individuals in Internet space (Kellerman 2014, Table 2.1). Under dual-space conditions, people are involved in spatial practices within both spaces. In physical space, these practices stretch mainly locally, but they may include also some out-of-town travel, whereas over the Internet spatial practices by users may extend globally. Furthermore, physical and virtual spatial practices may also take place simultaneously in dual-space. For example, an individual may physically commute by local metro, while simultaneously sending messages, or posts and tweets, globally, through the Internet. Individuals further have the choice between moving themselves physically to their workplaces through commuting in physical space, or they may opt for moving their information virtually while working from home (telework). Individuals may also choose to alternate daily between the two mobility options of commuting and telework.

The Web may be viewed as social space, similar to physical space viewed as social space, in some additional ways. Like physical social space the Web constitutes a resource and a production force, for instance in its provision for online shopping. Also like physical social space, Web applications may be looked upon, by their very nature, as constituting texts and as symbols, for both individuals and organizations, and they may further serve as organizational frameworks, notably in Intranet systems within work places and multi-location companies, as we will note in the following chapter. In addition, the Internet may also be considered as constituting an imagined landscape, a place and even as a social value (Dodge and Kitchin 2001; Kellerman 2016).

Another social theory, the notions of which may be extended for the understanding of dual-space, is structuration theory, originally developed by Giddens (1984), and later extended by Löw (2008). Giddens (1984) claimed for a duality of social structures and human agency, operating within time and space, while altering their significance. In her extension of this theoretical perspective, Löw (2008, 25–26) suggested that 'as the form of organization of the juxtaposed, spaces epitomize simultaneities. In this sense spaces are, first, an expression of the possibility of pluralities; second, they point to the possibility of overlapping and reciprocal relations; and third, and for this very reason, they are always open and indefinite with respect to future formations'. This multiple interpretation of space points to the flexibility of the spatial organization of the social, despite the strong material connotation of physical space.

We suggest that the flexibility of social space, expressed through its simultaneous pluralities, overlapping, and openness, can be considered as being even stronger with regard to Internet space, which by its virtual and metaphorical nature is more flexible in both its formation and change. In the dual-space society consisting of both physical and Internet spaces in joint operation, one may assume these flexibilities to be of even wider significance. Such an extensive flexibility for dual-space may permit Internet users to enjoy several options: easily change their social contacts; simultaneously participate in several social networks, sometimes adhering to contradicting views; and benefit from a wider choice and selection of commercial vendors in both spaces.

Löw (2008, 31) further noted the difference between duality and dualism, in that 'the term duality denotes a twoness, not an opposition or dichotomy as implied by the term dualism'. She further noted that Giddens' (1984) duality of structure and human agency is expressed mainly in human routines that shape social processes. Löw (2008) extended these notions into her proposed 'duality of space', treating 'spaces as products of action which at the same time have structuring power' (Löw 2008, 33). This duality may also apply to Internet space (Figure 5.1). Internet users function within given rules of action and within structured websites, while their aggregate virtual actions may reshape the rules of expression and conduct of people over the Internet, and may bring about changes in the functioning of websites.

The duality of space, as proposed by Löw (2008), denotes space as a product of actions with structuring power, and, as we noted, it may pertain to both physical space and Internet space separately. As such, the duality of space should not be mixed with dual-space. We suggest that these two spatial notions, the duality of space and dual-space, mean jointly the following: each of the two spaces per se, the physical and the virtual, constitutes a product of action with some structuring power involved in it. In addition, the two spaces, the physical and the Internet, are jointly and simultaneously, lived and experienced by their users (Figure 5.1). Theoretically, then, the contemporary routine spatial experiences of individuals comprises simultaneously three dualities: two dualities of space production, separately for physical and Internet spaces, and a lived duality for their operation within the two spaces jointly.

Our observations so far have implied that the dual-space of joint existence and action within physical and Internet spaces involves complex actions, structures, and transitions, performed and experienced by contemporary individuals in their daily routines, since they operate under given structures within the two spaces, while simultaneously affecting them. The possible dominance of any of the two spaces on the other one depends on the nature of any given activity. We will discuss this complexity more particularly in the following section, when focusing on specific physical space and Internet spatialities, as expressed through a variety of daily performances.

5.3   DUAL-SPACE SPATIALITIES

The dual-space society, based on hybrid space, as presented in the previous section, implies the existence and emergence of spatialities. Generally, the notion of spatiality was suggested by Soja (1989, 7) to constitute simultaneously 'a social product (or outcome) and a shaping force (or medium) in social life' (see also Löw 2008). This kind of double role for spatiality resembles the logic of structuration theory that we noted in the previous section. Spatiality may apply to a rather wide array of existential dimensions of humans in space, including mainly their use of space, its experiencing, and their acting within it. Thus, every single existential event, performed or experienced by a person in space, may be considered as an outcome of previous events and/or of existing norms. Side by side with its being an outcome, such an event may contribute, solely by itself, or aggregately with other similar events, to the forming and shape of future events. In addition to Soja's (1989) approach to spatiality, viewed as reflecting a vertical axis of past and future events, Holloway and Valentine (2000) suggested a horizontal axis for spatiality, as relating to the mix between the local and the global in social ties, as well as to socio-spatial everyday practices.

We propose that the notion of spatiality, whether interpreted as constituting simultaneously an outcome and a shaping force, and/or as relating to the geographical extent of social ties and everyday practices, may also apply to human performance in Internet space. Spatiality for the Internet can be applied to actions taking place in Internet space, as well as to Internet use, and even for Internet experiencing. The virtual, in general 'may be experienced "as if" lived for given purposes' (Shields 2003, 49), and this applies the other way around as well, since 'our *experience* of the Web is fundamentally spatial' (Weinberger 2002, 35). The major *a priori* difference between physical space and Internet space in terms of human performance within them is that human existence in physical space constitutes one of the most basic given conditions of life, whereas presence and performance in cyberspace are rather matters of choice, requiring individuals to enter into Internet space through, normally paid-for, Internet subscriptions.

Side by side with the duality between physical and Internet spaces, which constitutes the essence of dual-space, people who are present within it may operate under double spatialities: those of physical and those of Internet spaces. These spatialities may differ from each other, given the difference in the basic spatial conditions for each of the two spaces: friction of distance for physical space, and instant transmissions of information for Internet space

Table 5.1   *Social performances for Internet and physical space spatialities*

Social performances	Internet spatialities	Possible Internet restrictions	Physical space spatialities	Dependencies in physical space	Relationships between spatialities in dual-space
Continuous					
Presence	Virtual	Low bandwidth	Bodily	N/A	Simultaneity (co-presence)
Personal identity	Flexible	Identification coding	Defined	Legal specifications	Simultaneity
Personal status	Autonomous	Norms and constraints	Autonomous	Norms and constraints	Simultaneity
Experience	Imaginative and metaphorical	Low-quality website design	Bodily	Bodily and mental conditions	Symbiosis
Changing					
Interaction	Disembodied	Low bandwidth	Embodied	Face-to-face	Complementarity
Social networking	Egalitarian open-code networking	Censored connectivity	Non-egalitarian networking	Social and political structures	Complementarity

Source: Partially for identity, experience and interaction, see Kellerman (2014: Table 1.1).

(Figure 5.1). We will demonstrate these differing spatialities for physical and Internet spaces, as well as the relations among them, along seven human performances, divided into two classes (Table 5.1 and the following sub-sections). First are four continuous, and rather basic, human performances: presence; personal identity; personal status, and experience. These four performances provide the basis for three additional and rather changing human performances: interaction, social networking, and acting. As we will note, in the following sub-sections, the relationships between the spatialities of physical space and Internet space may range from complementarity through simultaneity to symbiosis, depending on the type of performance.

Human routine social performances in dual-space, for all of the seven performance types, may reinforce or change socio-spatial structures in both physical and Internet spaces, as proposed at the time for physical space (Giddens 1984; Löw 2008). A most relevant example might be the technological ability for people to accelerate their driving speeds in physical space, and their ability to do so also for information transmission in Internet space. Both accelerations have been made possible by carmakers and Internet infrastructures, respectively, because of the cumulative performances of individuals, ever yearning for faster mobilities.

5.3.1   Presence

Presence implies the existence of place, whether physical and/or virtual, and the numerous meanings of 'place' as a basic spatial notion have been outlined elsewhere (Kellerman 2016). We mentioned in the previous section the presence or being of humans in physical space as one of the most basic elements for human existence. As such, presence in physical space may also be considered as the most basic spatiality. Presence of an individual in a specific place may be attributed to her/his previous movement ending up in that place, and the current presence, in turn, may bring about some future movement leading to another place. Humans physically staying in a physical space is not dependent on any other elements, whereas human movement in a physical space is dependent on numerous conditions. One of the most basic such dependencies for human mobility is the level of people's personal autonomy, which will be discussed in the sub-section devoted to personal status.

The being or presence of humans over the Internet constitutes a virtual spatiality, facilitated through IP numerical addresses assigned uniquely to every communications device connected to the Internet. Once such an IP address is assigned to a device in use, human personal virtual presence can then be expressed through all possible modes: audibly, visually, textually, and virtually. Audial communications can take place through VoIP conversations, and visual communications can be created through video conversations, using applications such as Skype or WhatsApp. Virtual presence can further be expressed via textual communications performed through chats over Web 2.0 applications, such as WhatsApp or Viber, originally developed for smartphones, through emails, or through some specific textual communications available through websites. Internet presence can further be expressed virtually through interactions with appliances using IoT. Any such virtual presence involves the simultaneous bodily presence of the communicating persons in physical space, whether being located in a fixed place or whether being on the move. This dual presence in physical and virtual space amounts to co-presence in dual-space. Such co-presences may variously emerge when Internet users communicate with fellow Internet users, attend events remotely, view places virtually, consult information, and contact things (Kellerman 2016).

Virtual presence within co-presence contexts may impose differential uses of human senses. Virtual audial communications with people requires the use of hearing, coupled with the use of vision for video conversations. Remote event attendance requires the use of both vision and hearing, whereas communications with places, or the watching of places remotely, involves vision only. Working with textual information requires the use of vision only, albeit the use of hearing may be required for music and films, as special classes of information. Finally, co-presence with things involves the use of vision for the activation of smartphone or PC screens.

It turns out that despite the seeming complexity of co-presence contexts vis-à-vis Internet space, the use of the Internet does not carry with it any meaningful operational or perceptional difficulties for most of its subscribers. Furthermore, Goby (2003) studied the relationship between the uses of personal physical and virtual spaces among 600 young Singaporeans, and showed that Internet users dwelling in larger residential spaces make more extensive use of the Internet and vice versa.

5.3.2 Personal identity

Personal identity refers to people's internal and external identities (Kellerman 2014). Our focus here will be mainly on their external identities, which may involve some spatialities. In physical space, these external identities refer mainly to one's name, fixed residential address, and phone numbers, with the two latter identity pieces being spatial and changeable. In Internet space, external personal identity may be expressed through one's name and email address, with the latter bearing a spatial connotation. However, email addresses have gained some extensive geographical flexibility, since they can be accessed globally through fixed and mobile connectivities.

Both physical and virtual identities provide people with some security and protection: in physical space, one's home secures physical properties, whereas in virtual space one's identity secures informational properties. Thus, Curry (2000, 14) stated: 'that privacy, whether in the form of security of place or of protection of information, is essential to the development of individual identity … if an individual's every thought and action were open to view, the result would be chaos'. Furthermore, for both physical space and Internet identities 'it can be argued that in the final instance individual identities are always social identities' (Häkli and Paasi 2003, 145). Internet users make simultaneous uses of their physical and virtual addresses in dual-space, and their possession and use of virtual identities do not seem to bring about any confusion with their physical space identities.

Our physical space identities may be clearly defined by domestic legal directions and requirements for name and address registrations, whereas our virtual identities are much more flexible. Thus, Internet users may easily choose fake names and multiple email addresses, something that we noted in the previous chapter as emerging for social networking platforms, notably for Facebook. Other online systems, such as banking, are less flexible in this regard, in their requirement of identification coding. The ability to use multiple identities in social networking permits users, notably adolescents, to experiment with their identities, so that about an estimated 50 percent of them pretended over the Internet to be someone else, notably when virtual communities function separately from those in real life (Valkenburg and Peter 2008). Furthermore, the use of fake and multiple identities may involve some cultural dimensions, as we noted in the previous chapter, with Internet users often preferring to disguise gender and race identities (Kennedy 2006).

More generally, it was argued that 'the networked self is much more public and much less private than the autonomous human subject who lies at the core of most traditional thought in the social sciences' (Warf 2013, 148; see also Turkle 1995). The fluid identity in Internet space has made some to prefer the notion of 'identification' over the more normative one of 'identity' (Hall 1996).

5.3.3   Personal status

The personal status of people as actors in physical and Internet spaces is expressed through the level of their personal autonomy, which refers to the individual autonomy of people with respect to their choices regarding desires, actions, or character, including their freedoms of expression, religion, and association (Friedman 2003, 4). Personal autonomy for the performance of personal mobility by individuals, notably by car in physical space and with the Internet in virtual space, is based on the value of freedom. It allows people to enjoy a wide autonomy in their personal mobility, as long as they do not cause any risk, damage, or nuisance to others (Kellerman 2006).

Personal autonomy, as expressed by levels of personal mobilities in both physical and Internet spaces, constitutes spatiality. Thus, 'true mobility can only be achieved autonomously – the distinction between moving and being moved, a passive and decidedly dependent (as opposed to autonomous) state' (Böhm et al. 2006, 4). Personal autonomy may routinely be experienced simultaneously in physical and Internet spaces, for instance when using a mobile phone while driving, or when surfing the Internet while riding a train. Thus, dual-space can be characterized by a simultaneous expression of personal autonomies in both physical and Internet spaces.

The degree by which one may realize her/his personal autonomy, in both physical and Internet spaces, may depend on a variety of individual and societal factors, such as personal character, social norms, and cultural preferences. Furthermore, the ability to move freely in space depends on the levels of immobility of people who provide transportation and communications services for other persons being on the move (Boltanski and Chiapello 2007; see also Massey 1993; Graham and Marvin 2001).

Personal autonomy in both physical and Internet spaces may be limited by social norms as well as by political restrictions. Some of these restrictions and norms, mostly those relating to the freedom of expression, may apply to physical and Internet spaces alike. For instance, the free expression for people may be restricted whether they use social networking platforms such as Facebook, or whether they talk in face-to-face social gatherings, attempting, for instance, to avoid 'shaming'. These restrictions might differ among countries, sometimes amounting to censorship. Another type of restriction relates to spatial privacy, which is honored through the avoidance of transgression of private physical or virtual properties. Thus, some balancing has always been sought between one's own personal autonomy, as applied to free mobility and expression, on the one hand, and fellows' personal autonomies, as expressed through the boundaries of their private space, or through their personal honor, on the other.

5.3.4 Experience

The undergoing of an experience in physical space constitutes, first, an external bodily event, which is followed by the creation and preservation of an internal mental impression. Thus, physical space experiences are regulated by bodily and mental conditions at the time of experiencing, and they can often be considered as spatialities, notably when locational or environmental dimensions are of particular significance for any experiencing.

Experiencing in Internet space does not constitute a bodily matter, since it is rather an imaginative and/or metaphorical one. It can be imaginative through visual (textual, graphic, still and streaming pictures) and/or audial (vocal and/or instrumental) signals transmitted through screens and speakers. Experiencing in Internet space can further be metaphorical in nature, due to the wide use of geographical terms for Internet operations. The visual and audial experiencing of Internet space depends on the quality of website design, as well as on the quality of the devices used for Internet connectivity. Despite the seeming lack of 'depth' of identity and history for websites, as compared to those attributed to places in physical space, websites may possess their own identities through their design and functionalities, and, thus, they may be experienced as places by their users (Kellerman 2016). Hence, Internet space may present some imaginative spatialities.

Experiencing through the Internet is more flexible than experiencing in physical space, in the sense that one may move from one screen, or experience stimulus, to another one, by a single click, whereas moving from one place to another in physical space involves coping with some friction of distance. Thus, the ease of movement through the Internet facilitates 'wider' or more extensive experiencing of Internet space as compared to those for physical space. On the other hand, however, Internet experiencing, being imaginative in nature, is shallower by the internal impression that it may construct, as compared to bodily physical space experiencing. Hence, Internet experiencing constitutes a 'different human experience of dwelling in the world; new articulations of near and far, present and absent, body and technology, self and environment' (Crang et al. 1999, 1).

Natural bodily experiencing in physical space coupled with imaginative and metaphorical ones taking place over the Internet might reach symbiosis when experienced in dual-space. This may emerge, for instance, when somebody undergoes a physical space experience, such as traveling, while being simultaneously exposed to Internet websites, of one sort or another, during their terrestrial travel.

5.3.5 Interaction

Following our discussions so far of the four continuous, and rather basic, human performances in physical, virtual and dual spaces, we move now to the exposition of three changing ones: interaction, social networking and action.

Whereas presence in any of the spaces constitutes a mere passive being in them, interaction among people pursued in them assumes the establishment of contact with at least one additional person, and such contacting constitutes a distinct class of human action. Interaction in both physical and virtual spaces constitutes a most meaningful spatiality, taking place either in single locations for face-to-face interactions, or in two locations for virtual ones between two communicating parties. As we noted for experiencing, face-to-face meetings constitute powerful interactions, since they include also body language gestures, which are lacking in virtual communications. However, virtual communications might be more extensive, in their frequency, as compared to face-to-face ones, as well as in the wider potential variety of parties involved. In many cases, it is normally easier and faster to carry out virtual communications as compared to face-to-face ones.

Boden and Molotch (1994) pointed to the crucial importance of face-to-face meetings for business conduct, in what they termed the 'compulsion of proximity'. Thus, they assumed that virtual contacts would be used only if face-to-face meetings cannot be carried out. Urry (2002) extended Boden and Molotch's notion of compulsion for proximity from business interactions to social ones, notably those engaging air travel, but this notion is applicable to local and domestic social ties, as well. Thus, 'virtual and imaginative travel will not simply substitute for corporeal travel since intermittent co-presence appears obligatory for sustaining much social life' (Urry 2002, 258).

In the dual-space society, face-to-face and virtual communications would then tend mainly to complement each other, so that, sometimes, virtual communications will be established prior to face-to-face meetings, and sometimes the other way around. In some cases, though, communications in dual-space might be pursued also simultaneously. For example, some people might be engaged in a face-to-face meeting, with some additional parties connected to that meeting via video communications.

As we noted back in Chapter 1, it was for Wellman (2001; see also Rainie and Wellman 2012), followed by Yu and Shaw (2008), to outline change phases in the conduct of social relations. In the first phase, face-to-face or door-to-door communications were the available norm, followed, in the second phase, by place-to-place contacts using cars and telephones, and culminating, in the third phase, with the contemporary person-to-person communications, in which both parties may communicate through location-free smartphones.

5.3.6   Social networking

By social networking, we refer to formal and informal group interactions, in both physical and Internet spaces, as we discussed in the previous chapter. Whereas interaction constitutes in most cases one-to-one communications, social networking is a one-to-many mode of communication.

The decline in the significance of the physical location of individuals for social relations, typifying the use of the Internet, notably via smartphones, followed earlier observations on the general weakening importance of distance vis-à-vis the emergence of digital communications systems (Cairncross 1997). However, a longitudinal study of interactions in Toronto (1978–2005), demonstrated that distance was still significant for human social relations, just before the massive adoption of online social networking, so that people preferred to establish contacts with fellows located within their geographical proximity, rather than in remote areas (Mok et al. 2010).

The spatiality of networks in physical space would normally involve clear locations for pre-organized group meetings, coupled with steady network memberships, based mainly on family, business, and/or social ties. Online networking, on the other hand, usually implies a flexible spatiality, even if all members of a network live in the same community, since network members may access their networks also when being located elsewhere (see McLean and Maalsen 2013, 252). The flexibility of online networking applies also to network membership, with joining and leaving of online groups, being easily pursued. It has become common for physical space networks, such as those of classmates, family members and workers, to be simultaneously organized and connected through online platforms, such as WhatsApp or Viber groups, so that ongoing communications are facilitated without any pre-organization. Thus, physical space and online meetings may sustain and complement each other in dual-space.

5.3.7   Action

As we discussed in the previous chapter, side by side with the roles of the Internet as an information source, and its provision for human interaction and social networking, the Internet has turned into an arena for the performance of a rather wide array of commercial and service activities, which have been traditionally carried out in physical space.

The spatialities of the Internet as the second action space for the obtaining of services consist of websites as virtual spaces, and these websites facilitate human actions as similarly as possible to those performed in equivalent facilities in physical space. This service space, which is offered by the Internet for numerous human needs, has brought about several emerging relationships between facilities in physical space, on the one hand, and the equivalent ones offered through the Web, on the other, such as those emerging for banking, shopping, governmental services, travel arrangements and so on.

Thus, facilities in the two spaces may complement each other, as we noted in the previous chapter for instance for shopping, when Internet information can complement shopping in a physical store, or vice versa. The action facilities in the two spaces may further compete with each other, as might be the case for some retail branches as well as for travel arrangements. In other cases, online facilities may even substitute equivalent services in physical space, as is the case, for example, for bank branches, possibly bringing about the closure of bank branches in physical space. We will return to this latter type of relationship between urban physical space and the equivalent virtual space in Chapter 9.

From the perspective of Internet users, the dual-space for action offers users, each time they need to perform any service activity, the option to choose between the two spaces for the service performance. This contemporary reality of operational choice between two spaces rather than between two locations in physical space, coupled with the varied and complex relations between the two action-spaces, present the two spaces as being in symbiosis with each other.

5.4   CONCLUSION

Physical space and Internet metaphorical space were originally viewed as two rather separate spaces. The development of GPS, broadband and mobile technologies have brought about the viewing of the two spaces as interfolding and converging into hybrid space. Later on, the conceptual focus in the study of spatial identities for digital codes moved from the metaphorical spatiality of the Internet to the identification of connectivities and spatial content in digital systems, thus turning them into spatial media. We argued in this chapter for the emergence of a dual-space society, based on the hybrid between physical and

Internet spaces, with the latter being a metaphorical one. This view approaches the Internet, as a leading digital system, from the perspective of human agency, thus focusing on people's spatialities while functioning within both physical and Internet spaces. This approach complements the viewing of selected digital systems as spatial media, since the latter constitutes a conceptual approach rather than a framework for the performance of everyday activities of the Internet as a digital system.

Dual-space constitutes an arena for spatial practices, with both physical and Internet spaces constituting separate dualities, as products of actions with structuring power. In order for Internet space to function dually with physical space, Internet users need three spatial conditions to be met by the Internet system: universal accessibility for the users to the system, universal reach of websites, and an instant pace for information transmissions. Dual-space implies several continuous conditions for individuals being in them: presence in the two spaces; personal identification; personal autonomy; and the experiencing of dual-space use. Changing performances within dual-space include interaction, networking and action. Each of these performances involves some physical space and Internet spatialities, and these spatialities are interrelated with each other in varying ways.

The dual-space society is not just the case for individual Internet users, or the demand side of the numerous uses facilitated by the Internet to its subscribers. It is also the case for the supply side of the system, namely for businesses and organizations functioning within hybrid space, as well. The dual-society dimensions for companies will be the focus of the following chapter. The notion of dual-space society may apply also to the terrestrial mobility of individuals in physical space, which is about to change dramatically in the near future via the upcoming introduction of autonomous vehicles (AVs). We will discuss the adoption of AVs and the urban impacts of this adoption in Chapters 8–9. The more efficient physical mobility to be offered by AVs, as compared to human-driven cars, will still not be able to compete with the instant and light-speed transmissions of information, which is facilitated by the Internet. Hence, it is difficult to assume that the contemporary reality of dual-space for human everyday operations will change in the near future.

6. The Internet and companies

The Internet is consumed as a powerful communications, business, and information tool, by commercial, industrial and service businesses, as well as by organizations and societies of all types. As such, the Internet is important for them, similar to its importance for individuals, as portrayed in Chapters 4–5. However, the Internet for businesses is not meaningful just for its consumption, thus presenting a demand side. The Internet for companies and organizations constitutes also a supply side, since companies serve as producers of products and services sold to individual customers, who are also Internet subscribers. Thus, the Internet per se may serve as a mediating channel between demand and supply, as being the two sides of transaction processes between companies and their customers. Thus, in this chapter, we will elaborate, first, on the penetration processes of the Internet into the operations of companies and organizations, notably small and medium-sized enterprises (SMEs), and the numerous uses of the Internet pursued by them.

Companies may consider the implementation of some organizational changes, following the adoption of the Internet, as a communications and informational tool. Such changes, as we will see, may be viewed as constituting the most advanced phase in the adoption process of the Internet. Organizational changes may be motivated by the ability of companies to increase their productivity with the Internet. Furthermore, such organizational changes resemble the experiencing dimension for individual users of the Internet, which we noted in the previous chapter, in that organizations, as entities with a kind of an organizational 'self', undergo a moment of change, similar to some personal change that might be involved in the experiencing process by individuals.

We may assume that by now companies and organizations have adopted the Internet, so that almost all of them are Internet-based, either in passive ways (presenting information on websites), or in active ones (facilitating direct sales through the Web). Hence, the consumption of the Internet by companies and organizations may be considered as spatially fully dispersed. This is not the case, however, for the production of the numerous Internet technologies, which present a different geographical pattern, being rather concentrated in specific cities located in several continents and countries. Therefore, following the exploration of the consumption side of the Internet by companies and organizations, this chapter will move to the highlighting of knowledge-based local economies, which specialize in the production of the rather numerous

Internet technologies, including: network, connectivity, navigation and application. Another dimension for Internet technology transfers is the provision of technological services for Internet users of all kinds, including the provision of infrastructure, content, and maintenance services. These Internet technological services are, by their very nature, dispersed, and located in major cities.

6.1 COMPANY INTERNET PENETRATION AND USES

The identification of phases for Internet penetration and adoption by companies has been sought for extensively, resulting in numerous proposed models for these phases. A variety of names have been suggested for similar phases, side by side with added phases accumulating along this research sequence (see Nambisan and Wang 1999; Overby and Min 2001; Teo and Pian 2004; and Cheong et al. 2009). These phase models are comparatively presented in Table 6.1. The Internet adoption phases that have been proposed by these models assume implicitly that the adopting companies have existed already prior to the availability of the Internet for them. Thus, the models refer mainly to the gradual adoption processes of the Internet by these rather veteran companies, presenting a continuum of adoption (Overby and Min 2001). However, there may also emerge other possibilities. For instance, companies that existed already prior to the introduction of the Internet, back in 1995, might have potentially adopted the Internet in fewer phases than those suggested by the models. In addition, newer companies, notably those established after 1995, and obviously companies that are being established these days, may have possibly adopted the Internet in advanced ways from the outset. In any case, we may safely assume that urban companies at large make use of the Internet, in any of the possible ways and five levels which are outlined in Table 6.1, and which are highlighted sequentially in the following paragraphs.

- **Phase zero: 'email adoption'**: Emailing was assumed to be the Internet service which was adopted first by businesses, in its constitution of a communications platform.
- **Phase one: 'information' or 'Web presence'**: This is a kind of 'passive' use of the Web, as an information platform, in addition the use of the Internet as a communications platform. It involves the creation of a company website, presenting some basic information on the company, in equivalence to traditional company printed brochures.
- **Phase two: 'work collaboration', 'interaction' or 'prospecting'**: From this phase on Internet adoption involves 'active' uses of the system. At first, the company websites may become more dynamic, in the sense that

information in them is frequently updated, and in their provision of an email contacting service for customers' service calls.

- **Phase three: 'transaction' or 'integration'**: In this phase, the Internet is used already for the conducting of company business, through e-commerce with other companies (B2B), as well as with end-customers (B2C).

- **Phase four: 'integration' or 'transformation'**: In this last phase, the Internet, through both the Web (possibly including also Intranets) and email networking, turns into a medium and tool for company business and organizational transformation, which may include, for instance, the dissemination of ERP (enterprise resource planning) systems.

These five phases and their business and organizational impacts, notably for SMEs, have been documented in numerous empirical studies, involving firms in numerous countries, and focusing mainly on companies being in earlier phases of their Internet adoption. These studies have argued for positive Internet effects for companies only once the adoption of the Internet has been eventually coupled with business and organizational transitions. For instance, it was shown for 799 Italian companies that the use of broadband during 1998–2004 yielded higher productivity levels only when accompanied by organizational change (Colombo et al. 2013). Similarly, a study of some 2,626 firms in Portugal showed that merely having a website did not imply high levels of Internet use. The study further showed that numerous companies used the Internet in order to attract customers (Oliveira and Martins 2011). A 2002 study of 264 SMEs in the Netherlands found that 198 firms out of them, or some 75 percent, established an Internet connection, but of these, the majority (93 percent) used the Internet for surfing only, and merely 23 percent made use of the Internet also for shopping (Sadowski et al. 2002). Similarly, studies of Singapore (Teo and Pian 2004) and Malaysia (Cheong et al. 2009) showed that most companies there used the Internet for phase two activities, thus presenting on their websites some detailed and updated business information, coupled with customer service. Similarly, a rather modest adoption of the Internet by civil society organizations, such as labor unions and environmental organizations, was reported for Hong Kong, as of the early 2000s (Chu and Tang 2005).

The Internet has facilitated yet another vital service for companies in their consumption of external producer services. This service is of significance mainly for firms located remotely from major urban centers, so that they tend to rely on Internet communications for the consumption of such services, as has been shown for New York State manufacturers (Macpherson 2008). A special case for Internet use by companies, in this regard, is their need for high-order knowledge intensive business services (KIBS), such as professional (e.g. higher level law and accounting), and scientific ones (e.g. specialized engineering). Such services tend to be located in metropolitan areas, and

Table 6.1   *Phases in Internet adoption by companies*

Phase	Nambisan and Wang (1999)	Overby and Min (2001)	Teo and Pian (2004); Cheong et al. (2009)
0			Email adoption
1	Information access	Information	Web presence
2	Work collaboration	Interaction	Prospecting
3	Core business transactions	Transaction	Business integration
4		Integration	Business transformation

Internet connectivity facilitates the provision of such services to remotely located companies. Thus, it was shown for the Quebec province in Canada that 'the further the distance between provider and user, the higher the probability that the provider assigns a high importance to electronic means of communication' (Shearmur and Doloreux 2015, 1665).

The Intranet was developed as an intra-organizational communications system, functioning similarly to the external Internet (Clarke and Preece 2005). The Intranet may permit, on the one hand, a wide exposure of internal information to company employees, but on the other hand, it can restrict access to specific files and emails to authorized personnel only. A company may further develop some websites within the Internet system, with restricted access to company employees only, whether all of them or merely selected authorized ones. Such websites are normally beyond the reach of the standard search engines, and thus constitute part of the so-called 'hidden Web', or 'deep Web'.

6.2   PRODUCTION OF INTERNET TECHNOLOGIES

As compared to the geographically universal consumption of Internet tools by companies and its gradual deepening, which we just noted, the production of Internet technologies, applications and contents, is rather concentrated in specific cities, which are located in several continents and countries, and these locations may differ by Internet technology types. Knowledge economies, in the most general sense, consist of a knowledge sector, or a mix of several of such knowledge sectors, which lead a local or a domestic economy. These knowledge sectors include mainly IT industries (hardware; software; applications); other high-tech industries (including biological and medical ones); fin-tech (finance technologies) business services; communications and information services; and research and development (R&D) activities pursued in other industrial and service branches, as well as those carried out within academic institutes.

Table 6.2   *Layers of Internet technologies*

Rank	Layer	Internet technologies	Technology type	Production locations
4	Application	Email systems; website design; smartphone apps	Software	*Email and web design*: ubiquitous *Apps*: specializing cities in Asia, Europe and US
3	Navigation and middleware	Browsers; search engines; payment systems; security systems	Software	*Leading high-tech cities*: Silicon Valley, New York, Boston, Stockholm, Tel Aviv, Singapore, London, Berlin
2	Connectivity	Access; server farms	Hardware	*Access provision*: ISPs *Server farms*: preference for cold countries
1	Network	Fiber-optic cables; routers; higher-generation mobile networks	Hardware	*Fiber-optics*: China, US, Japan and Italy *Routers*: China and Taiwan *Fifth-generation mobile networks*: US, Sweden, South Korea, China and Finland

Source: Following Casper and Glimstedt (2001, Table 1).

Knowledge economies too, like the sectors of manufacturing and service provision, imply a wide consumption of the Internet, and at its highest levels, and this is notably so when knowledge companies engage and specialize in the development of the Internet itself, including Internet applications, software, hardware, and websites. The location factors and patterns for knowledge and high-tech industries in general have been highlighted elsewhere (see e.g. Wilson et al. 2013), so that the following discussion will focus specifically on the location of Internet industries. However, we will still briefly address the location of high-tech industries in general, in the following discussion of the Internet navigation technologies, since these technologies constitute a sub-sector of the high-tech industry.

Casper and Glimstedt (2001) proposed a four-layer model for Internet technologies, which we will follow in our discussion here, and to which we will add the missing locational dimension (Table 6.2). Thus, Internet technologies consist, from bottom to top, of these four layers: network; connectivity; navigation and middleware; and application. The first two, and lower, Internet technology levels, consisting of network and connectivity, are hardware layers, whereas the two additional and upper Internet technology layers, those of navigation and application, are software ones. The software technologies can only begin to emerge once the infrastructures of network and connectivity are initially developed, but at later stages of development, all the four technologies are continuously integrated into the operations of the Internet. Let us examine each of these four layers of Internet technologies, with some special attention devoted to their locational dimension.

6.2.1   Network

The first layer of Internet technologies, namely networks, consists of hardware, which is not Internet-specific, such as PCs and servers for the hosting of LANs (local area networks), and these will not be discussed here. In addition to these general network technologies, the Internet network layer includes also Internet-specific technologies, mainly fiber-optic cables, which are required for the transmission of high volumes of information traffic, typifying notably streaming video information. However, such cables may be used also for fixed-line telephony (which may use the rather traditional copper wires). The Internet system requires an additional hardware device, routers, for two levels of its operation. First, and at the macro level, for the routing of system traffic, and second, and at the micro level, for home and office users, facilitating cable-less Wi-Fi Internet connectivity, so that several computers, tablets and smartphones can be connected to one wired PC. Network technologies further include higher-generation mobile networks, with the second generation permitting, at the time, the establishment of basic Internet connectivity, and higher generations, up to the fifth one, which is now being developed, for wider and faster volumes of information transmissions via smartphones.

The fiber-optic industry has become highly concentrated globally, and led by China, the US, Japan, and Italy, with China representing in parallel also the contemporary principal sources of demand for such wires (Cision 2017). Thus, in 2016, China produced some 41 percent of the world production of fiber-optic cables. The Yangtze Optical Fibre and Cable (YOFC) company was ranked first among fiber-optic production companies globally, producing some 13.4 percent of the global production in 2016, with its headquarters located in Wuhan. The American Corning company followed the Chinese YOFC, producing some 12.9 percent of the global production in 2016. Corning production took place mainly in Wilmington, Concord and Newton, all in North Carolina, US. The Furukawa Electric Company is the leading Japanese fiber-optic producer, being located in several places in Japan, with production taking place also in India and Morocco.

The manufacturing of routers is even more concentrated nationally, led by China and Taiwan, in which production is pursued for the mainly American companies of Netgear, Asus, D-Link, and Cisco (Bkav 2015). The development of the fourth generation of mobile networks was led by the US at the time. However, numerous companies, located in several countries, lead the development of the fifth generation, which is expected to begin by 2018–2019. These companies include the American Qualcomm and Intel companies, as well as the Singaporean Broadcom, the Chinese Huwai, the Swedish Ericsson, the Korean Samsung, and the Finnish Nokia (Clark and Kang 2018).

6.2.2   Connectivity

The second layer of Internet technology, consisting of Internet connectivity technologies, constitutes mainly of a hardware-based service supplied to Internet users, rather than of hardware or software manufacturing, which is the case for the other three Internet technologies. All subscribers, whether being individual users or companies of any kind, require access or connectivity to the Internet. This connectivity service is provided by ISPs (Internet service providers), mostly commercial and competitive ones, but sometimes also community-based ones (Foros and Hansen 2001). ISPs are located locally or regionally, depending on city size, as well as on specific ISP organizational structures (Nguyen 2002).

Connectivity technologies/services include also server farms, previously called Internet hotels. The farms host numerous powerful servers, which on their part, host and maintain large numbers of websites. Therefore, this service is required mainly by companies, which own and operate websites, rather than by individual customers. Server farms usually serve also as data centers for big data and cloud services. Server farms used to be located, in the early 2000s, almost solely in Pacific States of the US (Kellerman 2002), but recently preferences have emerged for farm locations in cold countries, such as Northern Canada, Sweden, Norway, Finland and Iceland. These unique locations have been chosen, given the heat that server farms create (Shehabi et al. 2011). In cold countries, the cold natural air may save on air-conditioning costs and heat, whereas the hot air produced by the servers can serve for the heating of homes and offices (PRI 2012).

6.2.3   Navigation

As we mentioned already, the third and fourth layers of Internet technology are software-based, as compared to the two lower levels of Internet technologies, which are hardware-based. Once networks and connectivity, the two basic Internet technology layers, are established, the next concern is to provide users with navigation and middleware tools. Thus, third-layer technologies include browsers, search engines, web payment systems, and Internet security systems.

It is mainly for large, and even the largest, Internet and information technology firms, such as Google and Microsoft, to handle the development and production of Internet navigation tools. Thus, the locations for the development for new technologies for navigation and middleware tools are clusters of high-tech industries at large. Such clusters have emerged, over the last five to six decades, in cities which enjoyed at the time a local availability of venture capital, or which were able to attract such venture capital. Such high-tech cities further include leading universities and qualified human resources, and they have been able to attract IT professionals for work and residence, given their general urban qualities (see e.g. Saxenian 1994; Wilson et al. 2013). Leading such cities are the Silicon Valley, New York, Boston, Stockholm, Tel Aviv, Singapore, London, and Berlin (see e.g. World Economic Forum 2017).

6.2.4   Application

The fourth layer of Internet technologies, application, has turned out to constitute the most lucrative one since the 1990s, as far as urban economies are concerned. In the first phase of Internet development, two major application activities were developed: domain registration, including the establishment of email systems, and website design. This early application phase emerged following the commercial introduction of the Internet in 1995, and prior to the introduction and massive adoption of smartphones and the numerous apps developed for their versatile usage, as of the early 2000s. Thus, since the introduction of smartphones and their fast adoption, the development of apps has become the frontier application activity. This new application frontier has turned the more veteran application activities of domain registration, the development of email systems, as well as the industry of website design, into ubiquitous urban activities, within the context of Internet service activities, rather than their being considered as Internet technology production activities.

Until 1999, it was for a single American company, Network Solutions Inc., to serve as the only domain name registrar for almost all domain names. Following regulation changes in the US, which accompanied the global spread and growth of the Internet system, this service has turned global. In 2018, some 2,519 registrars, or merely 566, when duplicates are excluded, were active all over the world, and were recognized by the ICANN (Internet Corporation for Assigned Names and Numbers). Leading nations among registration companies were the US with some 133 registrars, or 23.5 percent of the global total, and China with some 87 registrars, or 15.4 percent of the global total. Including Hong Kong, though, which was the third leading market of registrars with some 38 registrars, China reached 22 percent, closely competing with the US on the leadership in the number of registration companies (WHTop 2018).

Still, however, the worldwide distribution of domains, as of early 2017, was more in favor of the US. Thus, over 330 million domains existed worldwide by then, with some 43.4 percent of them carrying .com and .net suffixes, implying US registration, whereas only 6.5 percent of the global number of domains carried the .cn suffix, assigned for China (Verisign 2017). This division of domain names between these two countries reflects the cumulative registration of domains, including the earlier years of the Internet, when the US was the predominant nation in domain registrations.

Within China, there has emerged a decentralization of domain registrations, adding more cities as loci for domain registrations. This trend of geographical spread in domain registrations in China was attributed to a growing importance of market forces, as compared to previous government intervention in the industry (Zhen et al. 2015). Globally, it is safe to assume that domain registrars or their extensions are located in major cities. The establishment of email systems has become even more dispersed, as compared to domain registration, with computer professionals within companies and organizations being able to pursue the establishment of email systems by themselves within company domains.

The website (or web) design industry has undergone a process of decentralization, similar to domain registration. In the 1990s, the website design industry was mainly concentrated in San Francisco, New York, Los Angeles and London, in this order of centralization, reflecting the birth of the Internet in the US, and its early strong dominance in it. Furthermore, these cities offered three leading advantages for the website design industry. First, a well-developed telecommunications system built there, already prior to the introduction of the Internet, because of the location of the finance industry in these cities. This telecommunications system facilitated good communications with customers worldwide. Second, the existence of venture capital for newly established web design companies in these financial centers. Third, the local availabilities of computer specialists as well as artists, needed for the construction and design of websites, respectively (Kellerman 2002).

As of the early 2000s, these four cities lost their initial advantage for the website design industry. The global telecommunications system has been equipped with fast and globally stretching fiber-optic Internet telecommunications, downscaling the advantage of cities which were blessed first with fiber-optic cables. In addition, website production has become a routine professional specialty, not requiring venture capital anymore, so that website design has turned into a profession, which is being studied and its services offered worldwide. Thus, clients for the construction or the redesigning of their websites have now the choice between locally available web design companies, located in major cities, and remote ones, offering their services over the Internet.

As we mentioned already, the widening geographical distribution of Internet domain registration and web design suppliers has been coupled with the emergence of the app industry, which has focused on smartphone usage of the Internet, and this app industry is currently still concentrated in specific cities. Moriset and Malecki (2009) noticed such mixes of geographic dispersion and concentration as trends within the Internet industry.

The app industry has become a vast industry almost overnight. With the first app store (Apple App Store) opening up in 2008, it was merely a decade later, by the first quarter of 2018, when over 7 million apps were available for downloading for all smartphone operation systems. Of these apps, the Google Play Store offered some 3.8 million apps for Android-based mobile phones, the Apple App Store offered some 2 million apps, and these two leading app stores were coupled with over 1.3 additional apps offered by other virtual app stores (Statista 2018j).

The emerging app economy was viewed as consisting of three circles (Mandel and Long (PPI) 2017). First are the core app jobs, consisting of the app developers, who are by their profession either software engineers or computer security engineers. The second and wider circle of the app economy includes the indirect app economy jobs, including marketing, finance and other administrative duties, all required for app production and distribution. The third and widest circle of the app economy consists of spillover jobs, including professional services that benefit from the availability of apps to customers. Such third circle jobs of the app economy include a wide range of services, for instance bank tellers, law offices, building managers, and cable installers.

The locations for the spillover jobs of the app economy, as well as some of the indirect jobs, may be in cities without specific locational features, thus being most decentralized. However, and in the contrary, the urban location for the core sector of app development is most selective. The early and cumulative advantage of previous specializations in the high-tech industry in general, and in the Internet industry in particular, might explain some of the core locations (Zhen et al. 2015; Pon 2015). However, the rise of Asian cities, notably in China and South Korea, has to do with later developments of the high-tech industries, coupled with a rapidly growing demand for mobile services in these two countries, and further coupled with the emerging leaderships of these two countries in smartphone development and production.

Thus, as we will learn from the following city data, the application industry has undergone a geographical transition from the seniority of the US in the early Internet application industry, at the time, focusing on domain registration and web design, to an Asian dominance in the contemporary app industry, focusing on smartphone apps. In 2015, the US still enjoyed the largest number of developers worldwide located there, some 1,567 of them, and coupled with Canada (191), the total number of developers in North America stood at

1,758. The second largest country by the number of developers, China, had merely 776 developers, or merely a half of the number of American ones. However, if we add to the Chinese developers the developers of South Korea (395), Japan (351), India (289), Taiwan (256), Vietnam (173), and Hong Kong (158), the total for top East Asian countries in app development reached 2,398 developers or some 36.4 percent more developers than in North America. The global concentration of developers in Europe was similar in size to the North American one, reaching some 1,795 developers in 2015, and these European developers were divided among numerous countries: UK (456); Russia (321); Germany (307); Spain (239); France (219); Italy (137); and Finland (116). Four additional countries from other parts of the world were included in the list of 20 leading countries by number of developers, as presented by Caribou Digital (2016, Figure 4): Israel (196); Turkey (183); Australia (143); and Brazil (138). Weighing the number of developers by the number of Internet users, as calculated by Pon (2015) for a sample of countries worldwide, yielded the list of countries that specialized most in the app industry: Hong Kong (9.0); South Korea (7.96); Israel (3.5); and Switzerland (3.25).

The cities in which app developers were concentrated in 2014–2015 were presented by Pon (2015), based on a sample of 2,688 developers (see also Caribou Digital 2016, Figure 6, with a slightly different city distribution), and the 15 leading ones are presented in Table 6.3. These 15 cities included 50 percent of the developers worldwide, accentuating the strong concentration of the app industry globally. The leading city by the number of developers in 2015 was Seoul with some 11.8 percent of the global sample of developers. This attests to the leading role of South Korea in the app and smartphone industries. Seoul was followed by two additional Asian cities, Beijing and Tokyo, with 9.4 and 9.3 percent of the developers in each city, respectively. Six out of the fifteen globally leading cities were Chinese, and these cities consist of the largest high-tech specialized Chinese cities. The inclusion of rather veteran high-tech specialized cities was the case for the US, with three of its cities in the list of leading app cities: San Francisco, New York, and Seattle. Tokyo was joined by four European cities, led by Moscow, a non-EU city. The European leadership by Moscow attests to the significant role of language in the app industry, so that Moscow has served a wide international market of Russian speakers (Caribou Digital 2016).

Another study focused on the European app economy (Mandel and Long 2017). Totally, the European app economy (referring to the EU plus Switzerland and Norway) included in 2017 some 1.89 million jobs, as compared to some 1.73 million jobs in the US by then. However, weighing the app jobs by the total number of jobs points to a higher app intensity in the US, at the rate of 1.1 percent, as compared to just 0.84 percent in Europe. The leading European countries by app job intensity were again smaller countries,

Table 6.3   *Leading cities by number of developers 2014–2015*

Rank	City	Country	No. of developers	Sample percentage
1	Seoul	South Korea	318	11.8
2	Beijing	China	252	9.4
3	Tokyo	Japan	250	9.3
4	San Francisco Bay Area	US	162	6.0
5	Shanghai	China	88	3.3
6	Moscow	Russia	81	3.0
7	London	UK	78	2.9
8	Paris	France	69	2.6
9	New York	US	51	1.9
10	Shenzhen	China	49	1.8
11	Hong Kong	China, SAR (Special Administrative Region)	47	1.7
12	Berlin	Germany	32	1.2
13	Guangzhou	China	27	1.0
14	Hangzhou	China	26	1.0
15	Seattle	US	24	0.9

Source: Pon (2015, Figure 1; N=2,688).

as we just noted for the concentration of developers worldwide: Finland (2.2 percent); the Netherlands (2.2 percent); Sweden (2.0 percent); Norway (1.9 percent); and Denmark (1.6 percent). Thus, Scandinavian countries have led in the production of Internet apps, side by side with their long-standing leadership in individual Internet consumption, which has followed such leadership for previously invented telecommunications media, as we noted in Chapter 4.

Mandel and Long (2017) further presented the number of app employees in 30 leading European cities in 2017 (in EU countries plus Switzerland and Norway) (Table 6.4). The leadership of Moscow in the number of developers, which we just noted, was not included in this list, given the focus on EU countries and some additional European countries, but excluding Russia. By the very nature of the app economy, consisting of three circles of employment, the urban concentration of app employees was lower than the one that we noted for the tighter concentration of developers, comprising the core sector. Thus, London, the leading European city of the app economy, and the city that led at the time also in the web design industry in its early stages, included some 7.3 percent of the European app employees, as compared to Seoul, the leader by its number of developers, with some 11.8 percent of the developers worldwide

Table 6.4   *Top app employment (in thousands) in EU cities 2017*

Rank	Urban area	Country	App employment	Percentage of European total
1	London	UK	138	7.3
2	Paris	France	119	6.3
3	Amsterdam	Netherlands	89	4.7
4	Berlin	Germany	71	3.8
5	Munich	Germany	56	3.0
6	Stockholm	Sweden	47	2.5
7	Helsinki	Finland	37	2.0
8	Rotterdam	Netherlands	33	1.7
9	Oslo	Norway	29	1.5
10	Cologne and Dusseldorf	Germany	26	1.4
11	Milan	Italy	25	1.3
12	Prague	Czech Republic	23	1.2
13	Barcelona	Spain	22	1.2
14	Utrecht	Netherlands	22	1.2
15	Stuttgart	Germany	22	1.2
16	Manchester	UK	21	1.1
17	Copenhagen	Denmark	21	1.1
18	Madrid	Spain	21	1.1
19	Hamburg	Germany	20	1.1
20	Eindhoven	Netherlands	20	1.1
21	Lisbon	Portugal	19	1.0
22	Frankfurt	Germany	19	1.0
23	Birmingham	UK	19	1.0
24	Brussels	Belgium	16	0.8
25	Zurich	Switzerland	15	0.8
26	Vienna	Austria	15	0.8
27	Budapest	Hungary	15	0.8
28	Lyon	France	15	0.8
29	Oxford	UK	13	0.7
30	Bristol	UK	13	0.7

Notes: N=1.89 million in the EU, Switzerland and Norway. Urban areas are defined as 50 kilometers or 30 miles around a center city, except for Rotterdam with 45 kilometers only, to avoid overlap with Amsterdam.
Source: Mandel and Long (PPI) (2017, Figure 7).

in Pon's (2015) sample. This is true also for the second leading European city, Paris, which included some 6.3 percent of the European app employees, as compared to Beijing and Tokyo, with 9.4 and 9.3 percent of the global number of developers, respectively, as presented in Pon's (2015) sample.

The list of the 30 leading European cities by the number of app employees in 2017 is a rather diversified one, including cities from 16 out of the 30 countries, which were included in the study. Hence, the list included six German cities, five British ones, four Dutch ones, and two each from France and Spain. Other countries were represented by just one city for each country: Sweden, Finland, Norway, Portugal, Austria, Hungary, Switzerland, Belgium, Denmark, the Czech Republic, and Italy. This wide international spread attests mainly to the wide extent of the third, spillover circle, of the app economy. The list of cities also included smaller cities, as was also the case for the US, and this is in lieu of some local specializations, sometimes because of leading academic institutes located in them (e.g. Oxford and Utrecht).

6.3   CONCLUSION

In this chapter, we noted the wide distribution of Internet use among companies, which might possibly be even wider than the adoption of the Internet by individuals. However, the use of the Internet by companies may be varied by its depth and intensity. It may range from the mere use of the Internet for emailing, through a rather passive use of the Web by establishing an informative website only. The use of the Internet may then, at a third phase, possibly develop into informational exchanges by companies with their customers, followed by financial transactions with customers, and peaking by organizational transitions reflecting the use of the Internet.

We noted a rather different, and more concentrated, geographical pattern for the production side of Internet technologies, obviously carried out by companies. The production of Internet technologies consists of four layers: network; connectivity; navigation and application. The production and development of Internet network hardware is led by some specific countries, notably the US and China, whereas server farms, at the connectivity layer, are frequently located in cold countries. For the third level of navigation technologies, we noticed their concentration in cities specializing in high-tech industries in general, and located worldwide.

The fourth layer of Internet technologies, application, has been the most dynamic one. In the early stages of Internet penetration, it included the web design industry as well as domain registrations. These activities, coupled with the provision of access of subscribers to the Internet by ISPs at the connectivity layer, turned later into routine services with a rather ubiquitous urban spread.

Currently the application layer is focused on the smartphone app industry, which is concentrated in selected cities, some of which served already as Internet technology hubs in previous phases of Internet technology development. The change in the application technologies, from a focus on website design and domain registration to smartphone apps, has been coupled with a drastic geographical transition. The app industry is now being led by East Asian countries, rather than by the US, as has been the case in the earlier phases of Internet emergence. Thus, currently North America and Europe share similar shares of the app industry following the East Asian leadership.

This geographical change in the leadership of the Internet application industry refers mainly to the concentrated locations of app developers, and not to the economic and technological leadership, which might continue to be mostly American. Thus, we noted the transition in the leading countries and continents for the workers of the core app industry, from the US to Asia, notably China and South Korea. One may wonder, though, if a new and still unknown generation of application technologies that might possibly emerge in the future, will turn the smartphone app industry into a ubiquitous one, as far as the locations of app developers is concerned, with new geographical centers and concentrations, preferred by the, still unknown, future application industry.

7. The Internet for urban systems

Our discussions in the three previous chapters (4–6), on the uses of the Internet by people and companies, have assumed the use of the Internet for communications and information services by humans, for private as well as business uses. In this chapter, we move to yet another Internet-based dimension of cities, namely communications within and between urban systems, as well as communications between them and their human operators and users. These latter uses and operations by and for systems are based on the IoT technology, which we highlighted back in Chapter 3.

The very digitization of the operations and controls of urban systems originated before the introduction of the Internet and IoT, and has, therefore, been long recognized and interpreted. This trend of digitization for urban systems has received, over the years, numerous names, all of which focus on rather similar processes of digitization for urban systems. Major examples for these names include 'the city of bits' (Mitchell 1995); 'sentient cities' (Crang and Graham 2007); 'the automatic production of space' (Thrift and French 2002); 'the programmable city' (Kitchin 2011); 'the transduction of space' (Dodge and Kitchin 2005); and 'code/space' (Kitchin and Dodge 2011). These names for the digitization of urban systems, as well as the discussions related to them, refer mainly to large-scale city systems, such as citywide traffic control, water and sewage systems, airport control and management and so on. They further assume the dissemination of numerous codes or programmed software packages, which have been specifically developed for each urban system, bearing upon its unique requirements (Kellerman 2018b). The digitization of urban systems, coupled with the emergence of big data, have brought about the viewing of numerous cities as being 'smart cities' (e.g. Shelton et al. 2015; Dustdar et al. 2017; Kitchin 2014), a notion which we will explore in the following section of this chapter. Our explorations in this chapter will attempt to highlight the rather general technology that is currently used for digital connections with and of all major urban systems, the Internet/IoT.

Hence, this chapter will expose, first, the notion of smart cities, and the enhancement of smart cities through wide applications of the Internet and IoT. This exposure will be followed by specific elaborations on citywide uses of IoT. First, for the operations and controlling of two major urban utilities, electricity and water, notably through the adoption of smart meters, and second, for the smart regulation of urban traffic via sensor-based and IoT connected traffic lights. Finally, we will discuss the use of IoT for smart homes, which are remotely controlled by their residents.

7.1   SMART CITIES AND THE INTERNET

In Chapters 4–5 we discussed contemporary code-operated cities as being comprised of virtual Internet ones, offering urban services for individual urban users via dedicated websites, side by side with physical cities and the services which they offer. Our focus now turns to physical cities, which may too be Internet-operated ones. Such Internet-operated physical cities are usually called 'smart cities'. The term 'smart city' was first suggested as such, back in 1992, by Gibson et al. (1992; see also Batty 2017), just a couple of years prior to the commercial and universal introduction of the Internet in 1995. The smartness of cities by then referred to their growing dependence on codes/ computers for their very operations. The massive use of code for urban life, which has developed since then, has also included a growing role for digitized communications of urban systems, based on the specific codes of IoT. Urban smartness has been specifically attributed to numerous urban dimensions, led by the management of urban systems, and including also computing as used by urbanites and urban societies, and/or the development of smart city knowledge economies (Table 7.1). We will now take a brief look at each of these smart city dimensions.

The most common use of the term smart city refers to code-operated urban systems, including mainly utilities (water; electricity; sewage; and gas), transportation (traffic lights; metro; buses; and parking lots), environment (pollution of water, air and sound; and energy consumption), buildings (plants; offices; homes; malls; and schools), and city management (planning; mainte-nance; and taxing). Thus, the notion of smart city, for cities in general, and for urban systems in particular, focuses on the operations and control of the latter. Smart cities refer to the increasing extent to which urban places are composed of what Greenfield (2006) termed as 'everyware', implying the pervasive and ubiquitous dissemination of computing, as well as the wide use of digitally instrumented devices, which have both been planted into the fabric of urban environments (Kitchin 2014). The wide computing activities deployed in city systems reflects 'a coherent urban development strategy developed and managed by city governments seeking to plan and align in the long term the management of the various city's infrastructural assets and municipal services' (Dustdar et al. 2017, 3; see also Rathore et al. 2016, 65).

The notion of smart cities as referring to a ubiquitous dissemination of com-puterization may apply also to urban societies through some urban-specific uses of smartphones by city residents meant 'to engage with and navigate the city which themselves produce data about their uses, such as location and

Table 7.1   Smart city dimensions and their digitized components

Dimension	Digitized components
Systems	
Utilities	Water; electricity; sewage; gas
Transportation	Traffic lights; metro; buses; parking lots
Environment	Pollution of water, air and sound; energy consumption
Buildings	Plants; offices; homes; malls; schools
Management	Planning; maintenance; taxing
People	
Individuals	Local e-government; navigation apps; LBS; parking apps
Society	City use surveys (traffic and parking); housing surveys; facility-use surveys (shopping malls, sports)
Economy	
Knowledge economy	IT industries (hardware; software; applications); high-tech industries; business services; global finances and commerce; communications and information services; R&D

activity' (Kitchin 2014, 2). Such Internet activities, which involve specifically urban spaces, may include, for example, the use of municipal e-government, which we highlighted back in Chapter 4, the use of car navigation applications, such as Waze, as well as location-based services (LBS) offered through smartphones by changing locations of users, and parking apps. A wider social definition for smart cities relates to computerized activities of urban government vis-à-vis their city residents, noting 'the massive amounts of digital data collected about society as a means to rationalise the planning and management of cities' (Shelton et al. 2015, 13; see also Townsend 2013). Such data collection may include, for instance, traffic monitoring data and parking trends, as well as housing surveys, and facility-use surveys, such as those pursued for shopping malls and sports facilities.

The idea of smart cities and the increasing digitization of cities may further refer to local knowledge economies, which we elaborated in the previous chapter, regarding high-tech industries in general, and Internet technology production in particular. Thus, 'a smart city is one whose economy and governance is being driven by innovation, creativity and entrepreneurship, enacted by smart people' (Kitchin 2014, 2). The rationale of smart cities from this perspective, at least in some cases, 'largely coalesces around strategies for economic growth in an era of austerity' (Shelton et al. 2015, 16). In some other cases, though, an urban strategy would rather be to bring about 'a rich and active interplay of different stakeholders (primarily citizens, local businesses and authorities), effectively transforming the currently passive stakeholders into active ecosystem actors' (Dustdar et al. 2017, 3). Hence, knowledge economies may consist of a leading knowledge sector or of a mix of several of them, such as IT industries (hardware; software; applications); high-tech industries, including biomedical ones; high-level business services; global finances and commerce; communications and information services; and R&D activities taking place in academic institutes.

Viewing jointly the diversified interpretations for the term smart city, five characteristics were proposed for smart cities (Hollands 2008; see also Kitchin 2014):

1. Information technologies are widely disseminated within them.
2. Urban development is being led by the business sector, side by side with neoliberal urban governance.
3. Accent is put on social and human dimensions in the fostering of urban creativity.
4. Educational projects lead towards the emergence of smart communities.
5. Environmental and social sustainability are emphasized.

Smart cities may constitute newly built cities, or they may comprise upgraded existing ones. Examples for new cities, built *a priori* as smart ones, are Masdar (UAE), Songdo (South Korea), and Living Plan IT Valley (Portugal) (Shelton et al. 2015). Leading examples for veteran cities, upgrading into becoming smart ones, notably those making wide use of IoT, are: Suwon, Busan and Seoul (South Korea); Taipei (Taiwan); Mitaka (Japan); Singapore; Waterloo and Calgary (Canada); Glasgow (UK); New York and Chicago (US); Tehran (Iran); Amsterdam (the Netherlands); Nice (France); and Padova (Italy) (Talari et al. 2017). However, the wide interpretations and features, which have been attributed to the notion of 'smart city', imply that many, if not most, of the cities in the developed world may be recognized as smart ones, at least partially, in one way or another.

The Internet constitutes the obvious technology for people's use of smartphones, within the framework of smart cities. This is true also for the transmission of data that are collected about urban populations. Knowledge economies too imply a wide Internet use, mostly in their production activities, when engaged in the development of Internet applications, software, hardware, and websites. IoT has turned into an essential technology for the very operations of smart cities, notably as far as urban systems are concerned, so that utilities have become remotely operated and controlled, and interconnections are being established among urban systems. The adoption of IoT for smart city development involves the deployment of numerous wired and wireless sensors, installed in smart homes, in traffic lights, in central utility facilities, in environmental monitoring stations and so on. These sensors growingly reflect the development and use of artificial intelligence technologies, and they are connected to control centers through Wi-Fi, Bluetooth and mobile transmission networks of various generations (Rathore et al. 2016; Talari et al. 2017; Mehmood et al. 2017).

Two policies were proposed for European cities attempting to turn into smart ones, relating to their individual residents, as well as to their local institutions: encouragement of cooperation among city residents for the joint development of apps, and the creation of local cooperation among local governments, research institutes, universities, and companies (Komninos et al. 2013). On the other hand, however, Colding et al. (2018), as well as Bibri and Krogstie (2017) have warned of the growing complexities and energy consumption, which are involved in the growing incorporation of the Internet into urban systems. Local governments, which attempt to turn their cities into smart ones, lead such complexities, and these, jointly with high-energy consumption, may possibly bring about diminishing returns and even some destruction.

7.2   IoT-BASED URBAN ELECTRICITY AND WATER SYSTEMS

Urban Internet-based utilities in general, and electricity and water ones in particular, imply the installation of one or all of three systems and devices: remote management, smart grids and smart meters. Remote management makes it possible for operators of central control facilities to communicate through IoT and other media with control centers, or directly with some specific local systems, thus achieving better routine on-time management, as well as faster and more efficient crisis trouble shooting (Bedi et al. 2018). These communications channels may be extended by the inclusion of communications among customers, on the one hand, and suppliers-controllers, on the other, vis-à-vis IoT communications, transmitted over electricity grids, which, thus, turn into smart grids. Furthermore, the metering of electricity, water and gas consumptions can be pursued online and on time, using smart meters, thus saving the manual metering, and thus providing both suppliers and customers with on time information, notably as far as supply disturbances and over usages of utilities are concerned.

Of these three Internet upgrading options for urban utility systems, the installation of smart meters into households constitutes the most extensive and costly one, requiring the replacement of all manual meters with electronic IoT-based ones. This process is now in progress globally, with varying rates of completion among nations (Table 7.2). Thus, for electricity meters, in 2017 it was for Italy, Finland and Sweden to have the rollout of smart meters fully completed, whereas in the UK, it reached only the 20 percent level, and in Germany, the process has only begun. Likewise, China reached a 90 percent

Table 7.2   *Rollout for electricity smart meters in households in selected*
                 countries 2017

Country	Percentage
Finland	100
Italy	100
Sweden	100
China	90
US	50
UK	20

Sources: Finland, Italy and Sweden, My smart energy (2018); China, Research and Markets (2017); US, Rosenberg (2017); UK, UK Department for Business, Energy and Industrial Strategy (2018).

penetration level by 2017, whereas the US had only about 50 percent of its households equipped with smart meters for electricity by then. Obviously, therefore, there are cities which reached a complete rollout of smart meter installation, side by side with other ones which still await the beginning of installations.

The installation of smart meters for water consumption may be even more complex for several countries, notably for the US, in which there are some 50,000 water suppliers nationwide, as compared to the merely 3,000 energy suppliers throughout the country (Greguras 2018). A city that reached maturity in the installation of smart water meters is San Francisco, in which 98 percent of its water accounts are monitored by smart meters, as compared to merely 15–20 percent throughout California, a State that suffers severe water shortages (Greguras 2018). Smart water meters may obviously be useful for all of the numerous classes of water consumers, including homes, agriculture, gardening and manufacturing. However, IoT communications can be equally helpful for the controlling of other major water problems. Leading examples in this regard are flood protection, as is the case for the Netherlands (Rijcken et al. 2012), and the management of urban water quality, as is the case for China (Wang et al. 2013).

The use of IoT for the controlling and management of urban utility systems may be interpreted from numerous perspectives: human–machine relationships; utility customers; the utilities themselves; and the utility provision market. We will briefly outline each of these perspectives in the following paragraphs.

From the perspective of human–machine relationships, and as we noted already, IoT has facilitated communications among devices, as well as among urban utility systems. IoT has further provided for communications between humans, in their capacities as operators or users, on the one hand, and utilities, on the other. As Thrift (1996, 279) suggested, at the time, this latter capability constitutes part of a more general trend of human–machine relationships, which dates back to the 1960s: 'No longer is it possible to see the human subject and the machine as aligned but separate entities, each with their own specific functions.'

From the perspective of urban customers, the connection between people and machines, in this case human communications with utility provision machinery, involves a continuous metering of their utility usage, which Graham and Marvin (2001, 199) termed as 'the "pay per" revolution'. This revolution has implied the deep weaving of intelligent electronic systems into urban fabric, already before the introduction of sensor-based IoT communications (Virilio 1987, 16). We will discuss the citywide installations of Internet infrastructures, which include antennas, sensors, cameras and cables, in Chapter 9.

From the perspective of the utilities themselves, their IoT monitoring of operations and consumption imply their turning from highly fixed systems into mobile ones, through the continuous transmissions of information to and from them. These information transmissions, either from control centers and back to them, and/or by mobile operators using smartphones or tablets, relate to their routine functioning, as well as to their being remotely controlled. Thus, urban utilities, when being upgraded by IoT connectivity, rather than being replaced by newer pipe or cable grids, 'are transforming while still performing' (Lontoh 2016, 2).

From the commercial market perspective, the use of electronic metering may facilitate a change from a monopolistic provision of the public goods of urban utilities, to competition in the supply of such utilities to end customers, whether they be homes, offices, or industrial plants.

7.3   IoT AND TRAFFIC REGULATION

Urban utilities and urban traffic regulation share a similar dimension: the wide distribution of their consumers, buildings in the case of utilities, and traffic lights and cars in the case of traffic regulation. These citywide distributions of consumption for both utilities and traffic regulation are coupled with a rather centralized regulation and control, via control centers, which is common for both systems, but employed separately for each utility and for road traffic.

The basic element for road traffic control is *traffic lights*, also called t*raffic control signals/systems*, or simply *robots* (in South Africa). These light systems constitute the regulative means for traffic management in road intersections, using lights as signals. As McShane (1999, 379) noted: 'they are systems that attempt to impose a strong social control over the most fundamental of human behaviors, whether to move or be still'.

The development of traffic light systems represents simultaneous trends of growing traffic pressures, on the demand side, on the one hand, and the more constrained availability of roads and elevated exchanges, on the supply side, on the other. Hence, it has been for the invention of traffic lights and their enhancements, to serve as regulators between demand (traffic) and supply (roads). The development of traffic lights along the last 150 years, as of 1868, has been outlined elsewhere (Kellerman 2018a), and is summarized in Table 7.3. Transformations in traffic lights along the years present a five-phase process, which began with the installation of mechanical devices in road junctions for traffic management, through the introduction of traffic lights, the internationalization of traffic lights, and followed by their automation. Our interest here focuses rather on the fifth phase of road traffic regulation, namely 'autonomous, intelligent or smart systems', consisting of two recent developments for traffic regulation. First, the centralization of citywide traffic control pursued via control centers, and connected through IoT with traffic lights, and second, the sensor-based traffic lights, which communicate, also through IoT, with cars that approach road junctions.

The invention and development of computer technologies as of the 1950s, contributed to the continued enhancement of automated elements for traffic light systems. These developments facilitated higher reliability, the construction of complex central controlling centers, and the miniaturization of the controlling devices. Specifically, four technologies have constituted the core for these developments: new photography technologies; the Internet; remote sensing and artificial intelligence (see e.g. Saeed et al. 2011; Peshave et al. 2015; Gulić et al. 2016).

First among these four new technologies is enhanced photography technologies, which facilitate, for instance, wide-angle picture taking at road intersections, coupled with the development of image processing. Second, new information transmission technologies, notably the Internet and IoT, permitting instant transmission of pictures from road intersections to traffic control centers, as well as transmitting back, from control centers to traffic lights, proper operational changes accordingly. More recently, communications technologies between traffic lights and cars have been developed, the I2V (infrastructure to vehicle communications). Third, remote sensing technologies, facilitating the operation of sensors installed under the street surface, and used for the detection of cars approaching intersections. This latter type of transmitted information has implied a counter flow of information, through vehicle to infrastructure (V2I) communications. Fourth, the advancement of artificial intelligence technologies, bringing about the possibility for autonomous management of traffic by centralized controlling systems.

The first intelligent traffic light systems were probably the ramp meters, ramp signals, or metering lights, introduced for the first time in Chicago, US,

Table 7.3   *Milestones in the development of technologies for road traffic control*

Phase and year	Innovation	Place
Introduction of automobiles		
1886	First automobiles	Germany
1908	Introduction of Ford's T-model	US
I. Early devices for intersection regulation		
1868	Introduction of manual semaphore arms powered by gas	London
II. Manually operated traffic lights		
1914	First traffic lights in operation	Cleveland
1917	Yellow sign added	Detroit
1920	First four-direction light built	Detroit
1928	Twelve-bulb systems with red on top introduced	N/A
III. Automated traffic lights		
1922	First automated traffic lights in service	Houston
Mid-1920s	First controlled three-way, and lane reversal, intersections	New York
1925	Automatic control of CBD light systems introduced	Syracuse
1926	First staggered lights	Washington
1931	First lights for pedestrians	Stockholm
IV. Internationalization and universalization		
1922	First partial and manual lights in Europe	Paris
1926	League of Nations discusses colors in traffic lights	N/A
1931	First automated lights in Europe	London
1931	First staggered lights outside the US	Tokyo
V. Autonomous, intelligent or smart systems		
1963	Highway ramp metering/ monitoring	US
1970s	Development of advanced centrally controlling systems by time-of-day or through real time adaptivity	US

Phase and year	Innovation	Place
1984	First citywide intelligent or smart centralized traffic control system	Los Angeles
2015	Traffic light to vehicle communications introduced (I2V)	Numerous cities in the US

Source: Kellerman (2018a, Table 3.1).

in 1963. These lights were meant to provide for ramp monitoring, or the metering of cars attempting to access major highways, thus avoiding, or at least reducing, traffic congestions on such highways. Ramp monitoring systems have been adopted also in the UK, followed later also by other countries worldwide (Piotrovicz and Robinson 1995; Gould 2001).

The first autonomous citywide intelligent or smart system came into operations in Los Angeles in 1984, towards the Olympic Games there (LADOT 2012), and a decade before the universal introduction of the Internet. The system can be operated both manually and autonomously, and it controls some 4,600 intersections. The system makes use of over 20,000 loop detectors located at road intersections, coupled with over 500 closed-circuit television (CCTV) systems. The system has reduced travel time in Los Angeles by some 12 percent and has increased car speeds there by 16 percent. During the last thirty years, numerous cities worldwide constructed semi-autonomous or fully autonomous central controlling facilities for citywide traffic lights. It was reported for 2010 that Japan led this trend, coupled with Singapore, whereas in the US just 40 percent of traffic lights nationwide were connected to centrally controlled systems by then (Barry 2010).

The introduction of I2V communications has permitted properly equipped cars to be informed on the expected waiting time at road junctions, and as of 2016, this option has been available mainly for selected Audi and BMW car models. Such an option is of importance mainly for cars in which anti-idling systems are installed, systems that turn off car engines when waiting for signal changes at road intersections. Thus, I2V communications may facilitate an efficient use of anti-idling systems. In the US, I2V systems were installed by 2016 in road junctions in Las Vegas; Portland, Oregon; Eugene, Oregon; and in Salt Lake City (Geuss 2016). All the new systems for vehicle-to-vehicle communications (V2V), as well as those for two-way communications between cars and infrastructures (V2I and I2V) constitute crucial technologies for the operations of the upcoming AVs, which we will highlight in the following chapter.

It was noted, at the time, for the first generations of traffic lights, that they not only made it possible to manage existing intersection traffic, but that they added and attracted more traffic (McShane 1999). This two-way relationship between enhanced controlling efforts and growing volumes of traffic might be relevant for current and later improvements in traffic lights, as well, so that growing traffic may invite the development of new and enhanced technologies for its control. However, as we will note for AVs in the following chapter, future traffic volumes may tend to decrease with the adoption of AVs.

7.4   SMART HOMES AND IoT

'The smart home is firmly situated at the nexus between the digital and the human' (Strengers 2016, 61). Urban utility systems, which we discussed already, constitute utility suppliers, as well as partial producers, notably for electricity. As we noted, urban 'smartness' originated with the management and control of utilities. Urban homes, on the other hand, constitute utility consumers, unless they produce electric power, as is the case when electricity is produced by solar panels attached to people's home roofs. Still, however, the principle of 'smartness' may also apply to urban homes, as utilities customers: the ability to remotely operate and control them, notably as far as their energy consumption is concerned. Thus, 'a smart home is a residence equipped with a high-tech network, linking sensors and domestic services, appliances, and features that can be remotely monitored, accessed or controlled, and provide services that respond to the needs of its inhabitants' (Balta-Ozkan et al. 2013, 364). IoT is the communications technology that connects home appliances and systems with their remotely located residents. Smart home IoT is integrated within smart home technology (SHT), which makes use of sensors, monitors, interfaces, networked appliances and devices, as well as smartphones and tablets, for remote home controlling (Wilson et al. 2017).

Smart homes and SHT have emerged as of the early 2000s, following the growing environmental concerns for energy savings, side by side with the introduction and massive adoption of smartphones, equipped with Wi-Fi and 3G connectivities (Balta-Ozkan et al. 2013). Thus, smart homes permit the regulation and controlling of energy consumption in buildings, which in Europe amount to two-thirds of the total energy consumption, thus turning SHT into one of the ten priority areas for European energy policy (Killian et al. 2018; Wilson et al. 2017). SHTs further permit stricter home security controlling, including the use of remotely accessed cameras. In addition, smart homes facilitate enhanced assistance for the elderly, side by side with upgraded health services, which can be remotely provided at times of increasing importance attached to home treatments (Balta-Ozkan et al. 2013; Burrows et al. 2018; see also Chapter 4).

The penetration of smart homes so far has been modest, but it is growing, with a popular application for smart home technology being Internet-operated television sets (Wilson et al. 2017). Thus, in 2018 the penetration of smart homes was led by the US with some 22.8 percent of its households being remotely controlled and connected smart homes (rising from 3.7 percent in 2015), followed by Norway (22.2 percent), Estonia (17 percent), Denmark (15 percent) and Sweden (14.5 percent) (Statista 2018k). There are still barriers for a massive adoption of SHT. These barriers are led by the lack of a communication standard for smart homes, something which avoids the interoperability of devices (Kim et al. 2017), and which further implies a lack of regulatory policy (Balta-Ozkan et al. 2013). In addition, and as a survey in the UK revealed, potential adopters seemed to be aware of the possible benefits offered by smart home adoption, but smart home adopters could not clearly point to energy savings brought about by their adoption of smart home technologies (Wilson et al. 2017).

Thus, the potential ability of urbanites, mostly in developed countries, who own Internet-connected smartphones, to control their home appliances and devices, has not yet widely come into use, despite the popular tendency to download apps for a rather widening array of purposes. From the supply side, the still slow adoption of smart home technologies might stem from the lack of communications standards, avoiding the massive marketing of full home installation packages, coupled by the costs, to be borne by customers, of connecting numerous home devices and appliances to remote controlling systems. A wider use of SHT for assistance to the elderly and the sick population segments would require direct and indirect involvements by governmental welfare and health authorities.

7.5   CONCLUSION

In this chapter, we reviewed the digitization of urban systems, in addition to the digitization of activities of city dwellers, vis-à-vis a general communications technology, the Internet/IoT. The incorporation of numerous digital technologies into the wide fabric of cities has received the umbrella term of 'smart cities'. In recent years, IoT has been disseminated into diverse dimensions of urban life, including urban systems, governments, societies, and residents. Thus, most cities worldwide, notably in the developed world, include some or numerous smart systems or operations.

Urban Internet-based utilities in general, and electricity and water ones in particular, imply the installation of one or all of three systems: remote management, smart grids and smart meters. Of these systems, the installation of smart meters has been the most extensive one, with varying degrees of progress among nations. A second application of IoT for urban systems has been its dissemination into traffic regulation systems, turning IoT into a most significant element for the development of sophisticated traffic control systems. IoT permits two-way transmissions of visual and command information between traffic lights and control centers, and, more recently, it has further come to facilitate communications among cars, as well as between cars and traffic lights and sensors. These latter developments are crucial for the upcoming introduction of AVs. A third application of IoT technologies for urban systems is smart homes, which facilitate the remote controlling of home appliances by residents, notably for energy-rich ones. The possible massive adoption of smart home technologies still awaits the development of standard codes for their operations.

As we noted, the peaking of the urban Internet will be reached once AVs are fully adopted, possibly in some twenty to thirty years, in the 2040s–2050s. It is, thus, too early to speculate on possible integrations of human activities with urban systems that may emerge once urban traffic becomes fully driver-less and Internet-based. By that time, the Internet will probably not constitute anymore the only urban master-technology, since it will be joined by artificial intelligence, another leading technology required for the operations of AVs, with these two technologies possibly turning into a rather general and possibly unified urban technology. Smart cities by then may imply the emergence of numerous combinations between these two leading technologies, potentially developed for a variety of, as of yet unforeseen, urban uses.

8.   Autonomous vehicles (AVs) and the Internet

In the previous Chapters (4–7) we discussed the numerous uses and applications of the Internet for people, companies, and systems, all within urban contexts. All of these uses and applications have come already into operation so far. In this last chapter of Part II of the book we are about to explore a rather upcoming application of IoT, probably being the most extensive, daring and crucial one, namely communications by and to vehicles, thus turning them into driverless AVs. Driverless vehicles constitute a most daring human attempt in having all of the urban traffic, consisting of cars, motorcycles, buses and trucks, run completely automatically, with each vehicle being fully autonomous in its driverless operations, and all cars operating completely independently, without any central controlling facility for these fully autonomous vehicles. The AV project amounts, therefore, to the most extensive and most crucial implementation of IoT technology, and it deserves, therefore, some detailed attention.

Since AVs are expected to be commercially introduced first towards the mid-2020s, we will have to devote some attention to the challenges involved in the upcoming adoption process for AVs, side by side with the technological challenges, which will be met through their development. As we will note in the next chapter, the urban implications for an upcoming massive adoption of AVs are about to be immense for urban landscapes, as well as for city operations.

The rather wide-ranging Internet adoption process, spread over the last three decades, and turning cities into Internet-based ones, will reach its full range and saturation, as far as Internet dissemination within the numerous urban spheres is concerned, once AVs are introduced, possibly in 2022–2025. This culmination of Internet application will become even more striking, once AVs possibly turn into the normative mode for automobiles, probably in the 2040s–2050s. As we will see in this chapter, AVs are highly based, among other technologies, on IoT. The Internet is used already by human car drivers, notably for GPS-aided navigation, as well as for telephone calls, parking apps and Internet radio reception. AVs, however, will be rather Internet-based for their very operations, notably for their communications with other cars, as well as with traffic sensors, which will first complement and later replace, traffic lights.

In the first two sections of the chapter, we will attempt, first, to highlight the development of automation and autonomous operation for car technology towards the upcoming commercial introduction of AVs, followed by assessments of the prospects and obstacles towards their future potential mass adoption. These two insights will be followed by elaborations on the upcoming introduction of autonomous buses, trucks and drones.

8.1   IoT AND ADDITIONAL TECHNOLOGIES FOR AVs

The innovation of driverless cars will reach its fruition towards the commercial introduction of AVs, and this will occur once several technologies and their integrations reach maturity. These technologies include mainly IoT, GPS, photography, radar, computing, laser scanning, and artificial intelligence. The technological development of AVs has, therefore, to be outlined from a wider technological perspective rather than focusing on IoT only, as we have done so far, for other spheres of urban life and operations.

At the time, the US led the mass-adoption of human-driven private cars, beginning in the early twentieth century, soon after the commercial introduction of Ford's T-model (Kellerman 2006). In parallel, the US pioneered remote-controlled vehicles, first introduced in 1921, following the invention of autopilot technology for airplanes in 1912–1914, and the application of radio-wave technology for the control of moving mechanisms (Kröger 2016). The development and gradual introduction of automation for car systems are presented in Table 8.1, and are discussed in detail elsewhere (Kellerman 2018a).

Car automation technologies that have had a direct impact on the very emergence of the AV concept have been developed already as of the mid-1990s, and these technologies were mainly based on the more general information technologies. Leading among these technologies at the time were GPS-operated navigation systems, such as the current Google Maps and Waze ones, available first through separate appliances, followed later by smartphone applications for car navigation, and installed more recently also within driver screens, thus providing drivers with automated routing.

Car safety was also improved during the 1990s, through the introduction of the electronic stability program (ESP), providing for car stability in case of sharp steering actions. Side by side with automated navigation and safety technologies, entertainment for drivers and passengers has been enhanced as well, through the availability of digital audio systems for cars, presenting yet another dimension for a changing driving experience (Sheller 2007). Recent car radio systems may further enjoy Internet connectivity, thus offering car drivers radio channels from all over the world with high audial quality.

Table 8.1   Milestones in the automation of cars

Phase and year	Innovation	Place
Introduction of automobiles		
1886	First automobiles	Germany
1908	Introduction of Ford's T-model	US
I. Early autonomous cars		
1921	Remote-controlled vehicles first introduced	US
II. Early automation for cars		
1939	Automatic transmission first installed	US
1954	Automated guided vehicles (AGVs)	US
III. Computerized automation		
1968	Automotive electronic cruise control introduced	US
1978	Anti-lock braking system or anti-skid braking system (ABS) first installed	Germany
IV. On the way to AVs		
1990	First GPS navigation system for cars	Japan
1995	Electronic Stability Program (ESP) introduced	Germany
2003	First intelligent parking system	Japan
2003	Lane Keep Assist System (LKAS) introduced	Japan
2003	Forward Collision Warning (FCW) introduced	Japan
2013	Autonomous Emergency Braking (AEB) introduced	Italy
2017–2025	*Upcoming technologies*: Enhanced dynamic mapping and road databases; traffic-jam assistant; augmented reality (AR); parking companion; road departure protection systems; cameras replacing mirrors; V2X (V2V+V2I);highway chauffeur; valet parking	N/A
2022–2025	Expected commercial introduction of AVs	US? Europe? Japan?

Source: Kellerman (2018a, Table 6.1).

As of the early 2000s, several additional electronic technologies for driving safety have been developed, and these technologies warn car drivers or they may practically take over driving actions in cases of emergency. The main such technologies have been: autonomous safety systems, such as lane keep assist system (LKAS), intelligent parking, forward collision warning (FCW), and autonomous emergency braking (AEB) (Fagnant and Kockelman 2015). Still, however, contemporary human drivers maintain control over their cars under most circumstances, even when all of these currently available automated safety systems are installed and turned on in their cars.

The construction of early and rather experimental AVs date back to several competitive initiatives, notably the American DARPA (Defense Advanced Research Projects Agency) in 2004, and the Italian University of Parma VisLab in 2010, which followed several earlier experimental AV projects in the three geographical cores of automotive technology (North America, Europe, and Pacific Asia). The first experimental AV was the *Contidrom*, developed by the Continental carmaker in the US in 1969, followed by the Japanese *Tsukuba* intelligent car, tested in 1977, as well as by the European *PROMETHEUS* (PROgraMme for a European Traffic of Highest Efficiency and Unprecedented Safety) van, which was presented in 1994 (Kröger 2016; 2025AD 2017).

As we mentioned already, the AV project constitutes, by definition, a complex one, involving the invention and development of numerous technologies (Mitchell et al. 2010). Hence, the stimuli for the development and introduction of AVs are varied and involving three major industrial players: the IT industry, the autonomous technologies industry, and the car production industry. For the IT industry, led by the American Google, which has developed its own AV, and by Apple and Intel, working jointly with carmakers, AVs will bring about a heavier use of IT. This relates notably to the Internet, for V2X communications, as well as to other components of AVs involving enormous volumes of data transmission, storage and processing. IT for AVs relates also to passengers' travel time, which may be devoted by the previous drivers to Internet use, either for communications and entertainment, or for work.

For the developers of specific autonomous vehicle technologies, led by the Israeli Mobileye, now part of Intel, the fight against car accidents and the heavy death toll and material damage that they imply, has been first priority (Mobileye 2017). Finally, for car producers, led by the German Mercedes-Benz, the Japanese Nissan and the American Continental and Tesla companies, the adoption of AVs will mean an expansion of the car market to the non-driving populations, which currently do not purchase cars for numerous reasons: low income; living in highly congested urban areas; high age; physical disabilities; and personal choice.

AV prototypes, which may eventually lead to the commercial introduction of AVs, are now being developed and tested in the three global cores of car technology. In the US, such testing is performed mainly vis-à-vis the *Google Waymo*, the *Continental Farday Future*, as well as through Tesla and Uber projects. In Japan, experimentation is pursued, for instance, through Nissan's *Leaf* prototype. In Europe, for example, Daimler-Benz works on the development of autonomous trucks. For Daimler-Benz, its very being in the frontier of AV development, carries some special significance, since this company was also the first commercial car producer, back in 1886. (Alessandrini et al. 2015; 2025AD 2017). The American Tesla electric cars, equipped with Tesla's autopilot, constitute advanced, yet costly, commercially sold self-driving cars, albeit under driver's control (see also Mitchell et al. 2010 for a proposed small urban electric car).

The Google prototype constitutes a single-box two-seat car, thus being small and lightweight, and hence possibly less costly than traditional cars (excluding the cost of the autonomous operational systems for the car), whereas the prototypes being developed by carmakers are normally 2–3-box cars, looking similar to traditional cars. Google, as well as other newcomers to the car market, assume that future car bodies should be light in weight, since they will operate within an accident-free road environment. AVs should be small for other reasons, as well, notably in order for them to be suitable for on-demand transit, as well as for car sharing. Traditional carmakers, on the contrary, would prefer to keep the current car structure and size, thus keeping also their current prices.

During 2018–2025, several additional automated and autonomous systems for car operations will be introduced and installed in human-driven cars, many of them involving IoT applications, towards the introduction of AVs, which may probably come up sometime between 2022 and 2025. These systems may be used for partially autonomous cars, as well. These include:

1. *Enhanced dynamic mapping and road databases*: These data are required for advanced self-navigation by cars, rather than by Whumans, and they require IoT connectivity.
2. *Traffic-jam assistant*: This system is meant to take over car driving when cars are caught in traffic jams.
3. *Augmented reality (AR)*: A virtual system for the presentation of all rear and front views within a virtual frontal scene.
4. *Parking companion*: This technology carries out the finding of parking spaces, making use also of IoT, as well as the maneuvering of cars into available parking spaces. This technology is installed already in some current car models.
5. *Road departure protection systems*: A technology that will take over car driving under emergency circumstances.
6. *Cameras*: Photography technology should replace the traditional mirrors.
7. *V2X (=V2V+V2I)*: Internet-based communications among cars, and between cars and sensors installed in infrastructures (e.g. along roads and at traffic lights), so that AVs will keep a safe distance from each other, and will sense changing traffic lights, bus stops and so on. The US Congress considers legislation to enforce V2V, even for human-driven cars, in order to reduce car accidents.

8. *Highway chauffeur*: An advanced cruise control technology that will perform all the driving actions once cars reach highways.
9. *Valet parking*: Similar to the parking companion, this technology will drive the car safely into parking slots, albeit with remote activation (2025AD 2017).
10. *Central processing computer*: This computer will receive an enormous volume of information from all sensors, cameras, algorithms, monitors, radars, GPS, digital maps, and V2X, and will be able to process this rather varied information for the performance of car driving. The decision-making ability of this computer, or its artificial intelligence, has to be superior to the human one, notably regarding reaction time (Talebpour and Mahmassani 2016).
11. *Recognition of special road conditions*: Several special road conditions need automated solutions. For example, the recognition of icy roads and the setting of proper automated driving under such conditions, as well as the proper identification of pedestrians.

By 2016, several governments, led by the US, the UK, Germany, France, Switzerland, Israel, and Singapore, had regulated cars with automated driving systems installed in them as legal car drivers for experimental purposes. In addition, specially built driving parks for experimentation with AVs have been, or will soon be, constructed in California (US), China, the UK, Sweden, and Israel. So far, the road experimental testing of AV prototypes has brought about several car accidents, mainly in the US. The countries that have permitted AV road testing, jointly with Japan, also lead in the development of AV technologies. As AV development and experimentation will expand, one can expect that additional countries will join.

The gradual development of automated driving technologies has been systematically outlined through a six-level taxonomy proposed by the Society of Automotive Engineers International in its Standard J3016, pertaining to the degrees of automation in cars. These automation levels are: no automation (level 0); driver assistance (level 1); partial automation (level 2); conditional automation (level 3); high automation (level 4); and full automation (level 5) (SAE 2014; see also Heinrichs and Cyganski 2015) (Table 8.2). In the first three levels, the human driver monitors the driving process, whereas in the three latter ones, driving is increasingly executed and monitored by automated systems. Fully automated cars at level five constitute fully autonomous cars.

The advanced safety measures currently installed in human-driven cars, which we noted earlier in this section, are at level zero (just warning the drivers), or at level one (assisting the drivers). However, the technologies that will be installed in upcoming car models, but still prior to the introduction

Table 8.2   Levels of automation in car driving/operation

SAE level	Name	Narrative definition	Execution of steering and acceleration/ deceleration	Monitoring of driving environment	Fallback performance of dynamic driving task	System capability (driving modes)
Human driver monitors the driving environment						
0	No automation	The full-time performance by the *human driver* of all aspects of the *dynamic driving task*, even when enhanced by warning or intervention systems	Human driver	Human driver	Human driver	n/a
1	Driver assistance	The *driving mode*-specific execution by a driver assistance system of either steering or acceleration/ deceleration using information about the driving environment and with the expectation that the *human driver* perform all remaining aspects of the *dynamic driving task*	Human driver and system	Human driver	Human driver	Some driving modes
2	Partial automation	The *driving mode*-specific execution by one or more driver assistance systems of both steering and acceleration/deceleration using information about the driving environment and with the expectation that the *human driver* perform all remaining aspects of the *dynamic driving task*	System	Human driver	Human driver	Some driving modes

SAE level	Name	Narrative definition	Execution of steering and acceleration/deceleration	Monitoring of driving environment	Fallback performance of dynamic driving task	System capability (driving modes)
Automated driving system ('system') monitors the driving environment						
3	Conditional automation	The *driving mode*-specific performance by an *automated driving system* of all aspects of the *dynamic driving task* with the expectation that the *human driver* will respond appropriately to a *request to intervene*	System	System	Human driver	Some driving modes
4	High automation	The *driving mode*-specific performance by an *automated driving system* of all aspects of the *dynamic driving task*, even if a *human driver* does not respond appropriately to a *request to intervene*	System	System	System	Some driving modes
5	Full automation	The full-time performance by an *automated driving system* of all aspects of the *dynamic driving task* under all roadway and environmental conditions that can be managed by a *human driver*	System	System	System	All driving modes

Source: SAE International Standard J3016, 2014 (with permission to copy as is).

of full AVs, will be either at level two (partial automation) or at level three (conditional automation).

It is still unclear whether the first commercial AVs will be equipped with automation technologies at level four, followed by gradual enhancements towards level five in later car models, or whether the first commercial AVs will be already fully automated, and, thus, autonomous (level 5). It is further unclear whether the first commercially sold AVs will be autonomous only, or whether they will permit also human driving, side by side with an automated option (Katrakazas et al. 2015). In Tesla's electric cars, there are installed already level five driverless components, but the readiness of these cars for fully automated, or autonomous, level five operation, has not yet been announced (as of 2017). Such an announcement will require governmental certification and specific and explicit autonomous car licensing.

It is assumed that commercial marketing of AVs for the private car market will begin as early as 2022–2025 (Fagnant and Kockelman 2015), and that some twenty years later, in the 2040s, AVs will become the primary means of transport (Bertoncello and Wee 2015; Claudel and Ratti 2015). In the transitional decades, highway lanes may possibly be separated into those allocated for human-driven cars and those allocated for driverless cars (2025AD 2017). However, technological and legal obstacles, which we will note in the following section, may cause some delay in the introduction of AVs.

The contemporary race towards the full development of AVs, and eventually its following commercial introduction, has brought about technological developments for motorcycles as well, potentially leading towards a future development of autonomous motorcycles. Thus, in early 2017, the Japanese Honda introduced its *Riding Assist* motorcycle that facilitates automated self-balancing, so that the motorcycles never fall over (Sorokanich 2017). This automated balancing is achieved through a 'stretching' of the vehicle when circumstances call for it. This balancing further enables motorcycles to follow autonomously their walking owners/drivers.

8.2   PROSPECTS AND PITFALLS FOR AV ADOPTION

It is obviously still impossible to tell whether the adoption process for AVs will be straightforward, continuous and fast, or whether it will rather present some hesitant or even discontinuous patterns of penetration. After all, even the less-revolutionary technology of hybrid cars, introduced some 15 years ago, has only slowly and very partially, been adopted (Guerra 2015), though it does not involve any radical changes in driving habits, as compared to the adoption of AVs. Thus, the levels of automation for the operation of the first generations of AVs, as well as AV diffusion and adoption, will depend largely on the co-evolution of social readiness for the transition to the new car technology and operation, as has been the case for past adoptions of new technologies (see e.g. Geels 2005). During the 2020s–2040s, an interactive process may emerge between the introduction of early AV models, followed later by the introduction of advanced ones, on the one hand, and social reactions, in form of preferred adoption levels, on the other.

Generally, individuals' decisions regarding the possible adoption of any automated systems, mainly IT ones, not relating specifically to the adoption of AVs, may reflect rather varied attitudinal factors, and there are several leading factors in this regard. First among these factors is trust in the automated system (e.g. Parasuraman and Riley 1997; Ghazizadeh et al. 2012; Choi and Ji 2015), followed by the workload which its adoption may create or save (e.g. Parasuraman and Manzey 2010), and confidence (e.g. Parasuraman and Riley 1997). Perceived usefulness of the system, and its ease of use constitute a fourth leading factor (e.g. Davis 1989; Parasuraman and Riley 1997; Choi and Ji 2015), followed, finally, by social influence on the decision for its possible adoption (Venkatesh et al. 2003) (see also Madigan et al. 2016). These factors reflect the degree of the 'pull' power of new automated systems for their potential adopters, and they are in line with factors that have been suggested for the adoption of innovations in general (see e.g. Rogers 1995).

In the case of AV adoption, it might also be for some additional and rather specific reasons for individuals to oppose AV adoption following its introduction. Most significantly among such reasons may be a perception of AVs as 'threatening' people's future driving activities, as part of their culture. The need to cope with existing cultures when some automation process is introduced was identified long ago (see e.g. Sheridan et al. 1983). Normally, automation processes may transform the role of some workers from their being manual task performers to their turning into automation controllers (see Ghazizadeh et al. 2012; Endsley 1996). However, when AVs are adopted, the transformation in role of the previous drivers will be much sharper, since the controlling and active drivers will turn into passive passengers. Several theories have been developed for individual acceptance of newness in general (for a review see Venkatesh et al. 2003). Specifically for technology adoption, the TAM (technology acceptance model) (Davis 1989) and the UTAUT (unified theory of acceptance and use of technology) (Venkatesh et al. 2003) were proposed as multi-factor models for the assessment of technology adoption. The UTAUT model was applied in an extended way to the adoption of IT in cars (Oswald et al. 2012), as well as for the adoption of autonomous buses (Madigan et al. 2016). We will discuss this latter study in the following section devoted to autonomous buses.

The paces of AV adoption may not only differ individually among people, but they may further differ among countries. It is difficult to foresee as of yet, several years prior to AV commercial introduction, which countries will practically lead in AV adoption, notably since technological developments towards the introduction of AVs are still under way, and they take place in all of the three global technological cores (US, Europe, and East Asia). These technological efforts are coupled with AV experiments involving passengers seated in AVs, notably with people testing AVs as taxi service passengers. Such experiments take place already, notably through Uber services, or they are planned for numerous additional cities, such as Columbus, Pittsburgh, Boston, Tempe, and Las Vegas, in the US, Jerusalem in Israel, and Singapore. On-demand mobility might be helpful especially for last-mile travel between major metro or bus stations and riders' homes (Ohnemus and Perl 2016). In addition to these tests, AVs are used already routinely for military purposes, such as the unstaffed armored patrols performed by the Israeli army along the border with the Gaza Strip. However, these patrols are carried out within closed road systems, without interference with other traffic.

The current public attitude towards the possible future adoption of AVs, prior to their introduction, seems to be rather mixed, as numerous studies worldwide have attested (for reviews see Kyriakidis et al. 2015; Haboucha et al. 2017). However, studies focusing on people's attitudes to AV purchase or use are not sufficient for the general assessment of future AV adoption, since some practical use experience is an important factor in the perception of any newness, as well as for its evaluation by users for potential adoption (see Parasuraman and Riley 1997). Thus, for instance, a survey performed in Germany in 2014 has shown that less than 15 percent of car owners would consider the adoption of AVs (Heinrichs and Cyganski 2015). Similarly, a 2014 survey performed simultaneously in the US, UK and Australia, found much concern among respondents regarding self-driving cars (Schoettle and Sivak 2014). A 2016 follow-up survey by Schoettle and Sivak, performed among American drivers only, showed that some 46 percent of them prefer to retain full control of their driving (DeGroat 2016). On the other hand, however, the experimental *Navya* vehicles, which were tested within several European contexts, were accepted enthusiastically (Christie et al. 2016), whereas some additional surveys point to rather ambivalent views presented by potential future adopters (Fraedrich and Lenz 2016).

An American survey including some 2,167 respondents embraced an econometric perspective, in an attempt to assess the economic willingness of Americans to adopt the upcoming AVs (Bansal and Kockelman 2017). It was found that by 2045 some 24.8 percent of the American light-duty vehicles will be AVs (level 4), assuming an annual 5 percent drop in their prices until then, coupled with a rather constant WTP (willingness to pay). The share of AVs may reach 87.2 percent if one assumes an annual 10 percent decline in car prices, coupled with a 10 percent rise in WTP (see also Litman 2015). It was further predicted that around 98 percent of the US vehicles (both automated and human-driven ones) would be equipped with ESC (electronic speed control) by 2025, as well as with V2X, by 2030. More than half of the respondents were not willing to pay the additional costs required for levels 3–4 of car automation. However, as Bansal and Kockelman (2017, 61–62) noted, all of the responses in this survey were based on people's current knowledge of AVs, which brings one back to the rather social approach represented by the UTAUT model. Hence, the future personal decisions for AV adoption or rejection, following the introduction of AVs, will present blends of individual, social and economic considerations.

A wide 2014 international survey, based on 5,000 respondents from 109 countries found 'that respondents, on average, found manual driving the most enjoyable mode of driving, yet they found the idea of fully autonomous driving fascinating' (Kyriakidis et al. 2015, 135). Thus, some 22 percent of the respondents were not ready to pay any additional amount for AVs, but some 33 percent thought that AVs would be highly enjoyable. Respondents, notably from developed countries, were concerned with software hacking, and respondents in general expressed concern for legal and safety issues.

One may assume that the WTP for AVs will be highly affected by people's expectancies for enhanced job performance when embracing AVs, as well as by the ease of use that will be offered by AVs. These two considerations will be coupled with social influences, once AVs will be on the market. National cultures that tend to accentuate the adoption of IT technologies, as well as those emphasizing newness, may constitute an additional positive factor for AV adoption. Thus, in South Korea, which, as we noted already in Chapter 6, is a leading country in the development and adoption of smartphone and Internet technologies, people presented a relatively high WTP for car connectivity and wireless Internet, but not for lane keeping technologies (Shin et al. 2015). Similarly, a comparison between individuals in the US and in Israel, another leading country in the development and adoption of technological newness, found a higher tendency among Israelis to adopt AVs, when commercially introduced (Haboucha et al. 2017).

Another major market for AV adoption is company car fleets. The overall economic benefits of AVs for company car fleets, coupled with the current hesitation by individuals to adopt AVs in their future car purchases, might possibly lead to companies becoming the initial and pioneering AV purchasers, so that company cars will pave the road for individuals to join in private AV purchases. For companies, the provision of AVs to their employees would involve expectations for higher productivity of workers, including both employees who travel during work hours, and commuters, since travel time may be used for the performance of some additional work.

The decades 2020–2040 will constitute a transitional period, in which both human-driven and autonomous cars will move on the road simultaneously.

AVs will have to be smarter in this transitional period than those that will be introduced later on, as AVs will have to fully guess the behavior and possible reactions of human drivers located nearby but unequipped with V2V communications, as compared to later times, when all cars on the road will be fully communicative. Färber (2016) portrays an example for the transitional period, in which a human driver who has the right-of-way may attempt to yield it to an AV. Will the AV accept? As we mentioned already, authorities may opt for separate lanes to be allocated for AV traffic during this transitional period (see 2025AD 2017). However, even once all cars on the road are AVs, the problem of AV decision-making regarding non-computerized road users, notably bicyclists and pedestrians, will still persist.

Numerous problems have still existed in 2017 in the development process for AVs. These problems might slow down the count towards AV introduction until the mid-2020s, and they may further imply a potential delay in the possible massive adoption of AVs:

1. *High purchase prices for AVs*: This may be the case due to the rather costly technologies installed in AVs, possibly affecting AV pricing notably during the initial phases of adoption, when carmakers will need to regain the monies invested previously in heavy R&D efforts. Carmakers may have to consider, therefore, the offering of price tags that will assume risky volumes of sales.
2. *Differentiated AV certification by states and countries*: Legislation will be required for the certification of the advanced levels of AVs. Future gaps among states and countries in such certifications may cause trouble for car owners, notably in the US and the EU, since such gaps may restrict AVs in the crossing of international and interregional boundaries.
3. *Partial litigation, liability and perception of AVs by insurance companies*: The insurance industry will have to cope with a new and lower risk environment, which will present, in addition, several new challenges. A key question may be the identification of the insured and liable entity: are these the AV producers, their owners, or maybe rather their passengers? The problem of partially or fully uninsured cars may persist with AVs, as is the case with human-driven cars.
4. *Insufficient software security against hackers*: This is a crucial question, given the dependence of AV operation on V2X, and the fatal consequences of wrong operations potentially performed by AV systems, if attacked by viruses or by some misleading information.
5. *Privacy issues*: This issue may pertain to data sharing among AVs through V2V communications while on the road (Fagnant and Kockelman 2015). Orderly V2V communications is crucial for AV safe movements, so that the specific nature of V2V data transmission will have to be decided.

6. *Ethical aspects*: The development of AV technology involves also coping with ethical questions, notably as to the guiding of autonomous cars for their possible reactions in cases of approaching road accidents (Lin 2016; Gerdes and Thornton 2016). When a car accident develops, a particular AV may have two options for its reaction. It can give priority to its own passengers, causing them minimal damage, or it may give priority to other cars, if the total loss of life in the latter option will be lower. A survey found that people would prefer to use AVs programmed for the saving of their own passengers, rather than their being utilitarian. Thus, if such algorithms are adopted, then lifesaving through AVs will not be fully maximized (Bonnefon et al. 2016).

7. *Safety/security risk dimensions*: A major risk for AV accidents may emerge, as we noted already, at meeting points between AVs and non-computerized road users, notably pedestrians and bicyclists. Well-known is the auto-mated vehicle fatality, in which an automated test car with a non-driving observer, mistook an image, drove into a truck and brought about the death of the observer. Another safety concern, which we noted already, is the ability of AVs to accurately recognize snow and ice conditions, and to react cautiously to them. Enhanced safety measures for AVs may possibly mitigate but not eliminate risk, even though accident rates for AVs are pro-jected to be considerably lower than those occurring due to errors brought about by human drivers. AV maintenance standards constitute another aspect involving risk. This issue exists, of course, also for human-driven cars, but it might be more striking for AVs, given the complexity of their sophisticated operational systems.

8. *Partially human-driven cars*: Some types of cars, notably refuse collection vehicles, may still require partial human driving.

Another significant issue pertaining to the pace of AV adoption is the loss of the driving experience by individuals. During the transitional period of AV adoption, people will gradually lose their personal driving experiencing, so that some or many car drivers may reject this loss. This rejection may emerge since 'driving can be described as a practice that intertwines and *mixes* the human and the inhuman, the person and the thing, the material and the infor-mational' (Sheller 2007, 177). This issue of the loss of driving experience is part of a more general tendency of humans coping with novel procedures, which might lead to a rather slow adoption pace for AVs, or even to their possi-ble rejection. Prolonged objections and delays in the adoption of new mobility technologies, mainly due to people's hesitation to experiment with them and eventually adopt new personal experiences, occurred already several times in the past. Such was the case notably when new communications devices were introduced, for instance the rejection, at the time, of early mobile computers, as well as the prolonged objection to the use of videophones (Kellerman 2006).

In the long term, AVs may present a special promise for the populations of developing countries, in the facilitation of personal mechanized mobility by AVs for them. In recent years these populations have been able to achieve personal virtual mobility via the extremely wide adoption of mobile telephony (see Chapter 3), through a leapfrogging process, in which they were able to adopt mobile telephony without adopting first fixed-line telephony, which requires expensive cable infrastructures (Comer and Wikle 2008). Similarly, the populations of developing countries may experience a leapfrogging experience for the adoption of physical personal mobility, notably at the more advanced phases of the AV adoption process, when AV prices will be lower. By then, the wide adoption of AVs will remove the obstacle of the rather expensive human-driven cars. Furthermore, AV taxis, saving the cost of drivers and much of the energy consumption by cars (assuming that AVs will be electric cars), will provide another option for cheap semi-personal mobility for developing countries, side by side with the option of car sharing. These two latter options might be attractive by then for other markets, as well.

8.3   AUTONOMOUS BUSES

Autonomous buses (also called automated buses, driverless buses, self-driving buses, and robotic buses) constitute a most advanced collective automated road transport system (ARTS) (see Alessandrini et al. 2014). Passengers in numerous cities worldwide have tested autonomous buses for a number of years already. These cities include, for instance, Helsinki, Singapore, Paris, San Remon CA, Lausanne, Las Vegas, Tokyo, Washington DC, Wageningen and Ede in the Netherlands, and Perth. However, it has been only for the system which operates in the Rivium Business Park in Rotterdam (the Netherlands), consisting of low-speed buses which make use of separate lanes, to offer autonomous bus service on a permanent basis.

The testing of autonomous buses worldwide is of some importance, since ARTS may provide more frequent bus services, notably at off-peak hours, assuming similar or lower bus fares, as compared to traditional bus services, which require drivers for their operation. Hence, the public reactions to the testing of autonomous buses may contribute to the future shaping of routine service (see Alessandrini et al. 2016). It seems that the experimentation of autonomous buses in 2017 was in a more advanced phase, as compared to the still restricted testing of private light-duty AVs, which have been tested by professional observers, rather than by AV owners, or as taxis.

The buses which have been employed for urban tests are actually minibuses carrying some 10–12 passengers, and they are normally electric vehicles, used for short-distance lines, running at low speeds, and in most cases still using dedicated lanes. Furthermore, the experimental bus lines constitute, in many cases, special-purpose lines, such as in-campus shuttles, or they provide 'last mile' services, in their distribution of passengers to residential neighborhoods from major railway or bus stations. Still, in many if not in most of these experimental bus lines, a company attendee accompanies passengers while being on the ride. These features of the experimented autonomous bus services may explain the more advanced stage of autonomous busing, as compared to that of private AVs, which cannot be tested by potential buyers under such restricting terms of operation, unless they are tested as taxis.

The American Local Motors *Olli*, the French Induct Technology *Navia* (Arma), and the French *EasyMile* shuttle buses are leading examples of driverless buses. The EU has initiated an extensive experimentation of autonomous buses in numerous European cities, through its *Citymobil2* project. In Singapore, which has put driverless mobility high on its national priorities, full-size autonomous buses began their testing in 2017. The German Mercedes-Benz *Future Bus* and the Chinese *Yutong* driverless bus are leading examples of full-size buses being developed and tested (Souppouris 2016; O'Brian 2017; Poon 2016).

The European Citymobil2 project included, at the time, the surveying of passenger preferences between the two options of traditional human-driven buses and autonomous ones, with the latter ones potentially available for short-distance rides. The survey was carried out in twelve cities in seven countries, in spring 2013, with some 200 respondents in each city. However, the survey was not based on road experiences of the respondents, but rather on pictures of the autonomous buses presented to them (Alessandrini et al. 2014, 2016). The results showed that passengers will not prefer ARTS, if travel duration and fares are similar to those of traditional buses. A previous study performed several years earlier in Leeds (UK) found a preference for human-driven buses (Shires and Ibañez 2008). This survey further found that passengers would prefer ARTS if the service is provided for short-distance travel within a major facility, such as from some facility to its parking lot, and this finding was in line with previous ones (Delle Site et al. 2011).

The European Citymobil2 project further permitted the surveying of 349 passengers who experienced some real use of autonomous buses in Lausanne (Switzerland) (in 2015) and in La Rochelle (France) (in 2014–2015) (Madigan et al. 2016). Following their actual use of autonomous buses, the respondents were surveyed regarding the three major UTAUT parameters. First, performance expectancy, or the degree by which respondents believed that ARTS would enhance their job performance. Second, effort expectancy, or the degree of ease of use of ARTS. Third, social influence, or the degree of influence by important fellows on their use of the system. However, the cumulative explanatory power of these three variables on levels of expected uses of future system use was only 22 percent, so that possibly some additional factors, such as safety and hedonic motivation, comfort on-board and the traveled distance, might potentially be of importance (Madigan et al. 2016). This survey, jointly with the mixed attitude of individuals to the potential future purchase of AVs, which we discussed in the previous section, presents a clear need for careful and thorough preparations for AV adoption campaigns, prior to both public and private future introductions of AVs.

8.4   AUTOMATED AND AUTONOMOUS FREIGHT VEHICLES AND DRONES

Automated freight moving was first introduced back in 1954, through the automated guided vehicles (AGVs) (Savant 2017). These vehicles have been floor-borne ones, originally used for towing and hauling along cables. Later on, more contemporary technologies, such as laser, were adopted for the operations of AGVs, thus facilitating their more flexible movements, also widening their uses for logistics, such as for storage operations, and even for the moving of people between attractions within amusement parks. More recently, AGV vehicles and technologies have been adopted also for the enhancement of container mobility within harbors, thus bringing about the automated container terminals (ACTs), built in harbors worldwide (see e.g. Liu et al. 2002). The early development and implementation of AGVs, as compared to AVs, which have been in the process of development only recently, stem from the use of AGVs within closed areas of industrial plants and harbors, rather than on open roads. In addition, AGVs enjoy specially designated structures, fitting specific cargos, as compared to standard four-wheel trucks.

It seems that freight moving in the upcoming era of AVs will be divided between two types of autonomous vehicles: autonomous trucks and drones. Autonomous trucks (also called self-driving trucks, driverless trucks, or automated trucks) will be mainly big heavy-duty vehicles for long haul distances, whereas unmanned/unstaffed aerial vehicles (UAV), in the form of drones (also called unmanned/unstaffed aircraft systems (UAS)), will be used for package deliveries within cities, thus possibly replacing mainly small closed cargo vehicles.

Autonomous trucks were in 2017 in more advanced stages of testing and commercial use than autonomous buses, which we noted as being in a more advanced phase as compared to private light-duty cars. There might be two major reasons for this relatively leading advance. First, the current cost of the autonomous technologies for a single car may range between $5,000 and $10,000. When this cost is added to the cost of an average light-duty car, it might mean a close to doubling of its current retail price. However, when this amount is added to the price tag of a heavy-duty truck, currently ranging between $125,000–$150,000, the added cost is much less preventive. Second, the use of autonomous trucks saves the employment of several professional drivers for each truck, drivers who share the continuous long-distance driving of heavy-duty trucks (Sisson 2016).

It has been for the Rio Tinto Pilbara iron ore mines in Australia to introduce a routine use of autonomous trucks since 2008, still keeping, however, the autonomous operations of the trucks under remote controlling from Perth. The use of AVs in Rio Tinto enhanced the productivity of the mine operations, but simultaneously decreased drivers' employment. These implications may potentially pave the road for a possible reviving of unused mines, previously considered as uneconomic (Bellamy and Pravika 2011; Rio Tinto 2017). In addition to the routine use of autonomous trucks in Rio Tinto Pilbara, autonomous truck testing has been carried out worldwide. Thus, Mercedes-Benz tested its *Future Truck 2025* as of 2015 on German autobahns (2025AD 2017), Uber tested its Otto trucks with beer distribution in Colorado in 2016 (Trucks.com 2017), and Toyota and Scania jointly tested autonomous trucks in Singapore as of 2017 (Moon 2017). It is, therefore, too early to state whether European, American or Japanese autonomous trucks will take the lead in the commercial adoption of autonomous trucks (Trucks.com 2017).

Yet another contemporary autonomous vehicle is the aerial drone. Drones constitute unmanned/unstaffed tiny aerial vehicles (UAV), originally developed for military surveillance, and recently transferred for civilian uses, as well. Grounded operators communicate with drones via IoT. Both professionals and amateurs first used drones for aerial photography, and they were later fitted for a variety of other uses. Thus, drones have become helpful for the monitoring of road surface conditions (Hill 2014), for police monitoring of road safety and criminal actions, as well as for hotspot-monitoring following fire extinguishing (Zaleski 2016). Above all, however, drones have been extensively tested worldwide for last-mile parcel deliveries, mainly in cities (Murray and Chu 2015). For instance, Amazon tested drones in the UK, mainly for book deliveries, and so did Zookal in Singapore, Australia and Malaysia. Drones have further been tested for the delivery of medical supplies to a car-free island in offshore Germany by the Deutsche Post *Parcelcopter* service (Murray and Chu 2015). Drones have even been tested for pizza deliveries in New Zealand, as well as for home package deliveries by a shopping mall in Singapore.

The possible wide adoption of drones for parcel delivery, notably within cities, presents potentially cheaper and faster deliveries, as compared to freight vehicles, thus, possibly at least, reducing some terrestrial traffic. However, there are still several problems involved in the full commercial adoption of drones. Most importantly is air traffic safety, which has been a leading concern, for instance for the American FAA (Federal Aviation Administration), which released in 2016 its 'Part 107' regulations for drone operations (NLC 2016; see also Birtchnell 2017).

The concern for air traffic safety has been coupled with several additional obstacles. Drones are operated by batteries, and the current battery power permits the use of drones for short-distance deliveries only. In addition, in order for drones to reach the exact locations of addressees, as well as their avoidance of any flight obstacles, they require most accurate GPS signals (Murray and Chu 2015). Finally, there are issues of privacy involved in the use of drones within densely settled, notably urban, areas, with drones aimed at parcel deliveries, potentially taking uninvited aerial pictures. This latter issue requires a solution, as well as proper licensing, for both drone service providers and operators (Zaleski 2016; NLC 2016).

8.5   CONCLUSION

In this chapter we attempted to highlight the upcoming IoT-based AVs, as the ultimate autonomous mode for personal physical mobility. The upcoming introduction and the following adoption of AVs presents a critical use of IoT for their very operations, via V2X. Thus, AVs will eventually bring about a city that will be fully Internet-based, following the previous disseminations of the Internet and IoT into people's daily activities, as well as into the operations of urban companies and urban systems.

We exposed the development of AVs, and the technological challenges associated with it, as well as the potential adoption of AVs, given the problems involved with their acceptance and operation. AVs are being developed now simultaneously in the US, Europe and Japan, and are expected to be commercially introduced in 2022–2025, assuming the completion of developments of the relevant technologies, as well as the solving of numerous legal and ethical questions.

The pace of AV adoption is further still unclear, and is dependent on the readiness of individuals to cope with a major behavioral change. The introduction of fully automatic cars may touch directly upon the lives of individuals. AVs constitute a real revolution in their functioning without any type of human control, neither *in situ* by car drivers, nor by remote control centers, with thousands of them being on the road simultaneously. Following some two decades of the expected future adoption process, it is assumed that by the 2040s the traffic landscape will be mostly to fully automated. The development and testing for autonomous buses, trucks and drones, seem to be more advanced than are those for the light-duty private AVs.

PART III

Implications of urban Internet applications

9. Urban perspectives for the Internet-based city

In Part I of the book, we explored several traditional communications systems, which have developed in cities along the last two millennia, followed by the recently introduced and adopted digital Internet. The varied uses and applications of the Internet were outlined in Part II. In this third and last part of the book, we will attempt to outline several implications and outcomes for the extensive citywide applications of the Internet, which we explored in Part II, eventually reaching a level of saturation, once AVs are adopted. Thus, in this chapter, we will focus on the city per se as an entity that is Internet-based, as compared to our focus on rather specific uses and applications of the Internet in the city, that is, for people, companies, systems, and vehicles, as we did in the chapters of Part II.

In the following sections of this chapter, we will attempt to explore several basic dimensions and implications for the Internet-based city, presenting, first, its nature and operations as an Internet of Everything (IoE) city. This exploration will be followed by an exposition of the spatial dimensions of the Internet-based city, focusing on three dimensions: the possible spatial concentration or expansion of the Internet-based city, transitions in urban land-uses within the Internet-based city, and finally, the visible and invisible autonomously mobile Internet-based city. We will then move to the highlighting of Internet activities pursued by the residents of the Internet-based city, when operating within cities being Internet-based in a variety of their dimensions. Then we will move to an elaboration of some possible changes in the cultural significance of the physical city. Finally, we will focus on the major technological device used for the routine functioning of the Internet-based city, the smartphone.

In the following chapter, which will conclude the book, we will present jointly all the chapter summaries, followed by two concluding discussions. First, on the Internet as a general-purpose technology, notably as expressed within urban contexts, and second we will generally assess Internet applications versus Internet implications.

9.1   THE INTERNET OF EVERYTHING (IoE)

The Cisco Company (Evans 2012; Mitchell et al. 2013) coined the notion of the Internet of Everything (IoE), which constitutes an umbrella term, binding jointly all the three Internet connectivities: among people, between people and machines (via IoT), and among machines themselves (also via IoT). IoE includes, therefore, the three elements of people, machines and data, with the first two being transmitting entities, and the latter being transmitted ones. Furthermore, the comprehensiveness of IoE refers also to the spatial dimension, so that IoE includes Internet communications that takes place at all locations: at home, at work, at controlling centers, or for people and cars while being on the move. Internet communications is viewed as a process, assuring the proper and rather efficient transmissions of information.

Given the varied applications of the Internet within urban contexts, as well as the additional and upcoming use of the Internet for AV operations, Internet-based cities may be viewed as being IoE-based cities, with the comprehensiveness of Internet communications expressed through its being in use in cities by everyone and by everything, and being accessed everywhere and for everything.

9.2   BASIC OPERATIONAL FEATURES FOR THE URBAN INTERNET

Whether considered as IoE-based, or as Internet-based, it is possible to identify four features for present cities. These features arise from the extensive Internet applications for cities, and the even wider upcoming one, once AVs are adopted. These four features include connectivity; movability; controllability; and continuity. Since we noticed already the very existence of these features, we will only briefly highlight each of these characteristics separately in the following sub-sections.

9.2.1   Connectivity

The very idea of the connected city is not new, and it was foreseen before the wide adoption of the Internet (see e.g. Mitchell 1995). This vision is now being widely materialized, with the Internet serving as the leading urban communications technology. Thus, the Internet-based city is foremost the connected city. As we noted in Part II, everything and everybody in town can now be connected with something else or with somebody else, using the Internet technology. People can be reached everywhere and at any time by other people located everywhere. Using the same device that is used for communications, the smartphone, people can reach almost any desired piece of information, and they may further perform online a wide variety of urban activities (Kellerman 2014). People can further be connected, to their domestic appliances, and if their jobs call for it, they can be connected to urban systems, as well. Furthermore, devices, appliances and systems can become interconnected among themselves, thus being able to operate autonomously, in one way or another.

Virtual connectivity has turned into a basic feature of urban life and operations. Thus, and as we mentioned already, most urbanites, at least in developed countries, enjoy the use of smartphones for connections with fellow humans. Urban systems in many cities are still within the process of becoming fully connected with remote operators, as well as with each other. Under Internet connectivity, city operations and control may become more efficient, and possibly make the life of urbanites more pleasant, beyond people's extended personal communications and informational and service activities.

9.2.2   Movability

Connectivity implies movability, and human beings are simultaneously communicating and moving creatures. As we noted in Part I, people were able to move information from place to place verbally and in writing already before the introduction of electronic communications means (see Urry 2007). The wide adoption of the Internet has permitted the global movement of enormous amounts of information instantly and in all modes, audial as well as visual. An even more striking revolution has been the ability of fixed non-living entities, such as metros or utilities, to transmit and receive information through the Internet. This newly gained connectivity for these locationally fixed or materially moving entities has turned them into virtually moveable objects, despite their fixed and non-living nature. The gained communicative ability for non-living entities, operating mainly through sensors and artificial intelligence, implies change for individuals as well, in their ability to communicate with their appliances, and their upcoming ability to communicate with their future cars (AVs), as well. Both the fixed and the physically mobile components and residents of cities are on permanent virtual move, using the same communications technology of the Internet or IoT.

9.2.3   Controllability

By its much-dispersed nature, the Internet is not being governed or controlled by any centrally controlling authorities at any geographical scale, whether they be city, regional, or national governments, or whether they be global organizations, though censorship is being imposed on Internet contents and transmissions by numerous countries (Warf 2013). On the other hand, however, the universal use of IoT for the local or national controlling of any utilities has, obviously, its managerial advantages. Technologically, it is possible to apply the central controlling, which is being used for utilities and traffic systems using IoT, also for the central controlling of people's Internet communications and information activities. However, the open-code nature for Internet contents has become one of its cornerstones, so that it will be most difficult to apply such centralized controlling for the Internet, in the way it is being used by its human subscribers in free countries (see Lessig 2001).

9.2.4   Continuity

The lack of central controlling for the entire Internet operations in any given city enables its continued operations, thus avoiding the possible operation of any single mechanism, potentially aiming at its universal shutting down. This wide-scale continuity of operations stems from the Internet being a deconcentrated system, without a single central metropolitan, regional, or even national exchange facility. Furthermore, Internet traffic is extremely flexible, with routers choosing at any time the most efficient route for the transmission of any given package of codes for communications. The high speed of light, used in fiber-optic cables, makes no difference for simple users whether local transmissions of information are channeled directly or whether they are directed through international long-distance routes. Thus, at the 9/11 disaster in Manhattan, New York, back in 2001, all communications media in the Twin Towers area stopped operations, except for the router-based Internet traffic, and this despite of the destruction of a nearby Internet hotel. Therefore, the Internet enjoys a durable and permanent continuity even at times of emergency (see e.g. Kitchin and Dodge 2011).

Looking at the four basic features of the Internet-based city jointly, two of them constitute the most striking ones: connectivity and controllability. In other words, the Internet permits the connection of everybody and everything in town, but at the same time, it does not imply a centralized controlling of this wide-ranging connectivity (Figure 9.1). Each of these two most striking features of the Internet in town implies the existence of yet another basic feature. Thus, connectivity implies physical and/or virtual mobility for all of

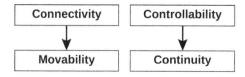

Figure 9.1   Basic features of the urban Internet

the connected people and things, and similarly, it is for the lack of centralized controllability for the urban Internet that guarantees its continued operations.

9.3   SPATIAL CONCENTRATION OR EXPANSION?

Dadashpoor and Yousefi (2018) reviewed some 80 articles, published between 1990 and 2017, which deal with possible spatial transitions in cities towards their centralization or, alternatively, towards their decentralization, because of the adoption of information and telecommunications technologies. They showed that some 42 percent of these articles focused on decentralization processes, with some additional 33 percent of the articles suggesting dual effects, whereas some other 16 percent emphasized centralization impacts, side by side with merely 9 percent of the articles arguing for negligible spatial effects possibly stemming from the adoption of IT. The centralization studies generally argued for the continued importance of face-to-face communications, whereas the decentralization studies mainly argued for the new spatial opportunities facilitated through the adoption of communications technologies.

From yet another perspective, the programming, production and transduction of urban space through code, as well as through digital technologies at large, may yield differing and even contradictory spatial patterns, when citywide utility systems of flow and mobility are compared with individual mobility activities (Kellerman 2018b). Thus, code has brought about the geographical concentration of Internet technological development, which we noted in Chapter 6, so that selected professionals and decision-makers, located in specific cities, carry it out. Code has further facilitated the centralization of utility operations by controllers, as well as the supervised autonomy for urban utility systems. However, the contrary has been true for urban activities performed by individuals using digital technologies, coupled with applications, developed mainly for smartphone use. Thus, the uses of the Internet by individuals, whether pursued from fixed or mobile devices and locations, are highly deconcentrated, with the operation and use of the Internet being decentralized to all users.

Digitized urban utility systems communicated via IoT, on the one hand, and individual Internet activities, on the other, are obviously interrelated. Individual activity in general cannot take place without the existence and support of urban utilities, notably electricity and water, so that, at the same time, the extent and velocity of urban systems reflects the number of locally active urbanites within any given city, as well as the extent of their individual activities. However, this relationship between aggregate human activities and their supporting utilities holds even when neither urban utility systems, nor urban activities, are digitized. Thus, code and digitization may affect the spread, quality, volume, and arena of both urban systems and individual activities, but not their very nature and their being interrelated.

Transitions in urban land-uses as well as in the organization of urban space can be further expected to emerge in light of the adoption of AVs, but these transitions will reach full maturity only once the adoption process of AVs reach maturity, that is, following the wide penetration of AVs. Thus, the urban scene may present major transformational trends only as of the 2040s, assuming that the commercial introduction of AVs begins in the early to mid-2020s (see section 9.5). By the 2040s, it might well be that some new, and as of yet unforeseen, societal and economic needs emerge, and these may be coupled with new opportunities for uses of urban space. However, as we will note below, these changes may possibly lead to opposing spatial directions: autonomously mobile cities may possibly become either more concentrated or more dispersed, as compared to contemporary ones. Such contradictory options for spatial growth will continue, therefore, the contradictory spatial effects that have been noted by the numerous studies on the spatial impacts of IT adoption so far.

The spatial changes in city structures, which may accompany the wide adoption of AVs, whether towards concentration or dispersal, may be in a scale similar to the vast urban expansion that accompanied the wide adoption of the traditional car in the previous century. This change has permitted longer commuting distances for suburban populations, and it further facilitated the development of suburban business centers (see e.g. Thrift 2004; Sheller 2007). Interestingly enough, this past trend of immense spatial growth, which was brought about by car adoption at the time, has not been caused by the adoption of personal virtual mobility media, notably the Internet and the mobile phone, so that the adoption of virtual mobility media was accompanied by a rather modest urban spatial change (Kellerman 2009). In light of these two differing volumes of past trends, the question is which dimensions of city structures and activities will be changed at times of full AV adoption, and what kind of spatial patterns will these changes present? AVs present, on the one hand, upgraded vehicles for corporeal mobility, but, at the same time, they will be based on the rather virtual IoT, and they will permit their passengers to be engaged with virtual mobility while riding the AVs.

The ability of passengers to work while being driven by AVs, may potentially bring about the expansion of exurbia, as workers may not mind traveling longer distances to their offices, located elsewhere in metropolitan areas (Heinrichs and Cyganski 2015; Guerra 2015). However, the opposite trend is also potentially possible. If parking lots are less required or not required at all anymore for apartment buildings, as we will see in the following section, and if the road system also needs less space, as we will see in section 9.5, cities and suburbs may become more condensed, with business centers possibly located close to metro stations.

The newly available space, devoted previously to parking lots, and freed due to AV adoption, notably in CBDs and other employment and business centers, may be used for other land-uses (Claudel and Ratti 2015). However, as we will note in the following section, numerous urban service facilities may close down, due to growing service provisions through the Internet. The freed urban space, coupled with the availability of more efficient mobility modes, may potentially bring about a re-concentration of office businesses in downtowns. However, as we noted already, the opposite, or a wider dispersal of employment areas may also become possible, as commuters will not mind traveling longer while working during travel time. Thus, it is difficult, as of yet, to foresee the possibility of new or renewed spatial organization of business facilities in metropolitan areas in the era of full AV adoption, since both re-concentration and continued spatial dispersion of businesses might possibly emerge (Heinrichs 2016).

9.4   TRANSITIONS IN URBAN LAND-USES

Several transitions in urban land-uses have emerged already since the introduction of the Internet, and additional ones may be expected, once AVs are widely adopted. We will explore here two transitions that are in effect already: the blurring between homes and work places, and the closure of physical stores and bank branches. We will then move to speculations on additional changes that may possibly emerge once AVs are adopted, focusing mainly on a possible decline in the need for parking solutions.

A leading kind of land-use transition constitutes the blurring of the traditional separation between home, or pleasure, and work activities, a trend which has been recognized already when access to the Internet was made first through fixed PCs only (see Kellerman 2006, 2012). This blurring has grown with the massive penetration of mobile access to the Internet, via smartphone and tablet versions of browsers, websites and applications. Portable Internet devices have made it possible for users to consume services without limitations of time and location in their routine daily life. This ease of universal access to services has brought about a vicious cycle between virtual services and real space facilities, expressed physically in the blurring between homes as pleasure foci and offices as work places. Thus, people can easily perform work duties at home, following their return from work or during weekends, and likewise they can pursue personal obligations through the Internet while being in their offices.

More striking in physical space are the recently growing closures of stores and bank branches. We noted back in Chapter 4 the growing worldwide popularity of online shopping and banking (Tables 4.1–4.2), and this trend has brought about increasing closures of physical stores as of 2010, mainly in the US, and mainly of stores specializing in apparel. These closures were coupled with the closing down of shopping malls, as well as with the collapse of store chain companies. The closure of some 6,700 stores was estimated for the US only for 2017 (Hannam 2017), and the trend for these closures has been termed by the media as constituting 'retail apocalypse' (e.g. Coresight Research 2018). Also in the US, some of the closed shopping malls have been turned into storage and shipping centers for online stores (Michel 2017). Similarly, bank branches have been closed down as well, with some 1,700 of them shut down in the US between mid-2016 and mid-2017, continuing a trend that began back in 2009, with an annual average closure rate of over 1 percent (Stackhouse 2018). Similarly across the EU some 9,100 branches closed down in 2016 (EBF 2017).

The possible continuation of these closure trends for brick-and-mortar stores and bank branches, and the possible expansion of this trend to other services traditionally offered by cities, may support a possible materialization of urban re-concentration rather than continued city dispersal in the Internet-based city. Alternatively, if urban residents continue to prefer suburban and exurban residences, the question is what will city streets look like when stores and other service facilities massively close down. The expansion of leisure activities is one option, and the emergence of new, and still unforeseen, types of services is another.

The decreased need for urban space for retail and other services will be coupled with some additional lower needs for urban space when AVs are widely adopted. Leading such change will be the possible reduction in the allocation of parking areas in cities. Repeated estimates, prepared for numerous countries, have pointed to an upcoming significant reduction in the number of cars in cities, once AVs are widely adopted. This reduction in the number of cars is expected, no matter if private purchases of AVs will be the preferred mode of adoption, or if rather taxis or shared AVs become the preferred modes for AV adoption. Thus, for instance, it was suggested that each AV which will be used in Austin, Texas, will be able to replace some eleven conventional cars, but simultaneously it will take 10 percent more time for each traveler to be met by ordered on-demand transit (Fagnant and Kockelman 2014; Fagnant et al. 2015). Another simulation, made for Lisbon (Portugal), assumed the operation of AV taxis side by side with a metro system, and it suggested that each AV would remove 9 out of 10 cars in the city, with a maximum of 5 minutes waiting time for ordered trips. If AVs are widely adopted without a metro service available in the city, each AV taxi will remove some five vehicles (ITF 2015). In Asia, it was estimated for Singapore that one-third of the current number of cars would suffice when AVs are fully adopted (Spieser et al. 2014). Finally, for Manhattan, New York, it was found that replacing the current taxi fleet with AV taxis will reduce the number of taxis to some 60 percent of their current number (Zhang and Pavone 2014; see also Correia and van Arem 2016).

These repeated estimates, which point to some of the most significant declines in the number of required cars when on-demand AV transit is introduced, suggest that urban traffic will change its tendency from its contemporary busy, congested and frequently hectic patterns. It further calls for governments to consider the introduction of subsidized AV taxi subscriptions, when AVs eventually become widely available, so that most urbanites will not have to buy cars, or at least not make use of them during weekdays, notably for commuting.

The estimates for drastically lower numbers of cars which will move on city streets will bring about no less dramatic changes in the urban parking scene. Thus, the parking shortages that typify contemporary city life may be relieved, at least partially, when AVs are widely adopted. The parking patterns for the lower number of AVs inside parking areas will be different than those of human-driven cars, since driverless AVs can park close to each other in depots rather than in parking lots, so that they would require only one-quarter of the parking spaces currently allocated in downtowns (Alessandrini et al. 2015) (Figure 9.2). This 'released' previous parking space may be immense. For example, in the CBD (central business district) of San Francisco in 2011, the number of off-street parking spaces reached 59,584, with additional separation spaces needed between cars, as well as access lanes required for accessing the parking spaces. This number of off-street parking spaces was coupled in San Francisco by some additional 23,873 on-street parking spaces with lower requirements of access space (NRMA 2014).

The reduced need for parking areas relates not only to parking spaces in downtowns and in other business districts, but it also applies to the parking

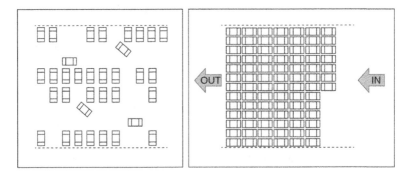

Figure 9.2   *Parking areas: (a) Parking lot for human-driven cars; (b) AV depot*

areas available next to or underneath residential buildings. Moreover, residents may not need parking spaces at all, if they opt for to making use of on-demand urban transit services for all of their travel needs. Otherwise, one AV may suffice for two-adult households, thus reducing the need for residential parking spaces.

City governments will have to adopt new regulations for a rather reduced number of required parking spaces for newly constructed buildings. As far as the residents are concerned, they too will have to get used to the idea that less or no parking spaces attached to their homes or apartments will not necessarily reduce the attractiveness of their properties when offered by them for future sales (Goodman 2016).

Another aspect of the reduced need for parking space will be the new uses that may possibly be preferred by house owners for their garages, which may lose their original purpose. As far as parking lots of apartment buildings are concerned, these may be turned into green recreational spaces for both adults and children. However, side by side with the possible reduction in the need for parking lots, apartment buildings will require special solutions in order for their residents to become accessible for package deliveries by drones (Goodman 2016).

9.5   THE VISIBLE AND INVISIBLE AUTONOMOUSLY MOBILE CITY

The penetration of the Internet so far into urban systems and actions has not yet affected the transportation systems of cities. However, the possible upcoming massive adoption of AVs may bring about some significant transitions in the landscapes of transportation and transmission systems in cities. We will focus here on the autonomously mobile city, dominated by Internet-based AVs, as well as by Internet-based traffic regulation systems.

Noyman et al. (2016) commented on cities in the AV age, noting that they will actually look similar to contemporary cities, at least as far as their road infrastructure is concerned. The gap between the upcoming availability and possibly fast adoption of the new mobility mode of AV, on the one hand, and the still unchanged road infrastructures of cities, on the other, reflects a more general trend. Technological development in general tends normally to evolve faster, as compared to the slower pace of change typical of urban planning and its following infrastructure construction. Thus, Noyman et al. (2016) found that AVs were referred to only by some 6 percent of the 68 transportation plans prepared for the 50 most populous metropolitan areas in the US. Incidentally, the urban plans that referred to AVs were prepared for the States in which the development and testing of AVs have taken place: California, Washington DC, Florida, Michigan, and Nevada. The US DOT (Department of Transportation) selected in 2016 the metropolitan area of Columbus, Ohio, to become an exemplary 'smart city', including also an upcoming use of AVs for first-mile/last-mile services accompanying public transportation systems (City of Columbus 2017). However, it seems that the city-state of Singapore has probably become the most advanced city worldwide in the testing of several types of AVs (notably taxis, buses and trucks) on its city roads, as we noted in the previous chapter, with an intention for its becoming also a pioneering city for future AV adoption, as well.

It is not necessarily required for future road systems, meant for AV use, to have a different structure than those of current road systems, since many AVs may have the same physical structure as traditional human-driven cars, namely 2–3 boxes for passengers, engine and baggage, riding on four vehicle bases. However, as we noted already in the previous chapter, fully electric taxis may potentially present a one-box structure for passengers only, with electric engines located underneath. In addition, one-box mini electric cars for 1–2 passengers may become popular, as well. A high popularity for smaller cars may possibly bring about the construction or marking of narrower road lanes.

Whichever the preferred structure for light-duty AVs, the major change in road systems for AVs will be in their traffic light systems. Since AVs will read sensors, traffic lights will turn into traffic control sensors, invisible to the innocent eyes of pedestrians and passengers. Moreover, even pedestrians will not need traffic lights anymore for road crossing, as they may be able to get some proper signals to their smartphones, informing them when road crossing is safe. In addition, the crossing of road junctions by AVs will not necessarily be regulated anymore by fixed time intervals. Sensors may rather provide for continuous traffic from a given direction, if clear traffic conditions at crossing directions at any given moment would permit it.

The future city, based on AVs, will produce the autonomously mobile city, which will be based on several elements. Autonomous mobilities include not merely the use of AVs, since automation is relevant also to numerous additional physical and virtual mobility modes, notably metros, the Internet and telephones, and these mobility modes operate differently through all of the four geographical spheres which are available for urban mobility: underground, ground, air and sea. Thus, the autonomously mobile city will consist of three layers in which automated mobility modes will operate: underground, ground, and air (Figure 9.3). The busiest of these layers is already, and will continue to be, by its very nature, the ground level of cities, with the underground and air layers serving as supportive mobility levels for the ground layer.

The supportive mobility for the urban ground sphere, offered by the underground and air spheres, is expressed in several ways. First, through the provision of some relief for ground mobility congestion, via underground metro services, and via aerial package delivery by drones. Second, under-

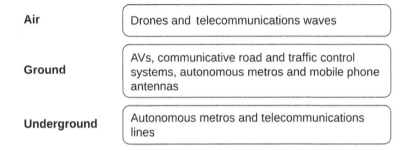

Air	Drones and telecommunications waves
Ground	AVs, communicative road and traffic control systems, autonomous metros and mobile phone antennas
Underground	Autonomous metros and telecommunications lines

Figure 9.3   The autonomously mobile city

ground mobility provides for enhanced environmental and safety conditions, through the underground installation of telecommunications cables, rather than their exposed installation on city surfaces. Third, the aerial sphere facilitates a unique provision for orthogonal photography by cameras installed in drones for municipal, police and other needs.

The physically lowest level of urban mobility infrastructures, the underground one, is also the oldest one among the three mechanized urban mobility layers, with the metros and telephone lines located there, being originally developed in or by nineteenth-century technologies.

The surface level of the autonomously mobile city constitutes its middle layer physically, lying between the underground and aerial ones. It is a middle one also historically, since the mobility modes currently functioning on city-grounds have been constructed through twentieth-century technologies, including paved roads, cars, traffic lights, and mobile phone antennas. The highest level of urban traffic is the aerial one, consisting of aerial mobility modes that are mainly based on twenty-first-century technologies. These include drones and C2X communications, coupled with late twentieth-century cable-free mobile communications for telephone and Internet services. These contemporary communications modes are supported by short-distance communications media, such as Bluetooth, as well as by additional communications technologies, such as GPS and cloud technologies. Helicopter services, which operate in some cities, offering transport services from downtowns to airports, constitute an exceptional mid-twentieth-century aerial mobility mode, and, given its high operational costs, their service is usually preserved for selected clients only.

The sequence for the emergence of mobility automation processes at the three city layers presents a different and more complex pattern, as compared to the chronological order of their initial non-automatic construction, which we noted as leading from the underground, through the surface to the air levels. Thus, the underground telephone cables have served already long ago automated telephone systems, which were first introduced in 1900, and were followed almost a century later by the Internet, so that enhancements and innovations in underground cable systems have mostly taken place at the cable terminals or exchanges rather than within the cable systems themselves. However, fiber-optic cables have begun to replace many of the original copper ones, as of 1983. The underground metros have begun automation processes later, becoming gradually automated only as of the 1980s.

On the surface, traffic lights became automated long ago, as of 1922, but cars will begin their road to full automation only as of the upcoming decade of the 2020s, or exactly a full century after the automation of traffic lights began. Whereas both the underground and surface mobility systems developed originally as non-automatic ones, becoming eventually automated, the aerial technologies present an original start as automated Internet-based mobilities. Thus, it was for mobile phones to become automated in the early 1980s, almost immediately following their introduction as a commercial communications service, whereas the twenty-first-century urban-civilian drones have been autonomous from their outset. Similarly, for the metro, telephone, and road line systems, no significant changes in the lines themselves were required, in order for them to serve the automated versions of the respective mobility modes. However, the possible emergence of wide uses and traffic by drones will be coupled by a need to establish skylines for them, and this presents a rather novel challenge, since such skylines have not existed for previously non-existent staffed personal aerial urban mobility modes.

Line networks of tracks for metros, as well as networks of roads for cars, both of which are meant for physical mobility, have been constructed at the underground and ground city levels respectively, but virtual mobility networks have operated in all of the three layers, through cables (underground), antennas (surface), and waves (air). For contemporary mobile individuals, virtual mobility, via the Internet, has become most vital, since the Internet facilitates a spatially continuous telephone and textual connectivity, applicable to people's corporeal mobility about the city, as well as to their communications pursued while staying in fixed locations anywhere throughout cities. In addition, Internet technologies have become of vital importance for the controlling or operation of all transportation modes. Thus, whereas the technologies for the mechanical operations of metros, cars and drones differ from each other, the communications systems, which they employ for their automated operations, are similar.

Once AVs are fully adopted, the autonomously mobile city will emerge. Given that AVs have not yet been introduced, it is still too early to attempt to fully portray the autonomous mobile city. However, one may note already now several new elements in both the looking and the functioning of the autonomously mobile city.

From an urban landscape perspective, it seems reasonable to assume the removal of all visual aids for drivers from the road system. These visual aids include mainly two elements. Traffic lights, as we noted already, will be removed, since AVs will 'read' sensors, rather than lights, and even traffic lights for pedestrians may possibly be replaced by some smartphone signals. Second, all the highway directional road signs with city names and road names and numbers will be removed, as AV routing will be directed by GPS, and road signs will not be necessary anymore. This applies also to most of the road signs on local streets, with the exception of road signs for the use of bicycle riders and pedestrians.

From a functional perspective, since the common technological thread among all the autonomous mobility systems will be their Internet-based communications and control technologies, one may expect attempts for, as of yet unforeseen, integrations among these mobility systems and their users, with the current wide usage of IoT constituting only a modest start in such a direction. Thus, it might be possible to coordinate the travel schedules of mobility modes for individual passengers. For instance, passengers will be able to order last-mile AV services to wait for them at a metro station following their arrival there by a specific train, and when reaching their homes, drones will be able to immediately drop off some dinner…

At the system level, it will be potentially possible to control the traffic of all AVs and metros more efficiently using GPS and satellites, similar to the already existing automated routing/navigation services, which serve simultaneously millions of individual drivers. On the other hand, however, the use of the Internet/IoT for the communications and control of all mobility systems may involve also the risk of wide and even fatal damages, to be potentially caused by hackers, as compared to the more modest damage and partial stoppage of services, sometimes caused by them in their criminal actions affecting Internet websites.

Side by side with the possibly upcoming emergence of the new and visible autonomously mobile city, the invisible landscape of the mobile city will expand, as well. Already before the introduction of the Internet, cameras were widely installed throughout cities. One system of such cameras was meant for traffic regulation, as part of remotely controlled traffic regulation. Other cameras were installed at numerous other locations, such as in stores, at the entrances of residential buildings, or in public parks and so on, all meant for enhanced security. The installation of cameras has expanded in recent years, attempting to cope with growing urban terror attacks. However, the wide scale of camera installations in the public sphere has also implied, at least implicitly, an expansion of personal surveillance (Graham 1998b). This is also the case for cars being recorded by traffic management and control cameras installed in road junctions, as well as for cars being monitored through GPS devices.

This invisible system, which serves the hidden visibility of people and cars will receive a second layer with the installation of sensors throughout cities, a phase which has already begun, in order to permit the safe moving of AVs, notably through road junctions. Road junction cameras and sensors communicate with traffic control centers through IoT and will communicate with AVs through V2I communications. Thus, it will be for rather invisible elements to operate and control city traffic and other urban systems, so that these invisible elements, notably sensors, will turn into crucial components for routine urban life. The use of the Internet for such communications will be still based on the lack of central Internet controlling, but it calls also for most careful assurances against prohibited uses by hackers and governments alike.

9.6   CHANGES IN THE CULTURAL SIGNIFICANCE OF THE PHYSICAL CITY

The introduction and wide adoption of mobile broadband implies instant access to cyberspace for its users, but it may further carry implications for the use and meaning of urban physical space by smartphone users. The constant availability of GPS for navigation and LBS for the consumption of urban services, while walking or driving through unknown cities, or through unknown parts of known cities, implies an efficient moving of people through urban space when aiming to reach specific addresses, thus saving time and effort in walking, driving, and searching. It further implies a live and ongoing integration of virtual and physical spaces, with the virtual space providing guidance for corporeal movements within physical space. However, this efficient crossing of physical space with the aid of tools located in virtual space turns the crossed streets, as well as urban space at large, into a kind of impediment rather than into an occasion for some cultural exploration of unknown city parts. Hence, this specific integration of virtual and physical spaces reduces one's urban experiences. Cities turn into a mere mosaic of places of production and consumption, ignoring the traditional role of cities as providing residents and visitors with passive or active experiences of human life at large, such as through the encounter with city rhythms at different times of the day and the week (see Allen 1999).

This loss of meaning of urban space for constant GPS users, who move about cities from one point to another, is not the only possible loss of exposure to the city by smartphone users. Another such loss, and maybe an even wider one, may develop when smartphone users move about the urban public sphere while being engaged with virtual space through their simultaneous interactions with apps, websites, chats, or emails, so that their attention to city landscapes is deteriorated, or sometimes even totally lost.

9.7   TRANSFORMATIONS IN ACTIVITIES CARRIED OUT BY URBANITES

In the core of the Internet-based city stand its residents. How has the newly basing of cities on the Internet affected the activities of their residents? The answer to this question is as varied as the urban applications of the Internet already are, and as they are about to be in the future. Thus, as far as the daily routine consumption of services is concerned, virtual services offered through the Internet serve as a potential alternative, or at least as a forceful competitor, with the traditional offerings of these services throughout the physical urban space. Thus, in this arena, the Internet serves growingly as a substitute for urban space, led by virtual retail and banking services.

This is not the case, however, when it comes to people's homes. Here, when IoT is installed into smart home systems, it facilitates the remote activation and operation of people's homes, and these systems are now in their take-off phase of adoption. The Internet, in this case, assists urbanites in the provision of efficient and convenient operations of home appliances. The smart home app is unique, as compared to the numerous apps installed in smartphones for users' assistance, and thus in its use of IoT for individuals.

Finally, the Internet may substitute urbanites in one of their major daily operational roles, namely in their functioning as drivers, once AVs are introduced and widely adopted. AVs will differ from the alternative and assistance functions offered by the Internet to its users for service provision and smart homes, respectively. AVs themselves will constitute the major users of IoT, rather than the previous drivers, who will make use of the IoT only in order to invite the vehicle and determine the ride destination.

Altogether, then, the Internet technology is already now in an advanced phase for constituting a partial *alternative* for physical cities, as far as service provision is concerned, side by side with its gradual provision of *assistance* for people's home operations through IoT. These two roles of the Internet as an alternative and as an assistance will be coupled with its future role as a *substitute* for urban human actions. These three roles of the Internet for residents of the Internet-based city, alternative, assistance and substitute, are not in conflict with each other, since they refer to three rather different human urban activities: service consumption, home operations and driving, respectively. The smart and joint uses of these Internet applications by urbanites may turn urban life into a continuously more efficient and pleasing experience.

9.8   URBAN OPERATION AND COMMAND VIA SMARTPHONES

The Internet-based city is embodied above all through the small pocket-fitting box – the smartphone. This small, and easy to operate, device provides for both traditional vocal communications, as well as for the activation of advanced digital urban and informational functions. It facilitates the provision of, among other things, urban facilities and services of markets, cafés, news, printing, radio, television, clock and telephone. These rather varied provisions imply the ability of smartphones to transmit and handle all information modes, whether textual, pictorial, streaming, or vocal. Smartphones further permit the remote control of homes, as well as the control and operations of urban systems, for the proper operators and controllers. Its connectivities facilitate fully mobile operations. The current, and even more so, the future operations of cities, will be gradually based on an invisible fixed infrastructure of sensors, whereas city operations and control by its residents and experts alike, is already now quite widely based on the rather mobile smartphones.

9.9   CONCLUSION

In this chapter we highlighted several implications and outcomes for the extensive citywide applications of the Internet, eventually reaching maturity once AVs are adopted. Contemporary cities have turned into IoE-based cities, in which people communicate with their fellows, as well as with machines, side by side with machine-to-machine communications. Thus, the Internet has turned into a fully comprehensive communications and information technology. The Internet-based city enjoys, therefore, four basic features. First, comprehensive connectivity for its residents, companies, homes and systems. Second, this connectivity brings about a rather growing movability for both its residents and their information. Third, Internet-based cities further enjoy a dispersed controllability, since Internet systems may operate both separately for each function and jointly for some interconnected systems. Fourth, the dispersed controllability assures a continuity of operation for the Internet, notably in case of malfunctioning by any Internet system.

The evidence for any changing overall spatial patterns of cities, whether possibly expanding or concentrating, is still mixed, and this is true also regarding speculations on any future transitions in urban spatial patterns, as well, once AVs become widely adopted. Thus, transitions in urban land-uses, stemming from the extending Internet use, notably for service provision, are also in an early phase of emergence, expressed presently through the blurring of differentiation between home-leisure activities and office-work ones, as well as by the growing closures of physical stores and bank branches.

Once AVs become massively adopted, it is estimated that the number of cars, and subsequently the number of needed parking spaces will be drastically lower. It is still unclear, however, if these two changes, coupled with the ability of commuters to work while riding AVs, will bring about further spatial expansions of metropolitan areas, or whether, in the contrary, CBDs will rather regain their past status as the leading employment foci, with released parking spaces there used for the construction of additional office buildings.

The massive adoption of AVs will bring about the emergence of the autonomously mobile city. This new formation of cities will be typified by a rather transformed urban mobility landscape, consisting of a much smaller number of cars, and a removal of visible traffic lights, as well as of directional signs on highways. Furthermore, if traffic becomes less congested and cars become smaller, then a reduced number of lanes will be needed on highways, coupled with their being shrunk by their lane width. So far, most metropolitan urban plans, at least in the US, have not yet taken into account the possible adoption of AVs. The common thread among all of the automated mobility modes in the autonomously mobile city will be their use of the same information technologies, the Internet and IoT, thus calling for possible future coordination among their operations.

The autonomously mobile city will consist of three layers in which automated mobility modes will operate: underground, ground, and aerial. The physically lowest level of urban mobility infrastructures, the underground, is also the oldest one among the three automated urban mobility layers, with metros, telephone and Internet lines located there, being originally developed using nineteenth-century technologies. The ground level constitutes the middle layer physically, lying between the underground and aerial layers. The ground level is also a middle layer historically, since the infrastructures that serve the mobility modes that function on city-grounds have been constructed with twentieth-century technologies, including paved roads, cars, traffic lights, and mobile phone antennas. The highest level of urban traffic is the aerial one, consisting of aerial mobility modes that are mainly based on twenty-first-century technologies. These include drones and C2X communications, coupled with late twentieth-century cable-free mobile communications for telephone and Internet services.

The use of smartphones for urban navigation, vis-à-vis GPS apps, brings about lower attention by people who move about cities, to the cultural richness that is offered by city buildings and road designs.

The Internet serves urbanites in varied ways. It may simultaneously replace the physical city for service provisions, side by side with it becoming an assistant in home operations, while having a future role as a substitute for human actions as drivers.

The small smartphone facilitates the pursuing of all the traditional and digital urban communications and information functions. Thus, the current, and even more so the future operations of cities is based, on the one hand, on an invisible fixed infrastructure of sensors, whereas on the other hand, its operations and control by its residents and experts alike, is based on the rather mobile smartphones.

10. Conclusion

We will begin this chapter with the summaries of the previous chapters, presented in sequence. We will then move to an interpretation of the Internet as a general-purpose technology, and finally, we will conclude the book with an evaluation of the general theme of the book as presenting Internet applications, followed by Internet implications, within an urban framework.

10.1   CHAPTER SUMMARIES

We noted in Chapter 1 three basic notions for the interpretation of the Internet within an urban context. First, information, as a wide spectrum, comprises data, information in a stricter sense of statements, knowledge and innovation. Second, spatial mobility refers also to people's communications through virtual mobility media, currently led by the Internet. Third, human connectivity, the levels and forms of which may differ by the chosen communications media. Devices too may communicate with each other, as well as with humans, through the IoT.

These three basic notions of information, spatial mobility and connectivity, present jointly the ability to move information to connected others, whether they be humans or devices. This human ability and its pursuance have always constituted one of the essential elements of urban life. Human connectivity and informational activities have been upgraded, and thus have become most extensive, as with the development of communications technologies and media, peaking with the emergence of the Internet and smartphones. As was further noted in later chapters of the book, these devices and media have facilitated full locational flexibility for human connectivity and informational activities. Furthermore, and as was shown too in later chapters, the Internet has further facilitated the instant transmission of all types of information to and from people wherever they are located and moving. Side by side with the expansion and upgrading of human connectivity, IoT has extended connectivity to non-living devices, as well.

Chapter 2 presented the leading urban facilities and services, which have been established for informational activities and connectivity in Western cities throughout history. These facilities and services have emerged cumulatively, rather than by way of newer facilities replacing previous ones. Each of these facilities and services has been shown to have its own functions, fulfilling needs for formal and informal informational activities.

One of these media and the newest among them all, the Internet, enjoys a rather special nature, given its comprehensive, multi-purpose and multi-modal nature. We have noted the inclusion of radio and television webcasts within the Internet, as well as vocal telephone communications. In addition, the Internet has brought about the emergence of virtual versions for all the previously developed informational facilities and services within it: markets, entertainment, books, newspapers, universities, and virtual meeting places. The Internet constitutes, therefore, a huge and global virtual informational and connectivity hub, somehow equivalent to the traditional role maintained by physical cities as hubs.

European countries and cities led the development of urban informational facilities and services until the introduction of telecommunications technologies, when the US emerged as a leader in both the innovation and adoption dimensions of informational newness.

We noticed in Chapter 3 the emergence of the Internet as a leading 'master technology', including smartphones and the IoT. As far as the Internet per se is concerned, we noted its comprehensive nature in its constituting both a communications and information system, facilitating the transmission, storage and retrieval of all forms and formats of information. Mobile phones turning into smartphones, and thus being connected to mobile broadband and GPS, constitute the leading medium for the use of the Internet in a rather location-free and mobile manner. Digital gaps in the adoption of the Internet still prevail at the global and international levels, whereas mobile phones have become widely adopted even at the global level. IoT development and use have flourished as of the late 1990s, and the technology has been applied at an enormously wide scale, expected to peak even further with the upcoming introduction of AVs.

The Internet has enabled the construction of a metaphorical virtual space, including sites, addresses, vehicles (search engines and browsers), and transmission systems (mobile broadband). Smartphones permit their users to reach this metaphorical space for a wide variety of uses from anywhere and at any time. The three technologies described in Chapter 3, the Internet, the smartphone and IoT, have reached an integration with each other from their users' perspective, in the sense that smartphones serve as always-there mobile terminals for Internet connectivity. This applies also to IoT connectivity between human users and their devices and services, pursued via smartphones. Connections among non-human devices are rather performed through servers, which further provide for connectivity between the Internet and IoT.

The growing communicational complexities presented by the Internet, including the IoT, bear also on the nature of digital divides and their measures. Digital divides should not be measured anymore merely along the traditional parameters of Internet and smartphone adoption levels, since these measures relate to individuals and their access to the Internet, but they do not expose of the possible emergence of complex smart systems in some cities or countries, as compared to other places where smart systems are still lacking. Such smart systems include mainly smart homes, smart cities, and smart cars. The emergence of such smart complexities implies the availability and use of sophisticated operational and control systems. Thus, wide adoption rates of mobile phones and the Internet by individuals do not imply by themselves the emergence of Internet-based cities, which involve the availability of complex control systems and technologies, as well.

Chapter 4 focused on urban services, which have become available to individuals virtually over the Internet. Leading among these virtual services are work; shopping; banking; government; travel; learning; health and networking. These eight services were compared with each other in Chapter 4, first by their varying nature and by their diversified significances in people's lives, and then by their differing global adoption rates.

Work extends for most adults over at least one-third of each weekday, and it is by far a leading human activity with major implications for people's present and future lives. This crucial significance and role of work for individuals may have possibly led to a continued global hesitation by workers to divert their physical locations while at work, fully or partially, from their offices to their homes. This preference for work in offices, as the major spatial focus for their work activity, has prevailed despite the growing performance of work activities by many workers through computers, so that their work can be pursued whether they are located at work or at home.

Studying in an online degree program is similar to work in its constituting a rather prolonged process, spanning along several years, and thus differing from online shopping, in which only a few minutes are required for the purchase of products and services online. Online study further requires a much more extensive investment by the customer-student, in terms of its financial costs, the extensive investment of time, and the required intellectual efforts, notably when studying virtually and thus individually, as compared to being part of a physically present group assembled together in a physical classroom. The intellectual effort involved in online study has frequently made it be considered as being inferior to face-to-face study, from the perspectives of students and universities alike. Another difference between learning and the purchase of goods and services is their durability, which for an academic degree is, at least partially, without expiration, as compared to the disposability or limited lifespan of most commercial products and services.

Shopping online is a more widely adopted service activity as compared to learning online. The adoption of online shopping is usually partial for each customer, because a preference for shopping in physical stores may still prevail for certain products, and shopping online may be split between browsing and shopping, with possibly just one of these two phases of a shopping session taking place online.

As compared to shopping online and the rather wide choice of merchants and merchandise, which typifies it, governmental services constitute a rather compulsory and uncompetitive type of services, forcing citizens to receive their governmental services normally from their own governments only, including services such as tax and fee payments, and submission and receipt of documents. The possible availability of governmental e-services may apply to governments at all geographical scales: local, regional and national.

Travel online differs from other 'e-' activities in that it does not constitute an end by itself, like work, shopping and banking, but it rather constitutes a preparatory phase for business or pleasure travel taking place in physical space.

E-health is not a fully automatic service, such as e-banking, travel online and e-government, other than for health management and health information seeking. For many health functions, e-health involves human intervention, such as the need for expert physicians or other medical workers, as well as specialized equipment, for telemedicine. Furthermore, in most cases telemedicine involves treatment at the patient's end to be performed remotely by nurses or technicians.

The Internet facilitates the management of wide social contacts, as well as the sharing of contents with them. These traits of online social networks stem from the very constitution of the Internet as an informational system. The barrier-free, constraint-free (in most countries) and cost-free virtual social networking has exhibited a tremendously fast adoption pace. However, the very use of social networking by individuals over the Internet does not automatically imply globally stretched networks established by all of them, and the attendance of all networks by a large number of subscribers. In developed countries, online social networking is as popular as other services obtained online, notably shopping, whereas among Internet users in developing countries, social networking is even more popular than in developed ones, whereas other online services are more weakly adopted, given the lower incomes there.

The geographical patterns of the worldwide adoptions of available online services are complex, so that the adoption processes are still in the making, some 22 years following the commercial and universal introduction of the Internet, back in 1995. Thus, an examination of the EU 2017 averages for the adoption of virtual services, taking into account the varied levels of economic development and Internet penetration levels of the EU member countries, reveals that only every second European consumed shopping, banking, travel, health, and social networking over the Internet. In addition, only one out of three residents in OECD countries consumed e-government services in 2016. The variations between the highest country-levels of adoption of e-service consumption and the lowest ones are wide in some cases. Banking constitutes the most striking case in this regard, with a level of adoption of merely 5 percent in Bulgaria, as compared to 93 percent in Iceland, attesting to differences in economic development, geographic location, and traditions of adoption of telecommunications means and services. Interestingly enough, the highest levels of adoptions for several services stood equally at 71 percent: government (in Denmark), travel (in Luxembourg), and health (in the Netherlands).

The US presented, for 2017, higher levels of adoption for Internet services, as compared to the EU average, but presenting, in some way, adoption rates that are similar to those of large European countries (UK, Germany and France). As for China, representing the rising Asian countries, as far as Internet adoption and use is concerned, the adoption levels for 2017 were more varied, ranging between high levels for shopping (83 percent) and learning (20 percent), and low ones for government (21 percent).

It seems that two services have reached wide levels of adoption at the global scale: shopping and social networking. However, whereas shopping online has become most popular in developed economies, social networking peaks in developing ones, thus pointing to the availability of Internet services for people living under varying economic conditions.

The global leadership in the adoption of Internet services was shared until a few years ago by the US and Scandinavian countries. The Scandinavian countries, with some of their populations being scattered in remote and cold areas, have long developed policies for the adoption of telecommunications newness. The US led globally in the adoption of Internet services, given it being the major inventing and introducing country for most of the new information technologies, and it being a country that enjoys a tradition of newness adoption. This leadership of the US has declined in recent years, attesting to a rather slow but still progressing maturing of the global Internet economy. The Nordic countries still lead in the adoption levels of numerous services, side by side with other small European countries (the Netherlands and Luxembourg). It seems, however, that in the upcoming years, it will rather be for Asian countries, notably South Korea and China, to take the lead in the adoption levels of Internet services, beginning with online shopping. The extremely fast and wide adoption of smartphones by the population in these two countries, side by side with their current leadership in smartphone R&D and production, may contribute to this direction.

It was claimed that cultural aspects have heavily influenced differences among countries in the adoption of the Internet and its use. Generally, the level of penetration of the Internet has depended on the social distance of countries from the US, the country that has been most reflected in the Internet. Thus, it was difficult at the time for the Japanese to adopt email communications, which permits rather 'horizontal', and open interactions by its users, without regard to hierarchical 'vertical' social structuring, which prevailed in Japan. It was further claimed that the level of adoption of emailing may differ from the adoption of online shopping, which on its part might be attractive when the time budget of individuals becomes restrained, thus making it possible for technology to overcome cultural-national values. Dominance of feminist and individualist values in countries may assist the adoption of the Internet there, as compared to countries with prevailing collectivist and uncertainty avoidance values, since emailing permits free networking, a routine which may be preferred by women.

Social virtual relations can take place physically and virtually through numerous platforms and in plenty of places, and they do not involve any financial transactions. The very nature of social relations developed online through social networks, as well as their potential impact on social relations in physical space, have been widely debated in recent years. This debate has taken place in parallel with the massive adoption of social networking by Internet users globally, so that societies worldwide are still in search of balances between physical and virtual social spaces and their interrelationships.

Chapter 5 was devoted to the relationships between physical and Internet spaces from the perspective of individual Internet users. The interface between the Internet and its users adopted from its outset a rather spatial terminology, for instance sites, browsing, home and so on. Physical space and the Internet metaphorical space were originally viewed as two rather separate spaces. Later on, the development of GPS, broadband and mobile technologies, have brought about the viewing of the two spaces as being interfolded and converging into a hybrid space. At a third phase of the study of the relationships between physical spaces and digital codes in general, the conceptual focus moved from the metaphorical spatiality of the Internet to the identification of connectivities and spatial content in digital systems, which may turn them into spatial media.

The dual-space society, which was presented in Chapter 5, is based on the hybrid between physical and Internet spaces, with the latter being a metaphorical one. This view approaches the Internet, as a leading digital system, from the perspective of human agency, thus focusing on people's spatialities while functioning simultaneously within both physical and the metaphorical Internet space. This approach rather complements the viewing of selected digital systems as constituting spatial media, since the latter approach is a conceptual one, rather than focusing on the everyday users of the Internet as a digital system.

Dual-space constitutes an arena for spatial practices, with both physical and Internet spaces constituting separate dualities, as products of actions with structuring power. In order for Internet space to function dually with physical space, Internet users need three spatial conditions to be met by the Internet system: universal accessibility to the system, universal reach of websites from their location of access, and an instant pace for information transmissions. Dual-space implies several continuous conditions to be met for the very being and acting by individuals in them: presence in the two spaces; personal identification; personal autonomy; and the experiencing of dual-space use. Changing performances within dual-space include interaction, networking and action. Each of these performances involves some physical space and Internet spatialities, and these spatialities are interrelated with each other in varying ways.

In Chapter 6, we moved from the Internet experiences of individuals to the adoption of the Internet by companies, as well as to the production of Internet technologies by them. We noted the wide distribution of Internet usage among companies, which might probably be even wider than the equivalent adoption rate of the Internet by individuals. However, the use of the Internet by companies may be quite varied by its depth and intensity. It may range from the mere use of the Internet for emailing, in a first phase of adoption, through a second phase involving a rather passive use of the Web by establishing an informative website only. In a third phase, it may possibly develop into informational exchanges with customers, followed, in a fourth phase, by financial transactions with them. The adoption of the Internet for companies may eventually peak, in a fifth phase, by a company undergoing organizational transitions reflecting a full use of the Internet.

When it comes to the geographical distribution of the production of Internet technologies, we noted a rather different, and more concentrated geographical pattern, as compared to the wide distribution of Internet usage by companies. The production of Internet technologies refers to four layers of Internet technologies: network, connectivity, navigation and application, each with its own geographical patterns of concentration.

Thus, the production and development of Internet network hardware is led by some specific countries, notably the US and China, whereas server farms, at the connectivity layer, are frequently located in cold countries. For the third level of navigation technologies, we noticed its concentration in high-tech cities worldwide.

The fourth layer of application has been the most dynamic one in recent years. In the early stages of Internet development, it included the web design industry as well as domain registration. These activities, coupled with the provision of access to the Internet by ISPs at the connectivity layer, have later turned into routine services with a rather ubiquitous urban spread. Currently the application layer is focused on the smartphone app industry, which is mainly concentrated in selected cities, some of which serve as Internet technology hubs for other phases of Internet technology development. This change in the focus of application technologies has been coupled with a drastic geographical transition, so that the very development phase of the app industry is being led by East Asian countries, rather than by the US, as has been the case for the earlier phases of the emergence of the Internet. Thus, currently North America and Europe share similar portions of the app industry following the East Asian leadership. The geographical change in the application industry leadership refers mainly to the concentrated locations of app developers, and not to the economic and technological leadership, which might be still American.

One may wonder if a new generation of application technologies, which might emerge in the future, will turn the current smartphone app industry into a ubiquitous one, as far as the locations of app production is concerned, with new geographical centers and concentrations to emerge, for the still unknown, future application industry.

In Chapter 7 we reviewed the digitization of urban systems, following our reviews of the Internet activities pursued by city dwellers and those adopted by urban companies, vis-à-vis the general communications technology of the Internet/IoT. The incorporation of numerous digital technologies into the wide fabric of cities received the umbrella term of 'smart cities'. Thus, in recent years, IoT has been disseminated into diverse dimensions of urban life, including urban systems, governments, societies, and residents, jointly constituting 'smart cities'. Thus, most cities worldwide, notably in the developed world, include some or numerous smart systems or operations.

Urban Internet-based utilities in general, and electricity and water in particular, imply the installation of one or all of three elements: remote management, smart grids and smart meters. Of these elements, the installation of smart meters has become the most extensive, with varying degrees of progress among nations in their installation. A second application of IoT for urban systems has been its dissemination into traffic regulation systems, turning IoT into a most significant element for the development of sophisticated traffic control systems. IoT permits two-way transmissions of visual and command information between traffic lights and control centers, and, more recently, it has further facilitated communications among cars, as well as among cars and traffic lights and sensors. These latter developments are crucial for the upcoming introduction of AVs. A third application of IoT technologies for urban systems are smart homes, which facilitate the remote controlling of home appliances by their residents, notably energy-rich appliances. The possible massive adoption of smart home technologies still awaits the development of standard codes for their operations.

The upcoming AVs, to be introduced in the 2020s, will be massively based on V2X IoT communications. Thus, the peaking of Internet use within urban contexts is expected to be reached once AVs are fully adopted, possibly in the 2040s–2050s. AVs will eventually bring about a city that will be fully Internet-based, following the previous disseminations of the Internet and IoT into people's daily activities, as well as into the operations of urban companies and urban systems. It is, thus, too early to speculate on possible integrations between human activities and urban systems, something that may emerge once urban traffic becomes fully driverless and Internet-based. By that time, the Internet will probably not constitute anymore the only urban master-technology, since it may be joined by artificial intelligence, another leading technology for the operations of AVs, and possibly turning into a widely applied urban technology. Smart cities by then may imply the emergence of numerous combinations of these two leading technologies, developed and applied for a variety of urban uses.

Chapter 8 attempted to highlight the upcoming IoT-based AVs, as the ultimate autonomous personal physical mobility mode. We exposed the development of AVs, and the technological challenges associated with it, as well as the potential adoption of AVs, given the problems involved in their acceptance and operation. AVs are being developed now simultaneously in the US, Europe and Japan, and are expected to be commercially introduced in 2022–2025, assuming the completion of development of the relevant technologies, as well as the solving of numerous legal and ethical questions. So far, the development and testing for autonomous buses, trucks and drones, seems to be more advanced than those for light-duty private AVs.

The pace of AV adoption is further still unclear, and is dependent on the readiness of individuals to cope with a major behavioral change, since the introduction of fully automatic cars may touch directly upon the lives of individuals. AVs constitute a real revolution in the functioning of vehicles without any type of human control, neither *in situ* by car drivers, nor by any remote controlling centers, with thousands of AVs being on the road simultaneously. Following two decades of an adoption process, it is expected that in the 2040s–2050s the traffic landscape will be mostly to fully automated.

In Chapter 9, we highlighted several urban implications and outcomes for the extensive and wide-ranging applications of the Internet, eventually reaching maturity once AVs are adopted. Contemporary cities have turned into IoE-based cities, in which people communicate with their fellows, as well as with machines, side by side with machine-to-machine communications. Thus, the Internet is on its way to turning into a fully comprehensive communications and information technology. The Internet-based city enjoys, therefore, four basic features: comprehensive connectivity for its residents, companies, homes and systems, which bring about a second feature, the rather growing movability available to both its residents and information. Internet-based cities further enjoy a third feature, namely dispersed controllability, since Internet systems may operate both separately for each function and jointly for some interconnected systems. This latter feature assures a fourth function of continuity of operation, notably in case of malfunctioning of any specific Internet system.

Evidence for the changing overall spatial patterns of cities, whether expanding or concentrating, is still mixed, and this may be true regarding future transitions in urban spatial patterns, as well, once AVs become widely adopted.
Similarly, transitions in urban land-uses, because of the extending Internet
use, are also in an early phase of change, led now by the blurring of differentiation between home-leisure activities and office-work ones, as well as by the
growing closures of physical stores and bank branches.

Once AVs become massively adopted, it is estimated that the number of
cars, and subsequently the number of needed parking spaces will be drastically
lower. It is still unclear, however, if these two changes, coupled with the ability
of commuters to work while riding AVs, will bring about further spatial expansion of metropolitan areas, or whether, in the contrary, CBDs will rather regain
their past status as the leading metropolitan employment foci, with released
parking spaces there used for the construction of additional office buildings.

The massive adoption of AVs will bring about the emergence of the autonomously mobile city. This new formation of cities will be typified by a rather
transformed urban mobility landscape, consisting of a much smaller number of
cars, and lacking visible traffic lights, as well as directional signs on highways.
Furthermore, if traffic becomes less congested and cars become smaller at the
AV age, then a reduced number of lanes will be needed on highways, coupled
with their being shrunk by their lane width. So far, most metropolitan urban
plans, at least in the US, have not yet taken into account the possible adoption
of AVs. The common thread among all the automated mobility modes in the
autonomously mobile city will be their use of the same information technologies, the Internet and IoT, thus calling for possible future coordination among
their operations.

The autonomously mobile city will consist of three layers in which automated mobility modes will operate: underground, ground, and aerial. The
physically lowest level of urban mobility infrastructures, the underground,
is also the oldest one among the three automated urban mobility layers,
with metro, telephone and Internet lines located there. The telephone cable
systems were originally developed through nineteenth-century technologies.
The ground level constitutes the middle layer physically, lying between the
underground and aerial ones. This ground level is a middle one also historically, since the infrastructures that serve the mobility modes that function
on city-grounds have been constructed using twentieth-century technologies,
including paved roads, cars, traffic lights, and mobile phone antennas. The
highest level of urban traffic is the aerial one, consisting of aerial mobility
modes that are mainly based on twenty-first-century technologies. These
include drones and C2X communications, coupled with late twentieth-century
cable-free mobile communications for telephone and Internet services.

Another implication of the growing use of the Internet by individuals within urban contexts, notably for navigation purposes, relates to people's exposure to city cultures, as expressed in the physical structures of cities. Thus, the use of smartphones for urban navigation, vis-à-vis GPS apps, brings about lower attention by people who move about cities, to the cultural richness offered by city buildings and road designs.

Looking generally at the varied uses of the Internet by people, per their traditional functioning within cities, the Internet serves urbanites in varied ways. In one way, the Internet replaces the physical city in its offering an alternative for urban service provisions. In a second way, the IoT is being turned into an assistant for individuals in its facilitation of remote home operations, whereas in a third way, it will, in the future, rather substitute human actions as car drivers.

The rather small smartphone has been developed into a complex and sophisticated device, providing for all the traditional and digital urban communications and information functions. Thus, the current, and even more so the future operations, of cities, is based, on the one hand, on an invisible fixed infrastructure of sensors, whereas its operations and control by its residents and experts alike, is based on the rather mobile and small-sized devices, the smartphones, on the other hand.

10.2 THE INTERNET AS A GENERAL-PURPOSE TECHNOLOGY (GPT)

A general-purpose technology (GPT) was defined as 'a single generic technology, recognisable as such over its whole lifetime, that initially has much scope for improvement and eventually comes to be widely used, to have many uses, and to have many spillover effects' (Lipsey et al. 2005, 98). As far as modern technologies are concerned, electricity, computers and cars have become leading examples in this regard. Soon following its commercial introduction, back in 1995, the Internet was recognized as a GPT (Harris 1998), notably given its ability to transmit data globally at low or no cost.

When the Internet is viewed from an urban perspective, then its general-purpose nature is highly evident, given its wide penetration into the operations of individuals, companies and systems, as well as its rather impressive number of applications. However, it still seems that the Internet will reach its full maturity as a GPT, once AVs become widely adopted, implying by then that there will not remain any single major urban system or activity that will be left without Internet communications for its operations.

The Internet and IoT have joined the veteran utilities of electricity, water, gas, sewage and telephony, all available in cities. The Internet has been adopted and used by city residents, as well as by almost all urban facilities, either through the wired telephone systems, or and growingly, through the wireless cellular and Wi-Fi systems. In its wide adoption and use by all urban partners, human and non-living alike, the Internet is most similar to electricity, which is a utility required by all urbanites, side by side with its use for all and rather varied urban facilities. As we noted in Chapter 7, the two systems of Internet and electricity can be combined by using the electricity grid also for Internet transmissions, thus turning the combined grid into a smart one. The universality of the electricity system, notably in developed countries, invites the developments of smart grids.

The two GPTs of electricity and Internet can be compared from other perspectives, as well. Of all major contemporary GPSs, the universal Internet, which transmits information, seems to be most similar to the universal electricity system, which transmits electric power. In both systems, the transmissions are invisible. However, whereas some if not most of the electricity infrastructures are visible, the Internet infrastructure is mostly invisible. Furthermore, electricity can be supplied also independently of the citywide electricity production and transmission systems, using generators or batteries, whereas the whole idea of the Internet, as a communications system, is that when a node is disconnected from the network it becomes meaningless for the system.

10.3   INTERNET APPLICATIONS VERSUS INTERNET IMPLICATIONS

The variety of urban dimensions into which the Internet has been disseminated so far, and those into which it will be disseminated in the near future are presented in Table 10.1. Side by side with the extensive spread of the urban applications of the Internet, the spatial effects or implications of the Internet within the urban arena seem to be more modest. This gap between the wide spectrum of Internet applications currently presented by Internet-based cities, on the one hand, and the still modestly changed spatial organization of these cities, on the other, presents a second phase out of three for the urban impacts of Internet dissemination within cities. Let us discover below these three phases.

In the first phase of Internet/IoT dissemination, relevant for all of urban dimensions, the Internet was mainly used as an advanced and rather comprehensive communications technology. This applies mainly, but not only, to individuals and companies adopting the Internet as of 1995 until the early 2000s. The Internet by then was accessed mainly through fixed PCs, operating prior to the introduction of broadband. Thus, communications through email and information gathering through the Web were largely separated from each other. In its communications function, the rather multimodal Internet communications technology has followed the nineteenth-century traditional, and merely vocal, telephone technology, coupled later by the derived visual fax technology. The

Table 10.1   Internet applications for urban dimensions and their spatial effects

Urban dimension	Internet applications	Spatial effects
Individuals	Facilitation for urban service provision	1. Dual-space society 2. Blurring between home and work 3. Closure of stores and bank branches
Companies	Email; websites; transactions; organizational changes	N/A
Internet technology production	Network; connectivity; navigation; application	Concentration in specific countries and cities
Urban systems (utilities; traffic lights; smart homes)	Remote control	N/A
AVs	V2X	1. Less parking spaces 2. Autonomously mobile city 3. City expansion or concentration?

telephone technologies have assisted and accompanied the spatial expansion of cities, which has been brought about mainly by cars (Kellerman 2006, 2012). As an advanced communications technology, the Internet has expanded and enhanced communications for individuals and companies alike, and has facilitated remote controlling via IoT for urban utilities and other systems. Thus, the aggregate urban spatial effects at this phase were modest.

At a second phase, the Internet has been used in a wider functionality, in its offering of integrated communications and informational applications. This integration of the Internet communications and information functions has been celebrated mainly with broadband transmissions, and notably through the introduction and adoption of smartphones, equipped with both mobile broadband and Wi-Fi Internet access, coupled with apps, which have facilitated a growing variety of activities to be pursued over smartphones. Thus, it has become possible for businesses to construct financial exchanges with their clients over the Internet, side by side with the even more extensive and striking informational online services offered by the Internet to individuals. Hence, the Internet has, in its second phase, turned into an alternative for physical urban space, and as such, the Internet has become a competitor for urban services, which we noted in the previous chapter.

A decade later, in the second decade of the twenty-first century, the combined use of the Internet as a communications and information technology in its current fully mobile options has brought about early signs of urban spatial change, in the form of store and bank closures. This trend may expand with the growth in the performance of Internet service activities by individuals, coupled with still unforeseen uses for the vacating urban physical facilities. This second decade of the twenty-first century has witnessed also a growing integration of IoT and smartphone technologies, so that smartphones have offered smart home applications, thus providing assistance to urbanites in the management of their households, as we mentioned in the previous chapter. Smartphones obviously assist human life in numerous other ways, with leading examples being fast written communications among people and groups, and road navigation.

In the third phase of the urban dissemination of the Internet, which will begin with the upcoming introduction of AVs, the Internet/IoT communications and information technologies will be installed in AVs, as well as in urban transportation infrastructures. However, the Internet is not going to constitute the only major technology for the workings of AVs, as it will function in AVs in combination with additional powerful technologies, notably artificial intelligence, jointly making possible the operation of autonomous driverless cars. This combination of Internet features with additional advanced digital technologies may bring about vast changes in the spatial organization of cities, first in its transport landscape, and later in a possible expansion, or alternatively, re-concentration of cities. This combination of powerful technologies will further substitute human driving, in addition to the roles of the Internet per se as offering an alternative to urban services, side by side with its provision of assistance in household management.

Generally then, at phase one of Internet adoption, with the Internet functioning mainly as a communications system, and following the existing telephony, the Internet has not brought about some significant urban spatial change, but it has rather expanded communications and information activities for individuals and companies. At phase two, the informational dimension of the Internet has been integrated with its communications function, being activated powerfully through smartphones. Thus, the Internet offered, in this second phase, a platform for urban service provision, and eventually spatial change has become evident through a closure of urban services in cities. Finally, and in an upcoming third phase, the combination of the Internet with artificial intelligence for the introduction of AVs may bring about, at least potentially, some major urban transitions, turning cities into autonomously mobile ones.

The Internet has been developed into a most comprehensive and flexible communications technology, side by side with it becoming an ultimate information technology, permitting the manipulation of all information modes. These two abilities or elements of the Internet have become fully integrated with each other, and they have further been applied for device communications. From an urban perspective, as we noted, the spatial outcomes of these joint powerful dimensions of communications and information are only now beginning to emerge, and they may reach full maturity only once cars become widely driverless. Once this occurs it is possible to portray some elements for the future and resulting mobility landscapes of cities, but it is still unclear how fully Internet-based cities will be structured. It is still questionable whether fully Internet-based cities will expand, or alternatively, if they will rather shrink spatially. In addition, only time will tell whether transitions in urban land-uses in the fully Internet-based city will be immense or just marginal.

Castells (2000) identified and developed, at the time, the notion of 'network society', consisting mainly of business ties among elite societal segments in cities globally. This rather segmented network society was based mainly on the 'space of flows' among cities. It seems that, following the adoption of AVs, cities will turn fully into spaces of flows, and this time mainly as far as flows of information within cities, rather than among them. However, in the ways that these intra-city spaces of flows have developed so far, these spaces are and will be composed of several, and rather separate, spaces of flows, including spaces of flows for people, for urban systems, and for cars. It is tempting to speculate on a future united Internet/IoT network to emerge for all of these elements within given metropolitan areas. However, as we noted already in the previous chapter, such a unified Internet system can turn out as being risky and potentially damaging for the continued operations of cities, as well as for the well-being of urbanites.

References

Adams, C. and Warf, B. (1997), 'Introduction: cyberspace and geographical space', *The Geographical Review*, 87, 139–145.

Agar, J. (2003), *Constant Touch: A Global History of the Mobile Phone*, Cambridge: Revolutions in Science.

Alessandrini, A., Alfonsi, R., Delle Site, P., and Stam, D. (2014), 'Users' preferences towards automated road public transport: results from European surveys', *Transportation Research Procedia*, 3, 139–144.

Alessandrini, A., Campagna, A., Delle Site, P., and Filippe, F. (2015), 'Automated vehicles and the rethinking of mobility and cities', *Transportation Research Procedia*, 5, 145–160.

Alessandrini, A., Delle Site, P., Gatta, V., Marcucci, E., and Zhang, Q. (2016), 'Investigating users' attitudes towards conventional and automated buses in twelve European cities', *International Journal of Transportation Economics*, 63, 413–436.

Allen, J. (1999), 'Worlds within cities', in D. Massey, J. Allen, and S. Pile (eds), *City Worlds*, London: Routledge, pp. 53–98.

American Printing History Association (2012), History of printing timeline, accessed 28 February 2018 at https://printinghistory.org/timeline/.

Aristotle. *Politics*, Jowett, B. (trans), accessed 30 April 2018 at http://classics.mit.edu/Aristotle/politics.html.

Ariunaa, L. (2006), 'Mongolia: mobilizing communities for participation in e-government initiatives for the poor and marginalized', *Regional Development Dialogue*, 27, 140–151.

Ash, J., Kitchin, R., and Leszczynski, A. (2018), 'Digital turn, digital geographies?', *Progress in Human Geography*, 42, 25–43.

Ashton, K. (2009), The 'Internet of Things' thing, *RFID Journal*, accessed 18 March 2018 at http://www.rfidjournal.com/articles/view?4986.

Atkinson, J., Black, R., and Curtis, A. (2008), 'Exploring the digital divide in an Australian regional city: a case study of Albury', *Australian Geographer*, 39, 479–493.

Atzori, L., Iera, A., and Morabito, G. (2017), 'Understanding the Internet of Things: definition, potentials, and societal role of a fast evolving paradigm', *Ad Hoc Networks*, 56, 122–140.

Augé, M. (2000), *Non-Places: Introduction to an Anthropology of Supermodernity*, J. Howe (trans), London: Verso.

Bachmair, B. (1991), 'From the motor-car to television: cultural-historical arguments on the meaning of mobility for communication', *Media, Culture and Society*, 13, 521–533.

Balta-Ozkan, N., Davidson, R., Bicket, M., and Whitmarsh, L. (2013), 'Social barriers to the adoption of smart homes', *Energy Policy*, 63, 363–374.

Bansal, P. and Kockelman, K.M. (2017), 'Forecasting Americans' long-term adoption of connected autonomous vehicle technologies', *Transportation Research A*, 95, 49–63.

Barlow, J.P. (1994), The economy of ideas, *Wired*, accessed 12 March 2018 at https://www.wired.com/1994/03/economy-ideas/.

Barnouw, E. (1968), *The Golden Web: The History of Broadcasting in the United States*, Vol. 2: 1933–1953, New York: Oxford University Press.

Barry, K. (2010), Lag in intelligent transportation could hurt economy, *Wired*, accessed 19 June 2018 at https://www.wired.com/2010/02/us-lags-asia-in-its/.

Baskerville, P. (2018), The coffee timeline, *Quora*, accessed 28 February 2018 at https://espressocoffee.quora.com/The-Coffee-Timeline.

Batty, M. (1997), 'Virtual geography', *Futures*, 29, 337–352.

Batty, M. (2017), The age of the smart city, accessed 12 June 2018 at http://www.spatialcomplexity.info/archives/3295.

Bedi, G., Venayagamoorthy, G.K., Singh, R., Brooks, R.R., and Wang, K-C. (2018), 'Review of Internet of Things (IoT) in electric power and energy systems', *IEEE Internet of Things Journal*, 5, 847–870.

Bell, D. (1976), *The Coming of Post-industrial Society: A Venture in Social Forecasting*, second edition, New York: Basic Books.

Bellamy, D. and Pravica, L. (2011), 'Assessing the impact of driverless haul trucks in Australian surface mining', *Resources Policy*, 36, 149–158.

Benedikt, M. (1991), 'Cyberspace: some proposals', in M. Benedikt (ed.), *Cyberspace: First Steps*, Cambridge, MA: MIT Press, pp. 119–224.

Benkler, Y. (2006), *The Wealth of Networks: How Social Production Transforms Markets and Freedom*, New Haven: Yale University Press.

Bertoncello, M. and Wee, D. (2015), Ten ways autonomous driving could redefine the automotive world, *McKinsey & Company*, accessed 26 June 2018 at http://www.mckinsey.com/industries/automotive-and-assembly/our-insights/ten-ways-autonomous-driving-could-redefine-the-automotive-world.

Bibri, S.E. and Krogstie, J. (2017), 'Smart sustainable cities of the future: an extensive interdisciplinary literature review', *Sustainable Cities and Society*, 31, 183–212.

Birtchnell, T. (2017), 'Drones in human geography', in B. Warf (ed.), *Handbook on Geographies of Technology*, Cheltenham, UK and Northampton, MA, USA: Edward Elgar Publishing, pp. 231–241.

Bkav (2015), 1.4 millions of routers worldwide vulnerable to pet hole, accessed 3 June 2018 at https://www.bkav.com/documents/10180/48032/FullResearch _1.4percent20Millionpercent20Routerspercent20Vulnerablepercent20 topercent20Petpercent20Hole.pdf.

Boden, D. and Molotch, H.L. (1994), 'The compulsion of proximity', in R. Friedland and D. Boden (eds), *NowHere Space, Time and Modernity*, Berkeley: University of California Press, pp. 257–286.

Böhm, S., Jones, C., Land, C., and Paterson, M. (2006), 'Introduction: impossibilities of automobility', *Sociological Review*, 54, 3–16.

Boisot, M.H. (1998), *Knowledge Assets: Securing Competitive Advantage in the Information Economy*, Oxford: Oxford University Press.

Boltanski, L. and Chiapello, È. (2007), *The New Spirit of Capitalism*, G. Elliot (trans), London and New York: Verso.

Bolter, J.D. and Grusin, R. (1999), *Remediation: Understanding New Media*, Cambridge, MA: MIT Press.

Bonnefon, J-F., Shariff, A., and Rahwad, I. (2016), 'The social dilemma of autonomous vehicles', *Science*, 352, 1573–1576.

boyd, d.m. and Ellison, N.B. (2007), 'Social networking sites: definition, history, and scholarship', *Journal of Computer-Mediated Communication*, 13, accessed 1 May 2018 at https://academic.oup.com/jcmc/article/13/1/ 210/4583062.

Braman, S. (1989), 'Defining information: an approach for policymakers', *Telecommunications Policy*, 13, 233–242.

Breen, G-M. and Matusitz, J. (2010), 'An evolutionary examination of E-health: a health and computer-mediated communication perspective', *Social Work in Public Health*, 25, 59–71.

Breton, G. and Lambert, M. (eds) (2003), *Universities and Globalization: Private Linkages, Public Trust*, Paris: UNESCO and Université Laval.

Bruns, A. (2008), *Blogs, Wikipedia, Second Life, and Beyond: From Production to Produsage*, New York: Peter Lang.

Buda, N., Eliassen, F-E., and Szende, K. (eds) (2011), *Towns and Communication*, Vol. 1, Akron: University of Akron Press.

Burrows, A., Coyle, D., and Gooberman-Hill, R. (2018), 'Privacy, boundaries and smart homes for health: an ethnographic study', *Health and Place*, 50, 112–118.

Cai, G., Hirtle, S., and Williams, J. (1999), 'Mapping the geography of cyberspace using telecommunications infrastructure information', The First International Workshop on TeleGeoprocessing, accessed 7 May 2018 at https://

pdfs.semanticscholar.org/dc5c/d14f13622764a806ba50344c0d869b285fb4
.pdf.

Cairncross, F. (1997), *The Death of Distance: How the Communications Revolution Will Change Our Lives*, Boston: Harvard Business School Press.

Caribou Digital (2016), *Winners and Losers in the Global App Economy*, Farnham, UK: Caribou Digital Publishing, accessed 6 June 2018 at http://cariboudigital.net/wp-content/uploads/2016/02/Caribou-Digital-Winners-and-Losers-in-the-Global-App-Economy-2016.pdf.

Casper, S. and Glimstedt, H. (2001), 'Economic organization, innovation systems, and the Internet', *Oxford Review of Economic Policy*, 17, 265–281.

Castells, M. (2000), *The Rise of the Network Society*, second edition, Oxford: Blackwell.

Castells, M. (2009), *Communication Power*, Oxford: Oxford University Press.

Castells, M., Fernánddez-Ardèvol, M., Qiu, J.L., and Sey, A. (2007), *Mobile Communication and Society: A Global Perspective*, Cambridge, MA: MIT Press.

Chadwick, A. and May, C. (2003), 'Interaction between states and citizens in the age of the Internet: "E-government" in the United States, Britain and the European Union', *Governance*, 16, 271–300.

Cheong, T.Y., Sulaiman, A., and Parveen, F. (2009), 'Internet adoption among Malaysian companies', *Journal of Asia-Pacific Business*, 10, 166–185.

China Internet Watch (2018), Whitepaper: China Internet Statistics 2017, accessed 22 April 2018 at https://www.chinainternetwatch.com/whitepaper/china-internet-statistics/.

Choi, J.K. and Ji, Y.G. (2015), 'Investigating the importance of trust on adopting an autonomous vehicle', *International Journal of Human-Computer Interaction*, 31, 692–702.

Christie, D., Koymans, A., Chanard, T., Lasgiuttes, J-M., and Kaufmann, V. (2016), 'Pioneering driverless electric vehicles in Europe: the city automated transport system (CATS)', *Transportation Research Procedia*, 13, 30–39.

Chu, Y-W. and Tang, J.T.H. (2005), 'The Internet and civil society: environmental and labour organizations in Hong Kong', *International Journal of Urban and Regional Research*, 29, 849–866.

Cision (2017), Global and China optical fiber preform market 2017–2021 featuring 13 global and Chinese optical fiber preform enterprises, accessed 3 June 2018 at https://www.prnewswire.com/news-releases/global-and-china-optical-fiber-preform-market-2017-2021-featuring-13-global-and-chinese-optical-fiber-preform-enterprises-300533211.html.

City of Columbus (2017), SmartColumbus, accessed 27 June 2018 at https://www.columbus.gov/smartcolumbus/.

Clark, D. and Kang, C. (2018), 'Why companies and countries are battling for ascendancy in 5G', *New York Times*, 6 March, accessed 13 October 2018 at https://www.nytimes.com/2018/03/06/technology/companies-countries -battling-5g.html.

Clarke, K. and Preece, D. (2005), 'Constructing and using a company Intranet: "It's a very cultural thing"', *New Technology, Work and Employment*, 20, 150–165.

Claudel, M. and Ratti, C. (2015), Full speed ahead: How the driverless car could transform cities, *McKinsey & Company*, accessed 26 June 2018 at http://www.mckinsey.com/business-functions/sustainability-and-resource -productivity/our-insights/full-speed-ahead-how-the-driverless-car-could -transform-cities.

Coe, L. (2006), *Wireless Radio: A Brief History*, Jefferson: MacFarland.

Colding, J., Colding, M., and Barthel, S. (2018), 'The smart city model: a new panacea for urban sustainability or unmanageable complexity?', *Environment and Planning B: Urban Analytics and City Science*, DOI: 10.1177/2399808318763164.

Colombo, M.G., Croce, A., and Grilli, L. (2013), 'ICT services and small businesses' productivity gains: an analysis of the adoption of broadband Internet technology', *Information Economics and Policy*, 25, 171–189.

Comer, J.C. and Wikle, T.A. (2008), 'Worldwide diffusion of the cellular telephone, 1995–2005', *The Professional Geographer*, 60, 252–269.

Coresight Research (2018), What retail apocalypse? Reviewing trends in the US brick-and-mortar retail, accessed 4 July 2018 at https://www .fungglobalretailtech.com/research/retail-apocalypse-reviewing-trends-us -brick-mortar-retail/.

Correia, C.H. and van Arem, B. (2016), 'Solving the user optimum privately owned automated vehicles assignment problem (UO-POAVAP): a model to explore the impacts of self-driving vehicles on urban mobility', *Transportation Research B*, 87, 64–88.

Couclelis, H. (1998), 'Worlds of Information: the geographic metaphor in the visualization of complex information', *Cartography and Geographic Information Systems*, 25, 209–220.

Couclelis, H. (2004), 'Pizza over the Internet: e-commerce, the fragmentation of activity and the tyranny of the region', *Entrepreneurship and Regional Development*, 16, 41–54.

Coursera (2018), Take the world's best course, online, accessed 26 April 2018 at https://www.coursera.org/.

Crampton, J.W. (2009), 'Cartography: maps 2.0', *Progress in Human Geography*, 33, 91–100.

Crampton, J.W. (2014), 'New spatial media', *Open Geography* (2014), accessed 7 May 2018 at https://opengeography.wordpress.com/2014/06/06/new-spatial-media/.

Crang, M., Crang, P., and May, J. (1999), 'Introduction', in M. Crang, P. Crang, and J. May (eds), *Virtual Geographies: Bodies, Space and Relations*, London: Routledge, pp. 1–13.

Crang, M., Crosbie, T., and Graham, S. (2006), 'Variable geometries of connection: urban digital divides and the uses of information technology', *Urban Studies*, 43, 2551–2570.

Crang, M. and Graham, S. (2007), 'Sentient cities: ambient intelligence and the politics', *Information, Communication and Society*, 10, 789–817.

Credit Suisse (2018), 2017 online travel primer, accessed 25 April 2018 at https://www.credit-suisse.com/media/assets/microsite/docs/events/2017/private-internet-company-summit/cs-2017-online-travel-primer.pdf.

Crutcher, M. and Zook, M. (2009), 'Placemarks and waterlines: racialized cyberscapes in post-Katrina Google Earth', *Geoforum*, 40, 523–534.

Curry, M.R. (2000), 'The power to be silent: testimony, identity, and the place of place', *Historical Geography*, 28, 13–24.

Dadashpoor, H. and Yousefi, Z. (2018), 'Centralization or decentralization? A review on the effects of information and communication technology on urban spatial structure', *Cities*, 78, 194–205.

Davis, F.D. (1989), 'Perceived usefulness, perceived ease of use and user acceptance of information technology', *MIS Quarterly*, 13, 319–340.

Davis, J. (2010), 'Architecture of the personal interactive homepage: constructing the self through MySpace', *New Media and Society*, 12, 1103–1119.

DeGroat, B. (2016), Vehicle automation: most drivers still want to retain at least some control, *Michigan News University of Michigan*, accessed 26 June 2018 at https://news.umich.edu/vehicle-automation-most-drivers-still-want-to-retain-at-least-some-control/.

Delle Site, P., Fillip, F., and Giustiniani, G. (2011), 'Users' preferences towards innovative and conventional public transport', *Procedia – Social and Behavioural Sciences*, 20, 906–915.

Desjardins, J. (2018), Timeline: the history of the industrial Internet of Things, Visual Capitalist, accessed 21 March 2018 at http://www.visualcapitalist.com/timeline-industrial-internet-things/.

de Souza e Silva, A. (2006), 'From cyber to hybrid: mobile technologies as interfaces of hybrid systems', *Space and Culture*, 9, 261–278.

de Souza e Silva, A. and Frith, J. (2012), *Mobile Interfaces in Public Spaces: Locational Privacy, Control, and Urban Sociability*, London: Routledge.

de Vivo, F. (2007), *Information and Communication in Venice: Rethinking Early Modern Politics*, Oxford: Oxford University Press.

Ding, Y. and Lu, H. (2017), 'The interactions between online shopping and personal activity travel behavior: an analysis with a GPS-based activity travel diary', *Transportation*, 44, 311–324.

Dodge, M. and Kitchin, R. (2001), *Mapping Cyberspace*, London: Routledge.

Dodge, M. and Kitchin, R. (2005), 'Code and the transduction of space', *Annals of the Association of American Geographers*, 95, 162–180.

Dovbysh, O. (2013), The peculiarities of using digital technologies in rural areas in Russia, Paper presented at the World Social Sciences Forum, Montreal.

Drucker, S. (2005), 'Urban and suburban communication in the digital age', *Hofstra Horizons*, Fall, 10–13.

Dustdar, S., Nastić, S., and Šćekić, O. (2017), *Smart Cities: The Internet of Things, People and Systems*, Cham: Springer.

EBF (European Banking Federation) (2017), Banking in Europe: EBF publishes 2017 facts and figures, accessed 4 July 2018 at https://www.ebf .eu/regulation-supervision/banking-in-europe-ebf-publishes-2017-facts -figures/.

Electronics Notes (2018), Milestones in radio technology, accessed 7 March 2018 at https://www.electronics-notes.com/articles/history/radio-receivers/ radio-history-timeline.php.

Endsley, M.R. (1996), 'Automation and situation awareness', in R. Parasuraman and M. Mouloua (eds), *Automation and Human Performance: Theory and Applications*, Mahwah, NJ: Lawrence Erlbaum, pp. 163–181.

Ettlinger, O. (2008), *The Architecture of Virtual Space*, Ljubljana: University of Ljubljana.

Eurostat (2018), Individuals – Internet activities, accessed 22 April 2018 at http://ec.europa.eu/eurostat/en/web/products-datasets/-/ISOC_CI_AC_I.

Evans, D. (2012), The Internet of Everything: How more relevant and valuable connections will change the world, Cisco IBSG (Internet Business Solutions Group), accessed 2 July 2018 at https://www.cisco.com/c/dam/global/en _my/assets/ciscoinnovate/pdfs/IoE.pdf.

Fagnant, D.J. and Kockelman, K. (2014), 'The travel and environmental implications of shared autonomous vehicles, using agent-based model scenario', *Transportation Research C*, 40, 1–13.

Fagnant, D.J. and Kockelman, K. (2015), 'Preparing a nation for autonomous vehicles: opportunities, barriers and policy recommendations', *Transportation Research Part A*, 77, 167–181.

Fagnant, D.J., Kockelman, K., and Bansal, P. (2015), 'Operations of shared autonomous vehicle fleet for the Austin, Texas market', Proceedings of the TRB 94th annual meeting, accessed 27 June 2018 at http://www.caee.utexas .edu/prof/kockelman/public_html/TRB15SAVsinAustin.pdf.

Färber, B. (2016), 'Communication and communication problems between autonomous vehicles and human drivers', in M. Maurer, J.C. Gerdes, B. Lenz, and H. Winner (eds), *Autonomous Driving: Technical, Legal and Social Aspects*, Berlin: Springer Open, pp. 125–144.

Farman, J. (2012), *Mobile Interface Theory: Embodied Space and Locative Media*, New York: Routledge.

Feldman, M.P. (1994), *The Geography of Innovation*, Dordrecht: Kluwer.

Feldman, M.P. (2000), 'Location and innovation: the new economic geography of innovation, spillovers, and agglomeration', in G.L. Clark, M.P. Feldman, and M.S. Gertler (eds), *The Oxford Handbook of Economic Geography*, New York: Oxford University Press, pp. 373–394.

Felstead, A., Jewson, N., and Walters, S. (2005), *Changing Places of Work*, Basingstoke: Palgrave Macmillan.

Fischer, C.S. (1992), *America Calling: A Social History of the Telephone to 1940*, Berkeley: University of California Press.

Flexjobs (2017), The 2017 state of telecommuting in the US employee force, accessed 17 April 2018 at https://www.flexjobs.com/2017-State-of -Telecommuting-US/.

Foros, Ø. and Hansen, Ø. (2001), 'Competition and compatibility among Internet Service Providers', *Information Economics and Policy*, 13, 411–425.

Fraedrich, E. and Lenz, B. (2016), 'Societal and individual acceptance of autonomous driving', in M. Maurer, J.C. Gerdes, B. Lenz, and H. Winner (eds), *Autonomous Driving: Technical, Legal and Social Aspects*, Berlin: Springer Open, pp. 621–640.

Friedman, M. (2003), *Autonomy, Gender, Politics*, New York: Oxford University Press.

Geels, F.W. (2005), *Technological Transitions and System Innovations*, Cheltenham, UK and Northampton, MA, USA: Edward Edgar Publishing.

Gerdes, J.C. and Thornton, S.M. (2016), 'Implementable ethics for autonomous vehicles', in M. Maurer, J.C. Gerdes, B. Lenz, and H. Winner (eds), *Autonomous Driving: Technical, Legal and Social Aspects*, Berlin: Springer Open, pp. 87–102.

Geuss, M. (2016), Audi's new traffic light countdown seems basic, but it's a big step for autonomy, *Ars Technica*, accessed 19 June 2018 at http:// arstechnica.com/cars/2016/12/in-las-vegas-audis-now-talk-to-traffic-lights -so-you-can-count-down-to-green/.

Ghazizadeh, M., Lee, J.D., and Boyle, L.N. (2012), 'Extending the technology acceptance model to assess automation', *Cognition, Technology and Work*, 14, 39–49.

Gibson, D.V., Kozmetsky, G., and Smilor, R.V. (1992), *The Technopolis Phenomenon: Smart Cities, Fast Systems, Global Networks*, Lanham: Rowman and Littlefield.

Giddens, A. (1984), *The Constitution of Society: Outline of the Theory of Structuration*, Cambridge: Polity Press.

Giddens, A. (1990), *The Consequences of Modernity*, Cambridge: Polity Press.

Gilbert, M.R. and Masucci, M. (2011), *Information and Communication Technology Geographies: Strategies for Bridging a Digital Divide*, Vancouver: Praxis (e) Press.

Goby, V. (2003), 'Physical space and cyberspace: how do they interrelate? A study of offline and online social interaction choice in Singapore', *CyberPsychology and Behavior*, 6, 639–644.

Goodman, J. (2016), Autonomous cars will reshape residential communities, Builder, accessed 27 June 2018 at http://www.builderonline.com/land/planning/autonomous-cars-will-reshape-residential-communities_o.

Gopal, S. (2007), 'The evolving social geography of blogs', in H.J. Miller (ed.), *Societies and Cities in the Age of Instant Access*, Dordrecht: Springer, pp. 275–293.

Gould, C.J. (2001), The highways agency ramp metering pilot scheme, Association for European Transport, accessed 19 June 2018 at http://www.abstracts.aetransport.org/paper/download/id/1306.

Graham, M. (2003), 'Geography/Internet: ethereal alternate dimensions of cyberspace or grounded augmented realities?', *The Geographic Journal*, 179, 177–182.

Graham, S. (1998a), 'The end of geography or the explosion of place? Conceptualizing space, place and information technology', *Progress in Human Geography*, 22, 165–185.

Graham, S. (1998b), 'Spaces of surveillant-simulation: new technologies, digital representations, and material geographies', *Environment and Planning D: Society and Space*, 16, 483–504.

Graham, S. and Marvin, S. (1996), *Telecommunications and the City*, London and New York: Routledge.

Graham, S. and Marvin, S. (2001), *Splintering Urbanism: Networked Infrastructures, Technological Mobilities and the Urban Condition*, London: Routledge.

Greatest Achievements (2018), Radio & television timeline, accessed 7 March 2018 at http://www.greatachievements.org/?id=3659.

Greenfield, A. (2006), *Everyware: The Dawning Age of Ubiquitous Computing*, Boston: New Rides.

Greguras, F. (2018), Water and the Internet of Things: 2018, Water Online, accessed 17 June 2018 at https://www.wateronline.com/doc/water-and-the-internet-of-things-0003.

Griffiths, F., Cave, J., Boardman, F., Justin, R., Pawlikowska, T., Ball, R., Clarke, A., and Cohen, A. (2012), 'Social networks – the future for health care delivery', *Social Science and Medicine*, 75, 2233–2241.

Grosz, E. (2001), *Architecture from the Outside: Essays on Virtual and Physical Space*, Cambridge, MA: MIT Press.

Guerra, E. (2015), 'When autonomous cars take to the road', *Planning*, 81, 36–38.

Gulić, M., Olivares, R., and Borrajo, D. (2016), 'Using automated planning for traffic signals control', *Promet – Traffic – Traffico*, 28, 383–391.

Haboucha, C.J., Ishaq, R., and Shiftan, Y. (2017), 'User preferences regarding autonomous vehicles', *Transportation Research C*, 78, 37–49.

Häkli, J. and Paasi, A. (2003), 'Geography, space and identity', in J. Öhman and K. Simonsen (eds), *Voices from the North: New Trends in Nordic Human Geography*, Aldershot, UK: Ashgate Publishing, pp. 141–155.

Halford, S. (2005), 'Hybrid workspace: re-spatialisations of work, organisation and management', *New Technology, Work and Employment*, 20, 19–33.

Hall, S. (1996), 'Who needs identity?, in S. Hall and P. du Gay (eds), *Questions of Cultural Identity*, London: Sage, pp. 1–17.

Hannam, K. (2017), A record amount of brick and mortar stores will close in 2017, Fortune, accessed 4 July 2018 at http://fortune.com/2017/10/26/a-record-amount-of-brick-and-mortar-stores-will-close-in-2017/.

Hargittai, E. (1999), 'Weaving the Western web: explaining differences in Internet connectivity among OECD countries', *Telecommunications Policy*, 23, 701–718.

Harris, R. (1998), 'The Internet as a GPT: factor market implications', in E. Helpman (ed.), *General Purpose Technologies and Economic Growth*, Cambridge, MA: MIT Press, pp. 140–165.

Harvard University (2018), History, accessed 28 February 2018 at https://www.harvard.edu/about-harvard/harvard-glance/history.

Harvey, D. (1989), *The Coming of Postmodernity*, Oxford: Blackwell.

Hassa, S. (2012), 'Projecting, exposing, revealing self in the digital world: usernames as a social practice in a Moroccan chatroom', *Names*, 60, 201–209.

Heinrichs, D. (2016), 'Autonomous driving and urban land use', in M. Maurer, J.C. Gerdes, B. Lenz, and H. Winner (eds), *Autonomous Driving: Technical, Legal and Social Aspects*, Berlin: Springer Open, pp. 213–231.

Heinrichs, D. and Cyganski, R. (2015), 'Automated driving: how it could enter our cities and how this might affect our mobility decisions', *disP Service*, 51, 74–79.

Herring, S.C., Scheidt, L.A., Wright, E., and Bonus, S. (2005), 'Weblogs as bridging genre', *Information, Technology and People*, 18, 142–171.

Hill, D. (2014), 'Researchers have high hopes for drone use in transportation', *Civil Engineering*, 84, 38–39.

Hislop, D. and Axtell, C. (2007), 'The neglect of spatial mobility in contemporary studies of work: the case of telework', *New Technology, Work and Employment*, 22, 34–51.

Hochheiser, S. (2015), Electromechanical telephone switching, *Engineering and Technology History*, accessed 5 March 2018 at http://ethw.org/Electromechanical_Telephone-Switching.

Hodgetts, T. (2018), 'Connectivity as a multiple: in, with and as "nature"', *Area*, 50, 83–90.

Hollands, R.G. (2008), 'Will the real smart city please stand up?', *City*, 12, 303–320.

Holloway, S.L. and Valentine, G. (2000), 'Spatiality and the new social studies of childhood', *Sociology*, 34, 763–783.

Hongladarom, S. (2011), 'Personal identity and the self in the online and offline world', *Minds and Machines*, 21, 533–548.

Huh, W-k. (2006), 'A geography of virtual universities in Korea', Paper presented at the Annual Meeting of the IGU Commission on the Geography of the Information Society, Sydney.

Internet World Stats (2018), Facebook users in the world 2017, accessed 1 May 2018 at https://www.internetworldstats.com/facebook.htm.

ITF (International Transport Forum) (2015), Urban mobility system upgrade: how shared self-driving cars could change city traffic, accessed 27 June 2018 at http://www.itf-oecd.org/sites/default/files/docs/15cpb_self-drivingcars.pdf.

ITU (International Telecommunication Union) (2018), *Statistics*, accessed 5 March 2018 at https://www.itu.int/en/ITU-D/Statistics/Pages/stat/default.aspx.

Jacobs, J. (2018), The history of flat screen TV, Techwalla, accessed 11 March 2018 at https://www.techwalla.com/articles/the-history-of-flat-screen-tv.

Jacobs, W., Amuta, A.O., and Jeon, K.C. (2017), 'Health information seeking in the digital age: an analysis of health information seeking behavior among US adults', *Cogent Social Sciences*, 3, 1–11.

James, J. (2003), 'Sustainable Internet access for the rural poor? Elements of an emerging Indian model', *Futures*, 35, 461–472.

Jones, B.W., Spigel, B., and Malecki, E.J. (2010), 'Blog links as pipelines to buzz elsewhere: the case of New York theater blogs', *Environment and Planning B: Planning and Design*, 37, 99–111.

Katrakazas, C., Quddus, M., Chen, W-H., and Deka, L. (2015), 'Real-time motion planning methods for autonomous on-road driving: state-of-the-art and future research directions', *Transportation Research Part C*, 60, 416–442.

Kaufmann, V. (2002), *Re-thinking Mobility: Contemporary Sociology*, Aldershot: Ashgate Publishing.

Kellerman, A. (1984), 'Telecommunications and the geography of metropolitan areas', *Progress in Human Geography*, 8, 222–246.

Kellerman, A. (1993), *Telecommunications and Geography*, London: Belhaven Pinter; New York: Halsted.

Kellerman, A. (1999), 'Leading nations in the adoption of communications media 1975–1995', *Urban Geography*, 20, 377–389.

Kellerman, A. (2000), 'Phases in the rise of information society', *Info*, 2, 537–541.

Kellerman, A. (2002), *The Internet on Earth: A Geography of Information*, London and New York: John Wiley.

Kellerman, A. (2006), *Personal Mobilities*, London and New York: Routledge.

Kellerman, A. (2007), 'Cyberspace classification and cognition: information and communications cyberspaces', *Journal of Urban Technology*, 14, 5–32.

Kellerman, A. (2009), 'End of spatial reorganization?: Urban landscapes of personal mobilities in the information age', *Journal of Urban Technology*, 16, 47–61.

Kellerman, A. (2012), *Daily Spatial Mobilities: Physical and Virtual*, Farnham, UK: Ashgate Publishing.

Kellerman, A. (2014), *The Internet as Second Action Space*, London and New York: Routledge.

Kellerman, A. (2016), *Geographic Interpretations of the Internet*, Dordrecht: Springer.

Kellerman, A. (2018a), *Automated and Autonomous Spatial Mobilities*, Cheltenham, UK and Northampton, MA, USA: Edward Elgar Publishing.

Kellerman, A. (2018b), 'Digitized urban systems and activities: a reexamination', *Environment and Planning B: Urban Analytics and City Science*, 45, DOI: 10.1177/2399808318761397.

Kellerman, A. and Paradiso, M. (2007), 'Geographical location in the information age: from destiny to opportunity?', *GeoJournal*, 70, 195–211.

Kennedy, H. (2006), 'Beyond anonymity, or future directions for Internet identity research', *New Media and Society*, 8, 859–876.

Keough, S.B. (2010), 'The importance of place in community radio broadcasting: a case study of WDVX, Knoxville, Tennessee', *Journal of Cultural Geography*, 27, 77–98.

Killian, M., Zauner, M., and Kozek, M. (2018), 'Comprehensive smart home energy management system using mixed-integer quadratic-programming', *Applied Energy*, 222, 662–672.

Kim, J.E., Barth, T., Boulos, G., Yackovich, J., Beckel, C., and Mosse, D. (2017), 'Seamless integration of heterogeneous devices and access control in smart homes and its evaluation', *Intelligent Buildings International*, 9, 23–39.

Kinsley, S. (2014), 'The matter of "virtual" geographies', *Progress in Human Geography*, 38, 364–384.

Kitchin, R. (2011), 'The programmable city', *Environment and Planning B: Planning and Design*, 38, 945–951.

Kitchin, R. (2014), 'The real-time city? Big data and smart urbanism', *GeoJournal*, 79, 1–14.

Kitchin, R. and Dodge, D. (2011), *Code/Space: Software and Everyday Life*, Cambridge, MA: MIT Press.

Kline, D. (2013), *Technologies of Choice? ICTs, Development, and the Capabilities Approach*, Cambridge, MA: MIT Press.

Kluitenberg, E. (2006), 'The network of waves: Living and acting in a hybrid space', *Open* 11, accessed 13 October 2018 at http://socialbits.org/_data/papers/Kluitenberg%20-%20The%20Network%20of%20Waves.pdf.

Knight, J. (2006), *Higher Education Crossing Borders: A Guide to the Implications of the General Agreement on Trade in Services (GATS) for Cross-border Education*, Vancouver and Paris: Commonwealth of Learning.

Knorr-Cetina, K. and Bruegger, U. (2002), 'Global microstructures: the virtual societies of financial markets', *American Journal of Sociology*, 107, 905–950.

Komninos, N., Pallot, M., and Schaffers, H. (2013), 'Special issue on smart cities and the future Internet in Europe', *Journal of the Knowledge Economy*, 4, 119–134.

Kong, L. (2001), 'Religion and technology: refiguring place, space, identity and community', *Area*, 33, 404–413.

Kopomaa, T. (2000), *The City in Your Pocket: Birth of the Mobile Information Society*, Helsinki: Gaudeamus.

Kosnick, K. (2004), '"Speaking in one's own voice": Representational strategies of Alevi Turkish migrants on open-access television in Berlin', *Journal of Ethnic and Migration Studies*, 30, 979–994.

Kröger, F. (2016), 'Automatic driving in its social, historical and cultural contexts', in M. Maurer, J.C. Gerdes, B. Lenz, and H. Winner (eds), *Autonomous Driving: Technical, Legal and Social Aspects*, Berlin: Springer Open, pp. 41–68.

Kwan, M-P. (2001), 'Cyberspatial cognition and individual access to information: the behavioral foundation of cybergeography', *Environment and Planning B*, 28, 21–37.

Kyriakidis, M., Happee, R., and de Winter, J.C.F. (2015), 'Public opinion on automatic driving: results of an international questionnaire among 5000 respondents', *Transportation Research F*, 32, 127–140.

Lacohée, H., Wakeford, N., and Pearson, I. (2003), 'A social history of the mobile telephone with a view of its future', *BT Technology Journal*, 21, 203–211.

LADOT (Los Angeles Department of Transportation) (2012), Live traffic information – about us, accessed 19 December 2018 at http://trafficinfo .lacity.org/about-atsac.php.

Lakoff, G. and Johnson, M. (1980), *Metaphors We Live By*, Chicago: The University of Chicago Press.

Layne, K. and Lee, J. (2001), 'Developing fully functional e-government: a four-stage model', *Government Information Quarterly*, 18, 122–136.

Lefebvre, H. (1991), *The Production of Space*, D. Nicholson-Smith (trans), Oxford: Basil Blackwell.

Lessig, L. (2001), *The Future of Ideas: The Fate of the Commons in a Connected World*, New York: Random House.

Leszczynski, A. (2015), 'Spatial media/tion', *Progress in Human Geography*, 39, 729–751.

Leszczynski, A. and Elwood, S. (2015), 'Feminist geographies of new spatial media', *The Canadian Geographer*, 59, 12–28.

Li, J., Whalley, F., and Williams, H. (2001), 'Between physical and electronic spaces: the implications for organizations in the networked economy', *Environment and Planning A*, 33, 699–716.

Lin, P. (2016), 'Why ethics matters for autonomous cars', in M. Maurer, J.C. Gerdes, B. Lenz, and H. Winner (eds), *Autonomous Driving: Technical, Legal and Social Aspects*, Berlin: Springer Open, pp. 69–85.

Lindberg, D.C. (2007), *The Beginnings of Western Science*, Chicago: University of Chicago Press.

Lipsey, R., Carlaw, K.I., and Bekar, C.T. (2005), *Economic Transformations: General Purpose Technologies and Long Term Economic Growth*, New York: Oxford University Press.

Litman, T. (2015), Automated vehicle implementation predictions, Victoria Transport Policy Institute, accessed 27 June 2018 at http://www.vtpi.org/ avip.pdf.

Liu, C.I., Jula, H., and Ioannou, P.A. (2002), 'Design, simulation, and evaluation of automated container terminals', *IEEE Transactions on Intelligent Transportation Systems*, 3, 12–26.

Lontoh, S. (2016), What does the Internet of Things mean for the energy sector?, World Economic Forum, accessed 17 June 2018 at https://www .weforum.org/agenda/2016/06/what-does-the-internet-of-things-mean-for -the-energy-sector/.

Loo, B.P.Y. (2012), *The E-Society*, New York: Nova Science Publishers.

Löw, M. (2008), 'The constitution of space: the structuration of spaces through the simultaneity of effect and perception', *European Journal of Social Theory*, 11, 25–49.

Luo, H. (2015), From workplace to anyplace: telework in China – based on a mixed method research, Dissertation submitted to Yokohama National University.

Machlup, F. (1983), 'Semiotic quirks in studies of information', in F. Machlup and U. Mansfield (eds), *The Study of Information: Interdisciplinary Messages*, New York: Wiley, pp. 641–671.

Macpherson, A. (2008), 'Producer service linkage and industrial innovation: results of a twelve year tracking study of New York State manufacturers', *Growth and Change*, 39, 1–23.

Madigan, R., Louw, T., Dziennus, M., Graindorge, T., Ortega, E., Graindorge, M., and Merat, N. (2016), 'Acceptance of automated road transport systems (ARTS): an adaptation of the UTAUT model', *Transportation Research Procedia*, 14, 2217–2226.

Malecki, E.J. and Moriset, B. (2008), *The Digital Economy: Business Organization, Production Processes and Regional Developments*, London and New York: Routledge.

Mandel, M. and Long, E. (2017), *The App Economy in Europe: Leading Countries and Cities, 2017*, Washington DC: PPI (Progressive Policy Institute), accessed 5 June 2018 at http://www.progressivepolicy.org/wp-content/uploads/2017/10/PPI_EuropeAppEconomy_2017 .pdf.

Massey, D. (1993), 'Power-geometry and a progressive sense of place', in J. Bird, B. Curtis, T. Putnam, G. Robertson, and L. Tickner (eds), *Mapping the Futures: Local Cultures, Global Change*, London: Routledge, pp. 59–69.

McCarthy, J. (2017), Survey: 64 percent of patients use a digital device to manage health, Mobihealth News, accessed 29 April 2017 at http://www.mobihealthnews.com/content/survey-64-percent-patients-use-digital-device-manage-health.

McLean, J.E. (2016), 'The contingency of change in the Anthropocene: more-than-real renegotiation of power relations in climate change institutional transformation in Australia', *Environment and Planning D: Society and Space*, 34, 508–527.

McLean, J. and Maalsen, S. (2013), 'Destroying the joint and dying of shame? A geography of revitalized feminism in social media and beyond', *Geographical Research*, 51, 243–256.

McLean, J., Maalsen, S., and Grech, A. (2016), 'Learning about feminism in digital spaces: online methodologies and participatory mapping', *Australian Geographer*, 47, 157–177.

McShane, C. (1999), 'The origins and globalization of traffic control signals', *Journal of Urban History*, 25, 379–404.

Megan & Jessica (2012), Greek theatre timeline, Prezi, accessed 3 March 2018 at https://prezi.com/osszqjnq3nv3/greek-theatre-timeline/.

Mehmood, Y., Ahmad, F., Yaqoob, I., Adnane, A., Imran, M., and Guizani, S. (2017), 'Internet-of-Things-based smart cities: recent advances and challenges', *IEEE Communications Magazine*, September, 16–24.

Merisalo, M., Makkonen, T., and Inkinen, T. (2013), 'Creative and knowledge-intensive teleworkers' relation to e-capital in the Helsinki metropolitan area', *International Journal of Knowledge-Based Development*, 4, 204–220.

Merriam-Webster (2018), Connectivity, accessed 11 March 2018 at https://www.merriam-webster.com/dictionary/connectivity.

Meyrowitz, J. (1985), *No Sense of Place: The Impact of Electronic Media on Social Behavior*, New York: Oxford University Press.

Michel, R. (2017), The evolution of the digital supply chain, *Logistics Management*, accessed 9 February 2018 at http://www.logisticsmgmt.com/article/the_evolution_of_the_digital_supply_chain.

Mitchell, S., Villa, N., Stewart-Weeks, M., and Lange, A. (2013), The Internet of Everything for cities, Cisco, accessed 3 July 2018 at https://www.cisco.com/c/dam/en_us/solutions/industries/docs/gov/everything-for-cities.pdf.

Mitchell, W.J. (1995), *City of Bits: Space, Place, and the Infobahn*, Cambridge, MA: MIT Press.

Mitchell, W.J., Borroni-Bird, C.E., and Burns, L.D. (2010), *Reinventing the Automobile: Personal Urban Mobility for the 21st Century*, Cambridge, MA: MIT Press.

Mobileye (2017), Future of mobility, accessed 26 June 2018 at http://www.mobileye.com/future-of-mobility/.

Mok, D., Wellman, B., and Carrasco, J. (2010), 'Does distance matter in the age of the Internet?', *Urban Studies*, 47, 2747–2783.

Moon, M. (2017), Singapore hosts first full-scale autonomous truck platoon trial, *engadget*, accessed 27 June 2018 at https://www.engadget.com/2017/01/25/singapore-full-scale-autonomous-truck-platooning-trial/.

Moores, S. (2012), *Media, Place and Mobility*, Basingstoke: Palgrave Macmillan.

Moriset, B. and Malecki, E.J. (2009), 'Organization versus space: the paradoxical geographies of the digital economy', *Geography Compass*, 3, 256–274.

Morse, M. (1998), *Virtualities: Television, Media Art, and Cyberculture*, Bloomington: Indiana University Press.

Mossberger, K., Tolbert, C.J., and Franko, W.W. (2013), *Digital Cities: The Internet and the Geography of Opportunity*, New York: Oxford University Press.

Mumford, L. (1961), *The City in History: Its Origins, its Transformations and its Prospects*, New York: Harcourt, Brace & World.

Murray, C.C. and Chu, A.G. (2015), 'The flying sidekick traveling salesman problem: optimization of drone-assisted parcel delivery', *Transportation Research C*, 54, 86–109.

My smart energy (2018), My country, accessed 17 June 2018 at http://my-smart-energy.eu/my-country.

Nambisan, S. and Wang, Y.M. (1999), 'Roadblocks to web technology adoption?', *Communications of the ACM*, 42, 98–101.

Nguyen, J.V. (2002), Introduction to the ISP market, Informit, accessed 3 June 2018 at http://www.informit.com/articles/article.aspx?p=28284.

NLC (National League of Cities) (2016), *Cities and Drones: What Cities Need to Know about Unmanned Aerial Vehicles (UAVs)*, accessed 27 June 2018 at http://uavs.insct.org/wp-content/uploads/2016/09/NLC-Drone-Report.pdf.

Noyman, A., Stibe, A., and Larson, K. (2016), Autonomous cities and the urbanism of the 4th machine age: should AV industry design future cities? Changing Places Research Group, MIT Media Lab, accessed 27 June 2018 at https://pdfs.semanticscholar.org/fa09/f350f79e2a76fcf68415ca803619b5587015.pdf.

NRMA (National Roads and Motorists' Association) Motoring and Services (2014), Parking in the Sydney CBD: An International Comparison, accessed 1 March 2017 at https://www.mynrma.com.au/media/Parking_in_the_Sydney_CBD_An_International_Comparison.pdf.

O'Brian, C. (2017), Robotic buses leapfrog self-driving trucks in autonomy revolution, Trucks.com, accessed 27 June 2018 at https://www.trucks.com/2017/02/27/buses-european-self-driving-vehicle-revolution/.

OECD (Organisation for Economic Co-operation and Development) (2000), *Knowledge Management in the Learning Society*, Paris: Center for Educational Research and Innovation.

OECD (Organisation for Economic Co-operation and Development) Stat (2018), Government at a glance 2017 edition, accessed 22 April 2018 at https://ststs.oecd.org/index.aspx?DataSetCode=GOV.

Office for National Statistics (2014), Record proportion of people in employment are home workers, accessed 17 April 2018 at http://webarchive.nationalarchives.gov.uk/20160105210705/http://www.ons.gov.uk/ons/rel/lmac/characteristics-of-home-workers/2014/sty-home-workers.html.

Ohnemus, M. and Perl, A. (2016), 'Shared autonomous vehicles: catalyst of new mobility for last mile?', *Built Environment*, 42, 589–602.

OLC (Online Learning Consortium) (2016), Report: one in four students enrolled in online course, accessed 29 April 2018 at https://onlinelearningconsortium.org/news_item/report-one-four-students-enrolled-online-courses/.

Oliveira, T. and Martins, M.F.O. (2011), 'Understanding the determinant factors of Internet business solutions adoption: the case of Portuguese firms', *Applied Economic Letters*, 18, 1769–1775.

Open edX (2018), Open edX, accessed 26 April 2018 at https://open.edx.org/.

Oswald, S., Wurhofer, D., Trösterer, S., Beck, E., and Tsheligi, M. (2012), 'Predicting information technology usage in the car: towards a car technology acceptance model', in *Proceedings of the 4th International Conference on Automative User Interfaces and Interactive Vehicular Applications*, ACM, 51–58.

Overby, J.W. and Min, S. (2001), 'International supply chain management in an Internet environment: a network-oriented approach to internationalization', *International Marketing Review*, 18, 392–420.

Pal, S.K., Pandey, G.S., Kesari, A., Choudhuri, G., and Mittal, B. (2002), 'E-health: e-health and hospital of the future', *Journal of Scientific and Industrial Research*, 61, 414–422.

Paradiso, M. (2012), 'Benchmarking the quality of geoweb: information and tacit knowledge about restaurants in three Italian cities', *Tijdschrift voor Economische en Sociale Geografie*, 104, 18–28.

Parasuraman, R. and Manzey, D.H. (2010), 'Complacency and bias in human use of automation: an attentional integration', *Human Factors*, 52, 381–410.

Parasuraman, R. and Riley, V. (1997), 'Humans and automation: use, misuse, disuse, abuse', *Human Factors*, 39, 230–253.

Park, H. (2001), 'Cultural impact on Internet connectivity and its implication', *Journal of Euromarketing*, 10, 5–22.

Peshave, A., Rajenimbalkar, S., Puar, A., Gardare, V., Dodake, A., and Waydande, J. (2015), 'A review on autonomous traffic lights control system', *International Journal of Innovative Research in Computer and Communication Engineering*, 3, 10034–10037.

PewInternet (2013), Health online 2013, accessed 26 April 2018 at http://pewinternet.org/Reports/2013/Health-online.aspx.

Pew Research Center (2018), Internet/Broadband factsheet, accessed 21 March 2018 at http://www.pewinternet.org/fact-sheet/internet-broadband/.

Pick, J.R. and Nishida, T. (2015), 'Digital divides in the world and its regions: a spatial and multivariate analysis of technological utilization', *Technological Forecasting and Social Change*, 91, 1–17.

Pink, S., Ardèvol, E., and Landzeni, D. (2016), *Digital Materialities: Design and Anthropology*, London: Bloomsbury.

Piotrovicz, G. and Robinson, J. (1995), *Ramp Metering Status in North America: 1995 Update*, DOT-T-95-17, Washington DC: US Department of Transportation, accessed 19 June 2018 at https://rosap.ntl.bts.gov/view/dot/2703.

Polsson, K. (2017), Chronology of television, accessed 10 March 2018 at http://worldtimeline.info/television/.

Pon, B. (2015), 'Locating digital production: how platforms shape participation in the global app economy', Paper presented at the AAG 2015 Workshop on

Geographies of Production in Digital Economies of Low-Income Countries, accessed 5 June 2018 at http://cariboudigital.net/wp-content/uploads/2015/04/Pon-AAG-Platforms-and-app-economy.pdf.

Poon, L. (2016), Meet the high-tech buses of tomorrow, *Citylab*, accessed 27 June 2018 at http://www.citylab.com/tech/2016/12/meet-the-high-tech-buses-of-tomorrow/509417/.

Pósfai, M. and Féjer, A. (2008), 'The eHungary programme 2.0', *Innovation*, 21, 407–415.

Postman, N. (1999), *Building a Bridge to the Eighteenth Century*, New York: Alfred A. Knopf.

Postscapes (2018), Internet of Things (IoT) History, accessed 17 March 2018 at https://www.postscapes.com/internet-of-things-history/.

PRI (2012), Scandinavian countries are attractive sites for 'server farms', accessed 3 June 2018 at https://www.pri.org/stories/2012-06-01/scandinavian-countries-are-attractive-sites-server-farms.

Rainie, L. and Wellman, B. (2012), *Networked: The New Social Operating System*, Cambridge, MA: MIT Press.

Rashdall, H. (2010), *The Universities of Europe in the Middle Ages*, Cambridge: Cambridge University Press.

Rathore, M.M., Ahmad, A., Paul, A., and Rho, S. (2016), 'Urban planning and building smart cities based on the Internet of Things using Big Data analytics', *Computer Networks*, 101, 63–80.

Relph, E. (1976), *Place and Placelessness*, London: Pion.

Research and Markets (2017), China smart meter industry report, 2017–2021, accessed 17 June 2018 at https://www.researchandmarkets.com/reports/4436051/china-smart-meter-industry-report-2017-2021.

Rheingold, H. (1993), 'A slice of life in my virtual community', in L.M. Harasim (ed.), *Global Networks: Computers and International Communication*, Cambridge, MA: MIT Press, pp. 57–82.

Rijcken, T., Stijnen, J., and Slootjes, N. (2012), '"SimDelta" – inquiry into an Internet-based interactive model for water infrastructure development in the Netherlands', *Water*, 4, 295–320.

Rio Tinto (2017), Mine of the future, accessed 27 June 2018 at http://www.riotinto.com/australia/pilbara/mine-of-the-future-9603.aspx.

Roberts, J. (2001), 'The drive to codify: Implications for the knowledge-based economy', *Prometheus*, 19, 99–116.

Rogers, E.M. (1995), *Diffusion of Innovations*, fourth edition, New York: The Free Press.

Roland, M. (1951), *Recherches sur l'agora Grecque*, Paris: E. de Boccard.

Rosenberg, M. (2017), Smart meter ramp up, Energy Times, accessed 17 June 2018 at http://www.theenergytimes.com/policy-and-regulation/smart-meter-ramp.

Roszak, T. (1991), *The Cult of Information: A Neo-Luddite Treatise on High-tech, Artificial Intelligence and the True Art of Thinking*, second edition, Berkeley: University of California Press.

Sadowski, B.M., Maitland, C., and van Dongen, J. (2002), 'Strategic use of the Internet by small- and medium-sized companies: an exploratory study', *Information Economics and Policy*, 14, 76–93.

SAE (Society of Automotive Engineers International) (2014), Taxonomy and definitions for terms related to on-road motor vehicle automated driving systems, accessed 26 June 2018 at https://www.smmt.co.uk/wp-content/uploads/sites/2/automated_driving.pdf.

Saeed, Y., Khan, M.S., Ahmed, K., and Mubashar, A.S. (2011), 'A multi-agent based autonomous traffic lights control system using fuzzy control', *International Journal of Scientific & Engineering Research*, 2, 1–5.

Savant (2017), Frequently asked questions, accessed 27 June 2018 at http://www.agvsystems.com/faqs/.

Saxenian, A. (1994), *Regional Advantage: Culture and Competition in Silicon Valley and Route 128*, Cambridge, MA: Harvard University Press.

Schoettle, B. and Sivak, M. (2014), *A Survey of Public Opinion about Autonomous and Self-driving Vehicles in the U.S., the U.K., and Australia*, Report No. UMTRI-2014-21, University of Michigan, Transportation Research Institute, accessed 26 June 2018 at https://deepblue.lib.umich.edu/bitstream/handle/2027.42/108384/103024.pdf.

Schrag, Z.M. (1994), 'Navigating cyberspace – maps and agents: different uses of computer networks call for different interfaces', in G.C. Staple (ed.), *Telegeography 1994: Global Telecommunications Traffic*, Washington DC: Telegeography, Inc., pp. 44–52.

Schwanen, T., Dijst, M., and Kwan, M-P. (2008), 'ICTs and the decoupling of everyday activities, space and time: introduction', *Tijdschrift voor Economische en Sociale Geografie*, 99, 519–527.

Selim, H.M. and Chiravuri, A. (2015), 'Identification of factors affecting university instructors' adoption of hybrid e-learning', *International Journal of Innovation and Learning*, 17, accessed 3 May 2018 at https://www.inderscienceonline.com/doi/abs/10.1504/IJIL.2015.069633.

Shearmur, R. and Doloreux, D. (2015), 'Knowledge-intensive business services (KIBS) use and user innovation: high-order services, geographic hierarchies and Internet use in Quebec's manufacturing sector', *Regional Studies*, 49, 1654–1671.

Shehabi, A., Masanet, E., Price, H., Horvath, A., and Nazaroff, W.W. (2011), 'Data center design and location: consequences for electricity use and greenhouse-gas emissions', *Building and Environment*, 46, 990–998.

Sheller, M. (2004), 'Mobile publics: Beyond the network perspective', *Environment and Planning D: Society and Space*, 22, 39–52.

Sheller, M. (2007), 'Bodies, cybercars and the mundane incorporation of automated mobilities', *Social and Cultural Geography*, 8, 175–197.

Shelton, T., Zook, M., and Wiig, A. (2015), 'The "actually existing smart city"', *Cambridge Journal of Regions, Economy and Society*, 8, 13–25.

Sheridan, T.B., Vámos, T., and Aida, S. (1983), 'Adapting automation to man, culture and society', *Automatica*, 19, 605–612.

Shields, R. (2003), *The Virtual*, London and New York: Routledge.

Shin, J., Bhat, C.R., You, D., and Garikapati, V.M. (2015), 'Consumer preferences and willingness to pay for advanced vehicle technology options and fuel types', *Transportation Research C*, 60, 511–524.

Shires, J.D. and Ibañez, N. (2008), *CityMobil and DISTILLATE: Stated Preferences and Ranking Surveys*, Final report, Leeds: University of Leeds Institute for Transport Studies (ITS).

Shiu, E.C.C. and Dawson, J.A. (2004), 'Comparing the impacts of Internet technology and national culture on online usage and purchase from a four-country perspective', *Journal of Retailing and Consumer Services*, 11, 385–394.

Sisson, P. (2016), Autonomous trucks are coming to the mainstream sooner than you think, *Curbed*, accessed 27 June 2018 at http://www.curbed.com/2016/11/4/13518182/self-driving-cars-automated-trucks-freight-logistics.

Smith, R. (2004), 'Access to healthcare via telehealth: experiences from the Pacific', *Perspectives on Global Development and Technology*, 3, 197–211.

Soja, E.E. (1989), *Postmodern Geographies: The Reassertion of Space in Critical Social Theory*, London: Verso.

Soja, E.W. (1996), *Thirdspace: Journeys to Los Angeles and Other Physical and Imagined Places*, Cambridge, MA: Blackwell.

Sorokanich, B. (2017), Honda just invented a self-balancing motorcycle that never falls over, *R&T*, accessed 26 June 2018 at http://www.roadandtrack.com/new-cars/car-technology/news/a32162/honda-just-invented-a-self-balancing-motorcycle-that-never-falls-over/.

Souppouris, A. (2016), Singapore will trial a full-size autonomous bus, *engadget*, accessed 27 June 2018 at https://www.engadget.com/2016/10/24/singapore-autonomous-bus-trial/.

Spieser, K., Treleaven, K., Zhang, R., Frazzoli, E., Morton, D., and Pavone, M. (2014), 'Toward a systematic approach to the design and evaluation of automated mobility-on-demand systems: a case study in Singapore', in G. Meyer and S. Beiker (eds), *Road Vehicle Automation*, Cambridge, MA: Springer, pp. 229–245.

Stackhouse, J. (2018), Why are banks shuttering branches?, On the economy blog, Federal Reserve Bank of St. Louis, accessed 4 July 2018 at https://www.stlouisfed.org/on-the-economy/2018/february/why-banks-shuttering-branches.

Statista (2018a), Global mobile data traffic from 2016 to 2021 (in exabytes per month), accessed 16 April 2018 at https://www.statista.com/statistics/271405/global-mobile-data-traffic-forecast/.

Statista (2018b), Global markets with highest online shopping penetration rate as of 2nd quarter 2017, accessed 18 April 2018 at https://www.statista.com/statistics/274251/retail-site-penetration-across-markets/.

Statista (2018c), Average value of global online shopping orders as of the 4th quarter 2017, by device (US Dollars), accessed 18 April 2018 at https://www.statista.com/statistics/239247/global-online-shopping-order-values-by-device/.

Statista (2018d), Retail e-commerce sales as share of retail trade in selected countries from 2014 to 2017, accessed 18 April 2018 at https://www.statista.com/statistics/281241/online-share-of-retail-trade-in-european-countries/.

Statista (2018e), Quarterly share of e-commerce sales of total US retail sales from 1st quarter 2010 to 4th quarter 2017, accessed 18 April 2018 at https://www.statista.com/statistics/187439/share-of-e-commerce-sales-in-total-us-retail-sales-in-2010/.

Statista (2018f), Penetration of digital banking among Internet users in the United States from 2013 to 2018, accessed 22 April 2018 at https://www.statista.com/statistics/334063/penetration-digital-banking-internet-users-usa/.

Statista (2018g), Number of Internet users in China 2017, by activity (in millions), accessed 30 April 2018 at https://www.statista.com/statistics/277352/online-activities-in-china-based-on-number-of-users/.

Statista (2018h), Number of social network users worldwide from 2010 to 2021 (in billions), accessed 30 April 2018 at https://www.statista.com/statistics/278414/number-of-worldwide-social-network-users/.

Statista (2018i), Number of social network users in selected countries in 2017 and 2022 (in millions), accessed 30 April 2018 at https://www.statista.com/statistics/278341/number-of-social-network-users-in-selected-countries/.

Statista (2018j), Number of apps available in leading app stores as of the first quarter 2018, accessed 6 June 2018 at https://www.statista.com/statistics/276623/number-of-apps-available-in-leading-app-stores/.

Statista (2018k), Control and connectivity smart home household penetration in selected countries worldwide in 2018, accessed 16 June 2018 at https://www.statista.com/statistics/483772/global-comparison-home-automation-smart-home-household-penetration-digital-market-outlook/.

Stockwell, F. (2001), *A History of Information Storage and Retrieval*, Jefferson: McFarland.

Storper, M. (2000), 'Globalization and knowledge flows: an industrial geographer's perspective', in J.H. Dunning (ed.), *Regions, Globalization, and the Knowledge-Based Economy*, New York: Oxford, pp. 42–62.

Strengers, Y. (2016), 'Envisioning the smart home: reimagining a smart energy future', in S. Pink, E. Ardèvol, and D. Landzeni (eds), *Digital Materialities: Design and Anthropology*, London: Bloomsbury, pp. 61–76.

Takieddine, S. and Sun, J. (2015), 'Internet banking diffusion: a country-level analysis', *Electronic Commerce Research and Applications*, 14, 361–371.

Talari, S., Shafie-khah, M., Siano, P., Loia, V., Tommasetti, A., and Catalão, J.P.S. (2017), 'A review of smart cities based on the Internet of Things concept', *Energies*, 10, doi:10.3390/en10040421.

Talebpour, A. and Mahmassani, H.S. (2016), 'Influence of connected and autonomous vehicles on traffic flow stability', *Transportation Research C*, 71, 143–161.

Teo, T.S.H. and Pian, Y. (2004), 'A model for Web adoption', *Information and Management*, 41, 457–468.

Thrift, N. (1995), 'A hyperactive world', in R.J. Johnston, P.J. Taylor, and M.J. Watts (eds), *Geographies of Global Change: Remapping the World in the Late Twentieth Century*, Oxford: Blackwell, pp. 18–35.

Thrift, N. (1996), *Spatial Formations*, London: Sage.

Thrift, N. (2004), 'Driving in the city', *Theory, Culture and Society*, 21, 41–60.

Thrift, N. and French, S. (2002), 'The automatic production of space', *Transactions of the British Institute of Geographers*, 27, 309–335.

Tillema, T., Dijst, M., and Schwanen, T. (2010), 'Decisions concerning communication modes and the influence of travel time: a situational approach', *Environment and Planning A*, 42, 2058–2077.

Timeto, F. (2015), *Diffractive Technospaces: A Feminist Approach to the Mediations of Space and Representation*, Farnham, UK: Ashgate Publishing.

Townsend, A.M. (2013), *Smart Cities: Big Data, Civic Hackers, and the Quest for a New Utopia*, New York: W.W. Norton.

Trucks.com (2017), Self-driving trucks – autonomous vehicles, accessed 27 June 2018 at https://www.trucks.com/category/tech/autonomous-vehicles/.

Turkle, S. (1995), *Life on the Screen: Identity in the Age of the Internet*, New York: Simon & Schuster.

Tversky, B. (2000), 'Some Ways that Maps and Diagrams Communicate', in C. Freska, W. Brauer, C. Habel, and J.F. Wender (eds), *Spatial Cognition II: Integrating Abstract Theories, Empirical Studies, Formal Methods, and Practical Applications*, Berlin: Springer, pp. 72–79.

2025AD The Year of Automated Driving (2017), accessed 26 June 2018 at https://www.2025ad.com/technology/milestones-the-ad-timeline/.

Ugarte, P.P. (2015), Top 10 most gender equal countries in Latin America and the Caribbean, World Economic Forum Agenda, accessed 21 March 2018 at https://agenda.weforum.org/2015/11/top-10-most-gender-equal-countries-in-latin-america-and-the-caribbean-2/.

UK Department for Business, Energy and Industrial Strategy (2018), Smart Meters: Quarterly Report to end December 2017, accessed 17 June 2018 at https://assets.publishing.service.gov.uk/government/uploads/system/ uploads/attachment_data/file/694355/2017_Q4_Smart_Meters_Report.pdf.

Urry, J. (1999), Automobility, car culture and weightless travel, discussion paper, Department of Sociology, Lancaster University, accessed 11 March 2018 at http://www.lancaster.ac.uk/fass/resources/sociology-online-papers/ papers/urry-automobility.pdf.

Urry, J. (2000), *Sociology beyond Societies: Mobilities for the Twenty-first Century*, London: Routledge.

Urry, J. (2002), 'Mobility and proximity', *Sociology*, 36, 255–274.

Urry, J. (2003), *Global Complexity*, Cambridge: Polity.

Urry, J. (2007), *Mobilities*, Cambridge: Polity.

Valkenburg, P.M. and Peter, J. (2008), 'Adolescents' identity experiments on the Internet: consequences for social competence and self-concept unity', *Communication Research*, 35, 208–231.

Van Dijk, J. and Hacker, K. (2003), 'The digital divide as a complex and dynamic phenomenon', *The Information Society*, 19, 315–326.

Venkatesh, V., Morris, M.G., Davis, G.B., and Davis, F.D. (2003), 'User acceptance of information technology: toward a unified view', *MIS Quarterly*, 27, 425–478.

Verisign (2017), Verisign domain name industry brief: Internet grows to 330.6 million domain names in Q1 2017, accessed 6 June 2018 at https://blog .verisign.com/domain-names/verisign-domain-name-industry-brief-internet -grows-to-330-6-million-domain-names-in-q1-2017/.

Virilio, P. (1987), 'The overexposed city', *Zone*, 1, 14–31.

Wang, J. (2018), Capitalizing on the growth of Chinese mobile travel, accessed 25 April 2018 at https://www.itb-kongress.de/media/itbk/itbk_dl_de/itbk _dl_de_itbkongress/itbk_archiv_2016/etravel_1/LabDay2_Capitalizing _the_growth_of_chinese_mobile_travel_TravelDailyChina.pdf.

Wang, S., Zhang, Z., Ye, Z., Wang, X., Lin, X., and Chen, S. (2013), 'Application of environmental Internet of Things on water quality management of urban scenic river', *International Journal of Sustainable Development and World Ecology*, 20, 216–222.

Wang, Y., Lai, P. and Sui, D. (2003), 'Mapping the Internet using GIS: the death of distance hypothesis revisited', *Journal of Geographical Systems*, 5, 381–405.

Warf, B. (2006), 'Introduction', in B. Warf (ed.), *Encyclopedia of Human Geography*, Thousand Oaks, CA: SAGE, pp. xxv–xxviii.

Warf, B. (2009), 'Diverse spatialities of the Latin American and Caribbean Internet', *Journal of Latin American Geography*, 8, 125–145.

Warf, B. (2013), *Global Geographies of the Internet*, Dordrecht: Springer.

Warf, B. (2017), *E-Government in Asia: Origins, Politics, Impacts, Geographies*, Cambridge, MA: Chandos (Elsevier).

Weinberger, D. (2002), *Small Pieces Loosely Joined: A Unified Theory of the Web*, Cambridge, MA: Perseus.

Wellman, B. (2001), 'Physical place and cyberplace: the rise of personalized networking', *International Journal of Urban and Regional Research*, 25, 227–252.

WHTop (2018), List of ICANN registrars with reviews and ranks, accessed 6 June 2018 at http://www.whtop.com/tools.icann-accredited-registrars.

Wilk, R.R. (1999), '"Real Belizean food": building local identity in the Caribbean', *American Anthropologist*, 101, 244–255.

Wilkinson, C. (2015), 'Young people, community radio and urban life', *Geography Compass*, 9, 127–139.

Wilson, C., Hargreaves, T., and Hauxwell-Baldwin, R. (2017), 'Benefits and risks of smart home technologies', *Energy Policy*, 103, 72–83.

Wilson, M.W. (2014), 'Continuous connectivity, handheld computers, and mobile spatial knowledge', *Environment and Planning D: Society and Space*, 32, 535–555.

Wilson, M., Kellerman, A., and Corey, E. (2013), *Global Information Society: Knowledge, Mobility and Technology*, Lanham: Rowman and Littlefield.

World Economic Forum (2017), Step aside San Francisco: the best cities in the world for tech, accessed 4 June 2018 at https://www.weforum.org/agenda/2017/04/these-are-the-22-best-cities-in-the-world-for-tech/.

W³Techs (2013), Usage of contents languages for websites, *Online*, accessed 18 March 2018 at http://w3techs.com/technologies/overview/content_language/all.

Xu, X. (2017), *The Internet of Things: Projects-Places-Policies*, Dissertation in economic geography, Gothenburg: University of Gothenburg.

Yildiz, M. (2007), 'E-government research: reviewing the literature, limitations and ways forward', *Government Information Quarterly*, 24, 646–665.

Yu, H. and Shaw, S-L. (2008), 'Exploring potential human activities in physical and virtual spaces: a spatio-temporal GIS approach', *International Journal of Geographical Information Science*, 22, 409–430.

Zaleski, A. (2016), The urban drone invasion is nigh, Citylab, accessed 27 June 2018 at http://www.citylab.com/tech/2016/12/the-urban-drone-invasion-is-nigh/511496/.

Zhang, R. and Pavone, M. (2014), Control of robotic mobility-on-demand systems: a queueing-theoretical perspective, accessed 27 June 2018 at https://arxiv.org/pdf/1404.4391.pdf.

Zhen, F., Wang, B., and Wei, Z. (2015), 'The rise of the Internet city in China: production and consumption of Internet information', *Urban Studies*, 52, 2313–2329.

Zimmermann, K.A. and Emspak, J. (2017), Internet history timeline: ARPANET to World Wide Web. LiveScience, accessed 17 March 2018 at https://www.livescience.com/20727-internet-history.html.

Zook, M.A. and Graham, M. (2007a), 'Mapping DigiPlace: geocoded Internet data and the representation of place', *Environment and Planning B*, 34, 466–482.

Zook, M.A. and Graham, M. (2007b), 'The creative reconstruction of the Internet: Google and the privatization of cyberspace and DigiPlace', *Geoforum*, 38, 1322–1343.

Zook, M.A. and Graham, M. (2007c), 'From cyberspace to DigiPlace: visibility in an age of information and mobility', in H.J. Miller (ed.), *Societies and Cities in the Age of Instant Access*, Dordrecht: Springer, pp. 241–254.

Index